THEORIES OF ELECTROCHEMISTRY

THEORIES OF ELECTROCHEMISTRY

By

Prof. Sananda Chatterjee

Institute for Natural Sciences

Kolkata - 700 103

(West Bengal)

(India)

DPH

DISCOVERY PUBLISHING HOUSE PVT. LTD.

INDIA

Published by:
Namit Wasan
DISCOVERY PUBLISHING HOUSE PVT. LTD.
4383/4B, Ansari Road, Darya Ganj
New Delhi-110 002 (India)
Phone : +91-11-23279245; 23253475; 43596065
E-mail : discoverybooksindia@gmail.com
discoverypublishinghouse@gmail.com
namitwasan9@gmail.com
web : www.discoverypublishinggroup.com

***First Edition:* 2020**

ISBN: 978-93-88854-24-5

Theories of Electrochemistry

Printed at:
Infinity Imaging Systems
Delhi

Preface

Electrochemical theories and problems has been included in this book, with mathematical equations and electrochemical equations has been explained in detail.

The theories of electrochemistry explains different electrochemical laws and hypothesis.

The book also explains the different applications of these theories and hypothesis.

– Author

Contents

1

Resistance and Conductance

BASIC CONCEPTS AND TERMINOLOGY

Electricity: The term electricity refers to a form of energy or variety of phenomenon resulting from the accumulation of static charges or flow of charged particles.

Electric charge: The electric charge is the fundamental and conserved property of some subatomic particles which determines their electromagnetic interactions. It exhibits two states i.e., positive and negative.

In SI units, the electric charge is measured in Coulombs (C).

The smallest value of free charge known in nature is the charge of an electron or a proton, which has a magnitude of 1.602×10^{-19} Coulomb.

The charge on one electron is: -1.602×10^{-19}C.

Whereas the charge on a proton is equal to: $+1.602 \times 10^{-19}$C.

Electric field: It is an influence produced by an electric charge on other charges in its vicinity.

A charged particle experiences force when placed in an electric field. The electric field exerts a force on charged particles, accelerating them in the direction of the force, in either the same or the opposite direction of the electric field.

Hence some amount of work has to be done against this force to bring the charged particle to a certain point in an electric field.

Electric potential: The electric potential at any point in an electric field is defined as the energy required to bring a unit charge from an infinite distance to that point.

It is usually measured in volts (V). Volt can be formally defined as the ratio of energy in joules to the charge in coulombs.

The absolute electric potential cannot be measured. However, the difference in electric potential between two points can be measured and has more practical usage.

Electric potential difference or voltage: It is the energy required to move a unit charge between two specified points in an electric field. However, it is usually referred to as electric potential or some times as voltage.

$$\text{Electric potential difference (Voltage)} = \frac{\text{Energy required in joules}}{\text{charge in coulombs}}$$

One Volt (V) is equal to 1 Joule per 1 Coulomb.

$$1 \text{ volt (V)} = \frac{1 \text{ Joule (J)}}{1 \text{ Coulomb (C)}}$$

Electromotive force (emf): Formally it is same as electric potential difference. It is the potential energy divided by electric charge and is measured in volts.

It can be defined as the external work expended per unit of charge to produce an electric potential difference thereby causing the current to flow in the circuit.

Note: Though there are several different definitions given across the literature, the above explanation is sufficient in electrochemistry.

Current: Formally it is the flow of charged particles like electrons, protons, ions. The strength of current (I) is defined as the charge transferred in unit time. It is measured in amperes (A).

$$\text{Current (I)} = \frac{\text{Charge (Q)}}{\text{time (t)}}$$

One ampere (A) is defined as 1 coulomb of electricity transferred in one second.

$$1 \text{ Ampere (A)} = \frac{1 \text{ Coulomb (C)}}{1 \text{ second (sec)}}$$

ELECTRICAL RESISTANCE AND CONDUCTANCE

Resistance (R): The tendency of a material to stop the flow of current is known as resistance. It is measured in ohms (Ω).

According to Ohm's law, the resistance offered by a substance is directly proportional to its length (l), but inversely proportional to its cross sectional area (A).

$$R \propto \frac{l}{A}$$

In case of electrolytic solutions, 'l' represents the distance between two electrodes and the 'A' is the cross sectional area of the electrodes.

The above equation can also be written as:

$$R = \rho \frac{l}{A} \qquad (1)$$

Where ρ is the proportionality constant and is known as specific resistance or resistivity.

If A = 1 cm^2 and l = 1 cm, then R = ρ.

Therefore, the specific resistance can be defined as follows:

Specific resistance or resistivity (ρ): It is the resistance offered by a material or solution occupying one cm^3 volume.

It is measured in:

ohm. cm (in C.G.S system)

or

ohm. m (in S.I system)

Its unit can be derived as follows:

$$\rho = R.\frac{A}{l} = ohm.\ \frac{cm^2}{cm} = ohm.cm$$

Conductance (G): It is the tendency of a material to allow the flow of current through it. It is the reciprocal of resistance.

It is measured in ohm-1 = mho = Siemens.

$$\text{Conductance (G)} = \frac{1}{\text{Resistance (R)}}$$

By substituting, R from equation (1):

$$G = \frac{1}{\rho} \cdot \frac{A}{l} = \kappa \cdot \frac{A}{l} \qquad (2)$$

Where

$$\kappa = \frac{1}{\rho} = \text{specific conductance (or) conductivity}$$

From the equation (2),

$$\kappa = G.\frac{l}{A}$$

If A = 1 cm^2 and l = 1 cm, then κ = G.

Therefore the specific conductance can be defined as:

specific conductance or conductivity (κ): It is the conductance of a material or solution occupying one cm^3 volume.

It is measured in:

ohm-1. cm-1 = mho. cm-1 (C.G.S system) or Siemens. m-1 (S.I system)

* The specific conductance depends on the nature of substance or the electrolyte.
* It increases with increase in concentration of the electrolytic solution since the number of ions per unit area increases.

Cell constant (G*): The ratio of the distance between the electrodes, l to the cross sectional area, A of the electrodes is known as cell constant.

$$\text{Cell constant (G*)} = \frac{l}{A}$$

The cell constant can be determined by using following relations which can be derived easily from expressions discussed above.

RESISTIVITY AND CONDUCTIVITY

Electrical resistivity (also known as resistivity, specific electrical resistance, or volume resistivity) quantifies how strongly a given material opposes the flow of electric current. A low resistivity indicates a material that readily allows the movement of electric charge. Resistivity is commonly represented by the Greek letter ρ (rho). The SI unit of electrical resistivity is the ohm.metre (Ω.m) although other units like ohm.centimetre (Ω.cm) are also in use. As an example, if a 1 × 1 × 1 m solid cube of material has sheet contacts on two opposite faces, and the resistance between these contacts is 1 Ω, then the resistivity of the material is 1 Ω.m.

Electrical conductivity or specific conductance is the reciprocal of electrical resistivity, and measures a material's ability to conduct an electric current. It is commonly represented by the Greek letter σ (sigma), but κ (kappa) (especially in electrical engineering) or γ (gamma) are also occasionally used. Its SI unit is siemens per metre (S/m) and CGSE unit is reciprocal second (s^{-1}).

DEFINITION

Resistors or conductors with uniform cross-section

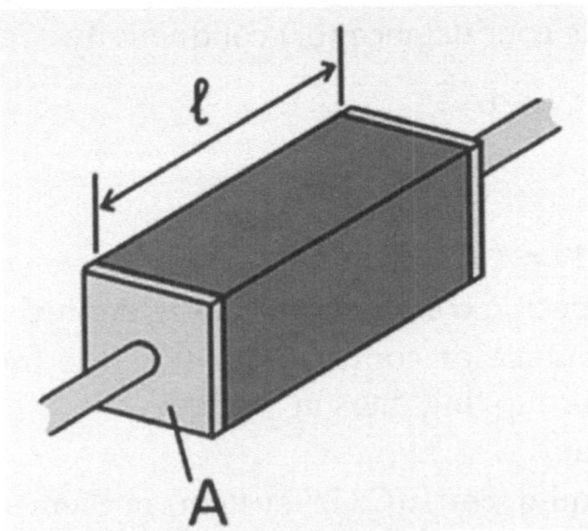

Fig. 1.1: A piece of resistive material with electrical contacts on both ends

Many resistors and conductors have a uniform cross section with a uniform flow of electric current, and are made of one material. (See the diagram to the right.) In this case, the electrical resistivity ρ (Greek: rho) is defined as:

$$\rho = \frac{A}{e}$$

where

R is the electrical resistance of a uniform specimen of the material (measured in ohms, Ω)

e is the length of the piece of material (measured in metres, m)

A is the cross-sectional area of the specimen (measured in square metres, m^2).

The reason resistivity is defined this way is that it makes resistivity an *intrinsic property*, unlike resistance. All copper wires, irrespective of their shape and size, have approximately the same *resistivity*, but a long, thin copper wire has a much larger *resistance* than a thick, short copper wire.

Every material has its own characteristic resistivity – for example, rubber's resistivity is far larger than copper's.

In a hydraulic analogy, passing current through a high-resistivity material is like pushing water through a pipe full of sand, while passing current through a low-resistivity material is like pushing water through an empty pipe. If the pipes are the same size and shape, the pipe full of sand has higher resistance to flow. But resistance is not *solely* determined by the presence or absence of sand; it also depends on the length and width of the pipe: short or wide pipes will have lower resistance than narrow or long pipes.

The above equation can be transposed to get Pouillet's law (named after Claude Pouillet):

$$R = \rho \frac{e}{A}.$$

The resistance of a given material will increase with the length, but decrease with increasing cross-sectional area. From the above equations, resistivity has SI units of ohm.metre. Other units like ohm.cm or ohm.inch are also sometimes used.

The formula R = $\rho e/A$ can be used to intuitively understand the meaning of a resistivity value. For example, if A = 1m² and e = (forming a cube with perfectly-conductive contacts on opposite faces), then the resistance of this element in ohms is numerically equal to the resistivity of the material it is made of in ohm-meters. Likewise, a 1 ohm.cm material would have a resistance of 1 ohm if contacted on opposite faces of a 1 cm×1 cm×1 cm cube.

Conductivity σ (Greek: sigma) is defined as the inverse of resistivity:

$$\sigma = \frac{1}{\rho}.$$

Conductivity has SI units of siemens per meter (S/m).

General Definition

The above definition was specific to resistors or conductors with a uniform cross-section, where current flows uniformly through them. A more basic and general definition starts from the fact that if there is electric field inside a material, it will cause electric current to flow. The electrical resistivity ρ is defined as the ratio of the electric field to the density of the current it creates:

$$\rho = \frac{E}{J}$$

where

ρ is the resistivity of the conductor material (measured in ohm.metres, Ω.m),

E is the magnitude of the electric field (in volts per metre, $V.m^{-1}$),

J is the magnitude of the current density (in amperes per square metre, $A.m^{-2}$), in which E and J are inside the conductor.

Conductivity is the inverse:

$$\sigma = \frac{1}{\rho} = \frac{J}{E}.$$

For example, rubber is a material with large ρ and small σ, because even a very large electric field in rubber will cause almost no current to flow through it. On the other hand, copper is a material with small ρ and large σ, because even a small electric field pulls a lot of current through it.

Causes of Conductivity

Band theory simplified

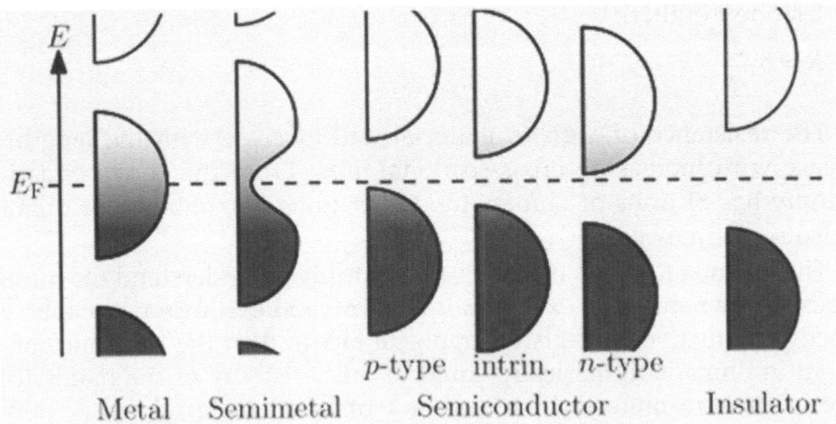

Fig. 1.2: Filling of electronic band structure in various types of material at equilibrium. In metals and semimetals the Fermi level E_F lies inside at least one band. In insulators and semiconductors the Fermi level is inside a band gap, however in semiconductors the bands are near enough to the Fermi level to be thermally populated with electrons or holes.

Quantum mechanics states that electrons in an atom cannot take on any arbitrary energy value. Rather, there are fixed energy levels which the electrons can occupy, and values in between these levels are impossible. When a large number of such allowed energy levels are spaced close together (in energy-space) i.e. have similar (minutely differing) energies then we can talk about these energy levels together as an "energy band." There can be many such energy bands in a material, depending on the atomic number (number of electrons) and their distribution (besides external factors like environment modifying the energy bands).The material's electrons seek to minimize the total energy in the material by going to low energy states, however the Pauli exclusion principle means that they cannot all go to the lowest state. The electrons instead "fill up" the band structure starting from the bottom. The characteristic energy level up to which the electrons have filled is called the Fermi level. The position of the Fermi level with respect to the band structure is very important for electrical conduction: only electrons in energy levels near the Fermi level are free to move around since the electrons can easily jump among the partially occupied states in that region. In contrast, the low energy states are rigidly filled with a fixed number of electrons at all times, and the high energy states are empty of electrons at all times.In metals there are many energy levels near the Fermi level, meaning that there are many electrons available to move. This is what causes the high electronic conductivity in metals. An important part of band theory is that there may be forbidden bands in energy: energy intervals which do not contain any energy levels. In insulators and semiconductors, the number of electrons happens to be just the right amount to fill a certain integer number of low energy bands, exactly to the boundary. In this case, the Fermi level falls within a band gap. Since there are no available states near the Fermi level, and the electrons are not freely movable, the electronic conductivity is very low.

In metals

A metal consists of a lattice of atoms, each with an outer shell of electrons which freely dissociate from their parent atoms and travel through the lattice. This is also known as a positive ionic lattice. This 'sea' of dissociable electrons allows the metal to conduct electric current. When an electrical potential difference (a voltage) is applied across the metal, the resulting electric field causes electrons to move from one end of the conductor to the other. Near room temperatures, metals have resistance. The primary cause of this resistance is the thermal motion of ions. This acts to scatter electrons (due to destructive interference of free electron waves on non-correlating potentials of ions). Also contributing to resistance in metals with impurities are the resulting imperfections in the lattice. In pure metals this source is negligible. The larger the cross-sectional area of the conductor, the more electrons per unit length are available to carry the current. As a result, the resistance is lower in larger cross-section conductors. The number of scattering events encountered by an electron passing through a material is proportional to the length of the conductor. The longer the conductor, therefore, the higher the resistance. Different materials also affect the resistance.

In ionic liquids/electrolytes

In electrolytes, electrical conduction happens not by band electrons or holes, but by full atomic species (ions) traveling, each carrying an electrical charge. The resistivity of ionic liquids varies tremendously by the concentration – while distilled water is almost an insulator, salt water is a very efficient electrical conductor. In biological membranes, currents are carried by ionic salts. Small holes in the membranes, called ion channels, are selective to specific ions and determine the membrane resistance.

Resistivity of various materials

- A conductor such as a metal has high conductivity and a low resistivity.
- An insulator like glass has low conductivity and a high resistivity.
- The conductivity of a semiconductor is generally intermediate, but varies widely under different conditions, such as exposure of the material to electric fields or specific frequencies of light, and, most important, with temperature and composition of the semiconductor material.

The degree of doping in semiconductors makes a large difference in conductivity. To a point, more doping leads to higher conductivity. The conductivity of a solution of water is highly dependent on its concentration of dissolved salts, and other chemical species that ionize in the solution. Electrical conductivity of water samples is used as an indicator of how salt-free, ion-free, or impurity-free the sample is; the purer the water, the lower the conductivity (the higher the resistivity). Conductivity measurements in water are often reported as *specific conductance*, relative to the conductivity of pure water at 25 °C. An EC meter is normally used to measure conductivity in a solution. A rough summary is as follows:

Material	Resistivityρ (Ω·m)
Superconductor	0
Metals	10^{-8}
Semiconductors	Variable
Electrolytes	Variable
Insulators	10^{16}

This table shows the resistivity, conductivity and temperature coefficient of various materials at 20 °C (68 °F, 293 K)

Material	ρ (Ω·m) at 20 °C	σ (S/m) at 20 °C	Temperature coefficient(K^{-1})
Carbon (graphene)	1×10^{-8}	-	-0.0002
Silver	1.59×10^{-8}	6.30×10^{7}	0.0038
Copper	1.68×10^{-8}	5.96×10^{7}	0.003862
Annealed copper	1.72×10^{-8}	5.80×10^{7}	0.00393
Gold[note 3]	2.44×10^{-8}	4.10×10^{7}	0.0034
Aluminium	2.82×10^{-8}	3.5×10^{7}	0.0039
Calcium	3.36×10^{-8}	2.98×10^{7}	0.0041
Tungsten	5.60×10^{-8}	1.79×10^{7}	0.0045
Zinc	5.90×10^{-8}	1.69×10^{7}	0.0037
Nickel	6.99×10^{-8}	1.43×10^{7}	0.006
Lithium	9.28×10^{-8}	1.08×10^{7}	0.006
Iron	1.0×10^{-7}	1.00×10^{7}	0.005
Platinum	1.06×10^{-7}	9.43×10^{6}	0.00392
Tin	1.09×10^{-7}	9.17×10^{6}	0.0045
Carbon steel (1010)	1.43×10^{-7}	6.99×10^{6}	
Lead	2.2×10^{-7}	4.55×10^{6}	0.0039
Titanium	4.20×10^{-7}	2.38×10^{6}	X
Grain oriented electrical steel	4.60×10^{-7}	2.17×10^{6}	
Manganin	4.82×10^{-7}	2.07×10^{6}	0.000002
Constantan	4.9×10^{-7}	2.04×10^{6}	0.000008
Stainless steel	6.9×10^{-7}	1.45×10^{6}	
Mercury	9.8×10^{-7}	1.02×10^{6}	0.0009
Nichrome	1.10×10^{-6}	9.09×10^{5}	0.0004
GaAs	1×10^{-3} to 1×10^{8}	1×10^{-8} to 10^{3}	
Carbon (amorphous)	5×10^{-4} to 8×10^{-4}	1.25×10^{3} to 2×10^{3}	−0.0005
Carbon (graphite)	2.5×10^{-6} to 5.0×10^{-6} //basal plane 3.0×10^{-3} ⊥basal plane	2×10^{5} to 3×10^{5}//basal plane 3.3×10^{2} ⊥basal plane	
Carbon (diamond)	1×10^{12}	$\sim10^{-13}$	
Germanium	4.6×10^{-1}	2.17	−0.048
Sea water	2×10^{-1}	4.8	
Drinking water	2×10^{1} to 2×10^{3}	5×10^{-4} to 5×10^{-2}	
Silicon[note 8]	6.40×10^{2}	1.56×10^{-3}	−0.075
Wood (damp)	1×10^{3} to 1×10^{4}	10^{-4} to 10^{-3}	
Deionized water	1.8×10^{5}	5.5×10^{-6}	
Glass	10×10^{10} to 10×10^{14}	10^{-11} to 10^{-15}	
Hard rubber	1×10^{13}	10^{-14}	
Wood (oven dry)	1×10^{14} to 1×10^{16}	10^{-16} to 10^{-14}	
Sulphur	1×10^{15}	10^{-16}	
Air	1.3×10^{16} to 3.3×10^{16}	3×10^{-15} to 8×10^{-15}	
PEDOT:PSS	1×10^{-3} to 1×10^{-1}	1×10^{1} to 1×10^{3}	
Fused quartz	7.5×10^{17}	1.3×10^{-18}	
PET	10×10^{20}	10^{-21}	
Teflon	10×10^{22} to 10×10^{24}	10^{-25} to 10^{-23}	

The effective temperature coefficient varies with temperature and purity level of the material. The 20 °C value is only an approximation when used at other temperatures. For example, the coefficient becomes lower at higher temperatures for copper, and the value 0.00427 is commonly specified at 0 °C. The extremely low resistivity (high conductivity) of silver is characteristic of metals. George Gamow tidily summed up the nature of the metals' dealings with electrons in his science-popularizing book, *One, Two, Three...Infinity* (1947): "The metallic substances differ from all other materials by the fact that the outer shells of their atoms are bound rather loosely, and often let one of their electrons go free. Thus the interior of a metal is filled up with a large number of unattached electrons that travel aimlessly around like a crowd of displaced persons. When a metal wire is subjected to electric force applied on its opposite ends, these free electrons rush in the direction of the force, thus forming what we call an electric current." More technically, the free electron model gives a basic description of electron flow in metals. Wood is widely regarded as an extremely good insulator, but its resistivity is sensitively dependent on moisture content, with damp wood being a factor of at least 10^{10} worse insulator than oven-dry. In any case, a sufficiently high voltage – such as that in lightning strikes or some high-tension power lines – can lead to insulation breakdown and electrocution risk even with apparently dry wood.

Temperature Dependence

Linear Approximation

The electrical resistivity of most materials changes with temperature. If the temperature T does not vary too much, a linear approximation is typically used:

$$\rho(T) = \rho_0[1 + \alpha(T - T_0)]$$

where α is called the *temperature coefficient of resistivity*, T_0 is a fixed reference temperature (usually room temperature), and ρ_0 is the resistivity at temperature T_0. The parameter α is an empirical parameter fitted from measurement data. Because the linear approximation is only an approximation, α is different for different reference temperatures. For this reason it is usual to specify the temperature that was measured at with a suffix, such as α_{15}, and the relationship only holds in a range of temperatures around the reference. When the temperature varies over a large temperature range, the linear approximation is inadequate and a more detailed analysis and understanding should be used.

Metals

In general, electrical resistivity of metals increases with temperature. Electron–phonon interactions can play a key role. At high temperatures, the resistance of a metal increases linearly with temperature. As the temperature of a metal is reduced, the temperature dependence of resistivity follows a power law function of temperature. Mathematically the temperature dependence of the resistivity ρ of a metal is given by the Bloch–Grüneisen formula:

$$\rho(T) = \rho(0) + A\left(\frac{T}{\Theta_R}\right)^n \int_0^{\frac{\Theta_R}{T}} \frac{x^n}{(e^x - 1)(1 - e^{-x})} dx$$

where ρ(0) is the residual resistivity due to defect scattering, A is a constant that depends on the velocity of electrons at the Fermi surface, the Debye radius and the number density of electrons in the metal. Θ_R is the Debye temperature as obtained from resistivity measurements and matches very closely with the values of Debye temperature obtained from specific heat measurements. n is an integer that depends upon the nature of interaction:

1. n=5 implies that the resistance is due to scattering of electrons by phonons (as it is for simple metals)
2. n=3 implies that the resistance is due to s-d electron scattering (as is the case for transition metals)
3. n=2 implies that the resistance is due to electron–electron interaction.

If more than one source of scattering is simultaneously present, Matthiessen's Rule (first formulated by Augustus Matthiessen in the 1860s) says that the total resistance can be approximated by adding up several different terms, each with the appropriate value of *n*.As the temperature of the metal is sufficiently reduced (so as to 'freeze' all the phonons), the resistivity usually reaches a constant value, known as the residual resistivity. This value depends not only on the type of metal, but on its purity and thermal history. The value of the residual resistivity of a metal is decided by its impurity concentration. Some materials lose all electrical resistivity at sufficiently low temperatures, due to an effect known as superconductivity. An investigation of the low-temperature resistivity of metals was the motivation to Heike Kamerlingh Onnes's experiments that led in 1911 to discovery of superconductivity. For details see History of superconductivity

CONDUCTANCE AND CONDUCTIVITY

The conductivity (or specific conductance) of an electrolyte solution is a measure of its ability to conduct electricity. The SI unit of conductivity is siemens per meter (S/m). Conductivity measurements are used routinely in many industrial and environmental applications as a fast, inexpensive and reliable way of measuring the ionic content in a solution. For example, the measurement of product conductivity is a typical way to monitor and continuously trend the performance of water purification systems. In many cases, conductivity is linked directly to the total dissolved solids (T.D.S.). High quality deionized water has a conductivity of about 5.5 μS/m, typical drinking water in the range of 5-50 mS/m, while sea water about 5 S/m[2] (i.e., sea water's conductivity is one million times higher than that of deionized water). Conductivity is traditionally determined by measuring the AC resistance of the solution between two electrodes. Dilute solutions follow Kohlrausch's Laws of concentration dependence and additivity of ionic contributions. Lars Onsager gave a theoretical explanation of Kohlrausch's law by extending Debye–Hückel theory.

Units

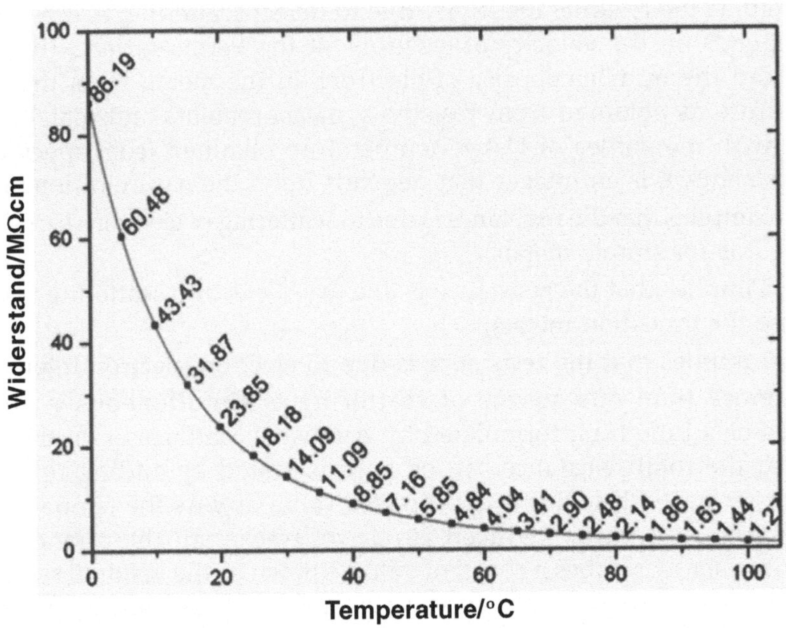

Fig. 1.3: Resistivity of pure water (in MW-cm) as a function of temperature

The SI unit of conductivity is S/m and, unless otherwise qualified, it refers to 25 °C (standard temperature). Often encountered in industry is the traditional unit of μS/cm. 10^6 μS/cm = 10^3 mS/cm = 1 S/cm. The numbers in μS/cm are higher than those in μS/m by a factor of 100 (i.e., 1 μS/cm = 100 μS/m). Occasionally a unit of "EC" (electrical conductivity) is found on scales of instruments: 1 EC = 1 mS/cm. Sometimes encountered is a so-called mho (reciprocal of ohm): 1 mho/m = 1 S/m. Historically, mhos antedate Siemens by many decades; good vacuum-tube testers, for instance, gave transconductance readings in micromhos. The commonly used standard cell has a width of 1 cm, and thus for very pure water in equilibrium with air would have a resistance of about 10^6 ohm, known as a megohm, occasionally spelled as "megaohm". Ultra-pure water could achieve 18 megohms or more. Thus in the past megohm-cm was used, sometimes abbreviated to "megohm". Sometimes, a conductivity is given just in "microSiemens" (omitting the distance term in the unit). While this is an error, it can often be assumed to be equal to the traditional μS/cm. The typical conversion of conductivity to the total dissolved solids is done assuming that the solid is sodium chloride: 1 μS/cm is then an equivalent of about 0.6 mg of NaCl per kg of water.

Molar conductivity has the SI unit S m^2 mol^{-1}. Older publications use the unit Ω^{-1} cm^2 mol^{-1}.

Measurement

The electrical conductivity of a solution of an electrolyte is measured by determining the resistance of the solution between two flat or cylindrical electrodes separated by a fixed distance. An alternating voltage is used in order to avoid electrolysis. The resistance is measured by a conductivity meter. Typical frequencies used are in the range 1–3 kHz. The dependence on the frequency is usually small, but may become appreciable at very high frequencies, an effect known as the Debye–Falkenhagen effect. A wide variety of instrumentation is commercially available. There are two types of cell, the classical type with flat or cylindrical electrodes and a second type based on induction. Many commercial systems offer automatic temperature correction. Tables of reference conductivities are available for many common solutions.

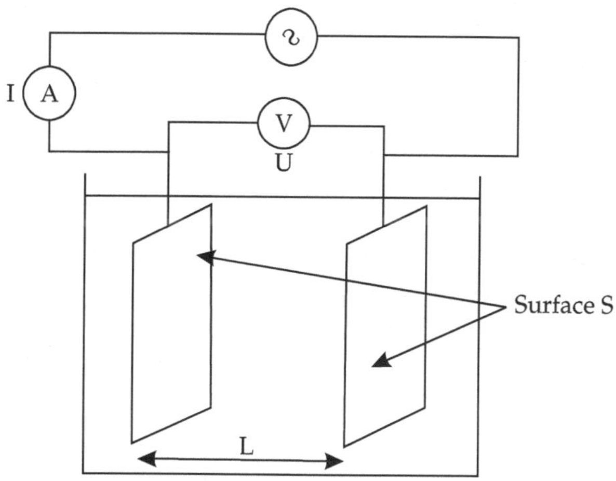

Fig. 1.4: Principle of the measurement

Definitions

Resistance, R, is proportional to the distance, l, between the electrodes and is inversely proportional to the cross-sectional area of the sample, A (noted S on the Figure above). Writing ρ (rho) for the specific resistance (or resistivity),

$$R = \frac{l}{A}\rho.$$

In practice the conductivity cell is calibrated by using solutions of known specific resistance, ρ^*, so the quantities l and A need not be known precisely. If the resistance of the calibration solution is R^*, a cell-constant, C, is derived.

$R^* = C \times \rho^*$

The specific conductance, κ (kappa) is the reciprocal of the specific resistance.

$$\kappa = \frac{1}{\rho} = \frac{C}{R}$$

Conductivity is also temperature-dependent. Sometimes the ratio of l and A is called as the cell constant, denoted as G^*, and conductance is denoted as G. Then the specific conductance κ (kappa), can be more conveniently written as

$\kappa = G^* \times G$

Theory

The specific conductance of a solution containing one electrolyte depends on the concentration of the electrolyte. Therefore it is convenient to divide the specific conductance by concentration. This quotient is termed molar conductivity, is denoted by Λ_m

$$\Lambda_m = \frac{\kappa}{C}$$

Strong electrolytes

Strong electrolytes are believed to dissociate completely in solution. The conductivity of a solution of a strong electrolyte at low concentration follows Kohlrausch's Law.

$\Lambda_m = L^0_m - K\sqrt{c}$

where Λ^0_m is known as the limiting molar conductivity, K is an empirical constant and c is the electrolyte concentration. (Limiting here means "at the limit of the infinite dilution".) In effect, the observed conductivity of a strong electrolyte becomes directly proportional to concentration, at sufficiently low concentrations i.e. when

$\Lambda^0_m > K\sqrt{c}$

As the concentration is increased however, the conductivity no longer rises in proportion. Moreover, Kohlrausch also found that the limiting conductivity of anions and cations are additive: the conductivity of a solution of a salt is equal to the sum of conductivity contributions from the cation and anion.

$\Lambda^0_m = \nu_+ \lambda^0_+ + \nu - \lambda^0_-$

where:

- ν- and ν are the number of moles of cations and anions, respectively, which are created from the dissociation of 1 mole of the dissolved electrolyte;
- λ^0_+ and λ^0_- are the limiting molar conductivities of the individual ions.

The following table gives values for the limiting molar conductivities for selected ions.

Limiting ion conductivity in water at 298 K			
Cations	**λ_+^0/mS m^{2}mol^{-1}**	**anions**	**λ_-^0/mS m^{2}mol^{-1}**
H^+	34.96	OH^-	19.91
Li^+	3.869	Cl^-	7.634
Na^+	5.011	Br^-	7.84
K^+	7.350	I^-	7.68
Mg^{2+}	10.612	SO_4^{2-}	15.96
Ca^{2+}	11.900	NO_3^-	7.14
Ba^{2+}	12.728	$CH_3CO_2^-$	4.09

An interpretation of these results was based on the theory of Debye and Hückel.

$$\Lambda_m = \Lambda^0_m - (A + B\Lambda^0_m)\sqrt{c}$$

where A and B are constants that depend only on known quantities such as temperature, the charges on the ions and the dielectric constant and viscosity of the solvent. As the name suggests, this is an extension of the Debye–Hückel theory, due to Onsager. It is very successful for solutions at low concentration.

Weak electrolytes

A weak electrolyte is one that is never fully dissociated (i.e. there are a mixture of ions and complete molecules in equilibrium). In this case there is no limit of dilution below which the relationship between conductivity and concentration becomes linear. Instead, the solution becomes ever more fully dissociated at weaker concentrations, and for low concentrations of "well behaved" weak electrolytes, the degree of dissociation of the weak electrolyte becomes proportional to the inverse square root of the concentration. Typical weak electrolytes are weak acids and weak bases. The concentration of ions in a solution of a weak electrolyte is less than the concentration of the electrolyte itself. For acids and bases the concentrations can be calculated when the value(s) of the acid dissociation constant(s) is(are) known. For a monoprotic acid, HA, obeying the inverse square root law, with a dissociation constant K_a, an explicit expression for the conductivity as a function of concentration, c, known as Ostwald's dilution law, can be obtained.

$$\frac{1}{\Lambda_m} = \frac{1}{\Lambda_m^0} + \frac{\Lambda_m C}{K_a(\Lambda_m^0)^2}$$

Higher concentrations

Both Kohlrausch's law and the Debye-Hückel-Onsager equation break down as the concentration of the electrolyte increases above a certain value. The reason for this is that as concentration increases the average distance between cation and anion decreases, so that there is more inter-ionic interaction. Whether this constitutes ion-association is a moot point. However, It has often been assumed that cation and anion interact to form an ion-pair. Thus the electrolyte is treated as if it were like a weak acid and a constant, *K*, can be derived for the equilibrium

$$A^+ + B^- \rightleftharpoons A^+B^-; K= [A^+][B^-]/[A^+B^-]$$

Davies describes the results of such calculations in great detail, but states that *K* should not necessarily be thought of as a true equilibrium constant, rather, the inclusion of an "ion-association" term is useful in extending the range of good agreement between theory and experimental conductivity data. Various attempts have been made to extend Onsager's treatment to more concentrated solutions. The existence of a so-called *conductance minimum* has proved to be a controversial subject as regards interpretation. Fuoss and Kraus suggested that it is caused by the formation of ion-triplets, and this suggestion has received some support recently.

Conductivity versus Temperature

Generally the conductivity of a solution increases with temperature, as the mobility of the ions increases. For comparison purposes reference values are reported at an agreed temperature, usually 298 K (~25 C), although occasionally 20C is used. It is often necessary to take readings from a sample at some other temperature, where it would be inconvenient to wait for the sample to heat or cool. So called 'compensated' measurements are made at a convenient temperature but the value reported is a calculated value of the expected value of conductivity of the solution, as if it had been measured at the reference temperature (usually 298 K (~25 C), although occasionally 20C is used). Basic compensation is normally done by assuming a linear increase of conductivity versus temperature of typically 2% per degree. Although generally satisfactory for room temperatures, and for purely comparative measurements, the further the measurement temperature is from the reference temperature, the less accurate such simply compensated measurements become. More sophisticated instruments allow programmable compensation functions, which can be specific to the ion species being measured, and which may include additional non-linear terms.

Applications

Notwithstanding the difficulty of theoretical interpretation, measured conductivity is a good indicator of the presence or absence of conductive ions in solution, and measurements are used extensively in many industries. For example, conductivity measurements are used to monitor quality in public water supplies, in hospitals, in boiler water and industries which depend on water quality such as brewing. This type of measurement is not ion-specific; it can sometimes be used to determine the amount of total dissolved solids (T.D.S.) if the composition of the solution and its conductivity behavior are known. It should be noted that conductivity measurements made to determine water purity will not respond to non conductive contaminants (many organic compounds fall into this category), therefore additional purity tests may be required depending on application. Sometimes, conductivity measurements are linked with other methods to increase the sensitivity of detection of specific types of ions. For example, in the boiler water technology, the boiler blowdown is continuously monitored for "cation conductivity", which is the conductivity of the water after it has been passed through a cation exchange resin. This is a sensitive method of monitoring anion impurities in the boiler water in the presence of excess cations (those of the alkalizing agent usually used for water treatment). The sensitivity of this method relies on the high mobility of H^+ in comparison with the mobility of other cations or anions. Conductivity detectors are commonly used with ion chromatography.

Conductance of Electrolytes

It is more convenient to focus attention on the conductance, L, rather than on resistance, R, The relationship is

$$R = 1/L$$

L is the conductance, is expressed, in mhos or ohm^{-1}. In terms of conductance equation 2 is written as

$$L = \kappa \frac{A}{I}$$

Where K is the specific conductance, i.e the conductance of a tube of material 1 cm long having a cross section of $1cm^2$. The units of K are mho cm^{-1}

The specific conductance of an electrolyte solution depends upon the equivalent concentration of the charged particle present and their nobilities. In order to remove at least part of the concentration dependence, a new quantity – the equivalent conductance L is introduced.

$$\Lambda = \frac{1000}{c}\kappa$$

Where c is the equivalent concentration. Therefore, if the electrolyte were completely dissociated (that is, each charged particle behaved independently), the physical meaning of equivalent conductance would be that it is the conductance of Avogadro's number of unit positive charge and unit negative charge placed in a conductance cell that is large enough to accommodate 1 liter of solution and in which the electrodes have an area of 1 cm^2 and are 1 cm apart.

Arrhenius explained that the equivalent conductance of the electrolytes is not independent of concentration but decreases with the increasing concentration because of only partial dissociation. According to this theory, complete dissociation of the ionic species occur only in the infinitely dilute solution and at any appreciable concentration only fractional dissociation occurs, the degree of dissociation can be calculated by the following equation

$$\alpha = \frac{\Lambda}{\Lambda_0} \quad (6)$$

Where Λ_0 is the equivalent conductance in an infinitely dilute solution. Although this theory is quite useful for the weak electrolytes, it has the inherent disadvantage of requiring of evaluation the Λ_0. For weak electrolytes the equivalent conductance decreases quite rapidly even in the dilute solutions and an accurate extrapolation to zero concentration cannot be achieved. This is in contrast to strong electrolytes, such as sodium chloride, for which a plot of Λ vs $\sqrt{c}$ yields a straight line, and Λ_0 can be obtained accurately by extrapolation to zero concentration.

The difference in Λ_0 for pairs of salts having a common ion is approximately constant. Kohlrausch prposed, that when complete dissociation exists in infinitely dilute solutions, each ionic species migrates independently. The Λ_0 can then be considered to be the sum of equivalent ionic conductances at infinite dilution, for each ionic species.

$$\Lambda_0 = \lambda_{0+} + \lambda_{0-} \quad (7)$$

Where λ_0^+ and λ_0^- are the equivalent conductances of the positive and negative ions, respectively, in infinitely dilute solutions. The differences between the equivalent conductances of the individual ionic species at infinite dilution, $\Delta\lambda_0$, where obtained from pair of strong electrolytes.

$$[\Delta\lambda_0 = \Delta\lambda_{0+} = (\lambda_{0K+} - \lambda 0_{Na+})] \quad (8)$$

From sodium chloride-potassium chloride, sodium nitrate-potassium nitrate, and so forth

$$[\Delta\Lambda_0 = \Delta\lambda_{0-} = (\lambda_0{}^{cl-} - \lambda_0{}^{NO_3})] \quad (8.1)$$

From sodium chloride-potassium chloride, sodium nitrate-potassium nitrate and were found to be constant. Although only the differences in equivalent conductances can be obtained numerically ($\Delta\lambda_0$) and not the individual conductances ($\lambda_0{}^{Cl-}$ and so forth). The Kohlrausch's additivity law can be ued to obtain Λ_0 for a weak electrolyte in the following manner.

$$\Delta_0{}^{CH_3COOH} = \lambda_0{}^{H+} + \lambda_0{}^{CH_3COO^-} = \Delta_0{}^{HCl} + \Delta_0{}^{CH_3COONa} - \Delta_0{}^{NaCl}$$

The extrapolated equivalent conductances, Δ_0 of hydrochloric acid, sodium acetate, and sodium chloride can be obtained easily since they are all strong electrolytes. Therefore, Kohlrausch's law permits the calculation of the equivalent conductance of a weak electrolyte (acetic acid)in an infinitely dilute solution.

Once Δ_0 for a weak electrolyte is obtained, the degree of dissociation of acetic acid at different concentrations can be calculated by using equation.

For a monoprotic acid, such as acetic acid, the dissociation reaction can be written as

$$CH_3COOH \rightleftharpoons H^+ + CH_3COO^- \quad (9)$$

And the dissociation constant as

$$K_a = \frac{(H^+)\,(CH_3COO^-)}{CH_3COOH} = \frac{(cx)(cx)}{c(1-x)} = \frac{cx^2}{1-cx} \tag{10}$$

Dissociation constants of weak electrolytes, obtained from conductance measurements and the Arrhenius theory, are constant at different concentrations. With hydrochloric acid for example, increase with the increasing concentration. In spite of these and other difficulties, the Arrhenius theory is still applied, but only to weak electrolytes.

The behavior of the strong electrolytes in conductance experiments has been successfully explained by Debye-Huckel theory of dilute solutions (0.01M). This theory treats the strong electrolytes as completely ionized particles. However, the independent motion of each ion is hindered by two effects:

1. The relaxation phenomenon of ionic atmosphere; and
2. Electrophoretic mobility.

A charged positive ion is, on the average, surrounded by an atmosphere of negative ions and vice versa. When the positive ion moves in one direction under the influence of electrical field, the ionic atmosphere is distorted. This distortion opposes the applied field and its results in a decrease in the current produced by the field.

The greater the electrolyte concentration, the greater the distortion of the ionic atmosphere; correspondingly the equivalent conductance decreases with the increase in the square root of concentration ($\sqrt{c}$).

The second effect stems from the fact that it moves with the ionic species. As the differently charged ions move in opposite direction, their solvent layers encounter a viscous drag, which decreases the mobility of ions. Again, this effect is more pronounced as the concentration of electrolyte increases. The Debye-Huckel theory also predicts square root concentration dependence for this effect.

The two effects enumerated are important only if the ionic concentration is appreciable.

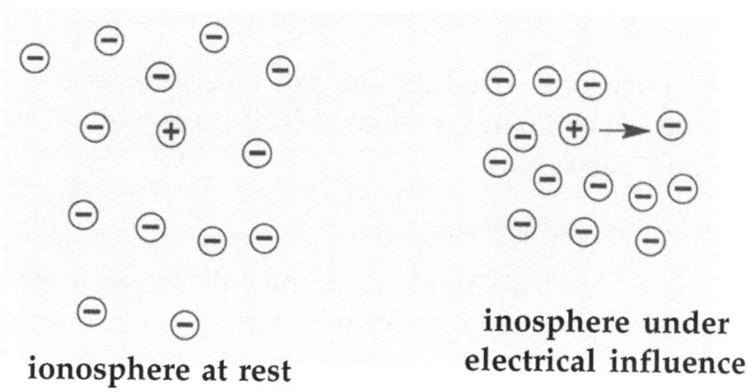

Fig. 1.5: Showing the influence of electrical charge in the ionosphere

For weak electrolytes the Debye-Huckel corrections are small, and they therefore can still be satisfactorily described in Arrhenius terms.

Moreover, at concentrations greater than 0.01M even the Debye Huckel theory cannot explain the conductance behavior of strong electrolytes. There are a number of theories, none of them completely satisfactory for description of the behavior in the more concentrated solutions. The qualitative picture is that, as the ionic concentration increases, more and more ion pairs and triplets are formed. This obviously decreases the independent movement of the individual particles in the electrical field, thus resulting in a decrease in the equivalent conductance with an increase in concentration.

These theories of Bjerrum and Fouss differ, however, from the old Arrhenius theory. An ion pair in only a temporary arrangement due to inelastic collisions, whereas an undissociated molecule is a permanent arrangement. The ion pair and higher ionic aggregations become especially important in solvents with low dielectric constants.

To understand the conductance behavior of different electrolytes in different concentration ranges, one selects the theory that explains the phenomenon in the simplest terms. No unified theory is available at present. However, the different theories try to account for the number of particles moving independently at any given concentration.

The relationship between the conductance of an independent ion and its mobility can be established unequivocally for infinitely dilute solutions for an applied potential, V, the flow of current is given by equation 1. Re-writing this equation in terms of equivalent conductance for infinitely dilute solutions we get

$$i = \Lambda_0 V = (\lambda_0^+ + \lambda_0^-)\, V = i^+ + i^- \qquad (11)$$

Where i^+ and i^+ are the currents carried by the positive and negative ions, respectively.

The mobility of an ion, u, is defined as the average velocity, v, under the influence of potential of 1 volt applied across a 1 cm cell.

$$u = \frac{v}{V} \qquad (12)$$

Since the current carried by the positive ions in one equivalent of electrolyte corresponds t o the passage of N/Z^+ ions with an average velocity of v^+ carrying eZ^+ charges.

$$i^+ = eZ^+ \frac{N}{Z^+} v^+ = eNv^+ = Fv^+ \qquad (13)$$

Where N is Avogadro's number, e is the unit charge, and F is the Faraday constant A similar equation can be written for i^-. Combining equations 11, 12 and 13 we get

$$u_0^+ = \frac{\lambda_0^+}{F} \text{ and } u_0^+ = \frac{\lambda_0^-}{F} \qquad (14)$$

It is assumed that the small ions are spherical and that their frictional resistance can be proved by Stoke's Law, the mobility can be given as

$$u = \frac{\zeta \in}{6\pi\eta} \tag{15}$$

Where $\in$ is the dielectric constant of the solvent, η is the coefficient of viscosity of the solvent, and ζ is the Zeta potential, which is related to the net charge at the shear surface, Q, of a sphere with radius r.

$$\zeta = \frac{Q}{\in r} \tag{16}$$

Therefore, if the $\in$ and η of a solvent are known one can predict the mobility of an ion in the given solvent for a set zeta potential from equation 12. Conversely, from the comparison of nobilities or equivalent conductance at infinitely dilute solutions of ions in different solvents, one can estimate whether the effective surface charge is the same or different in the different solvents.

THE CONDUCTANCE BRIDGE EXPERIMENT

The conductivities can be conveniently measured with a Wheatstone Bridge Circuit shown in the figure 1.6. In this circuit an audio frequency of 1 KHz has been used instead of D.C to avoid the polarization of the electrodes, which would lead to the electrode reactions in the conductance cell.

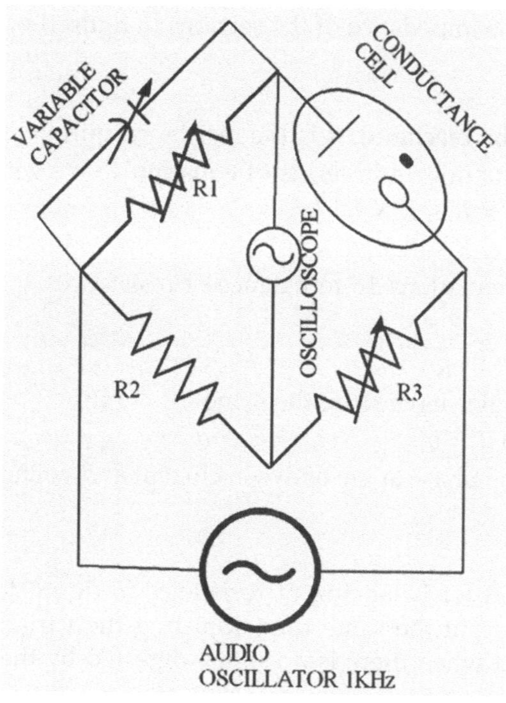

Fig. 1.6: Showing the Conductivity measurement by the Wheatstone Bridge Method

The platinum electrodes usually have a 1cm^2 surface area and are set a certain distance apart, but the geometry of the cell must be determined by calibration. The platinum electrodes extend to the top where they are sealed with the glass tube. The leads of the platinum electrodes either extend beyond the glass side arm so that they can be directly incorporated into the circuit or they dip into the pool of mercury. Under the latter condition the leads from the conductance bridge make contact with the mercury pools in both sides of the conductance cell. The conductance cell is filled with the electrolyte solution and thermostatic before measurement.

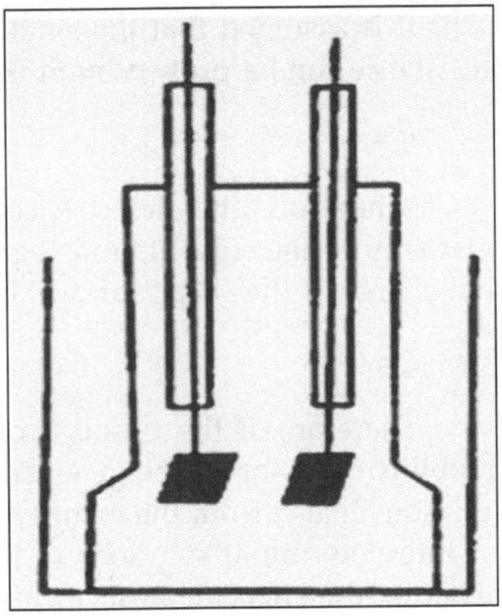

Fig. 1.7: Showing the Conductance Cell

A bridge is by an oscilloscope or any other detector device. The condition for balancing is that the potential as B should be the same as A or there should be no potential difference between A and B.

$$\frac{Z_1}{Z_2} = \frac{Z_x}{Z_3} \tag{17}$$

Where Z is the impedance of the sections in figure 1.6, the impedance is given by

$$Z = R + iX \tag{18}$$

Where X is the reactance, R is the resistance, and $i = \sqrt{-1}$

Rewriting equation 14 in terms of equation 15 we get

$$R_1R_3 - X_1X_3 = R_2R_x - X_2X_x$$
$$R_1R_3 - R_3R_1 = R_2X_x - R_xX_2 \tag{19}$$

In order for equations 16 to balance of resistances

$$\frac{R_1}{R_2} = \frac{R_x}{R_3} \text{ or } R_x = \frac{R_1R_3}{R_2} \tag{20}$$

the phase angles have to be the same

$$\theta_1 = \theta_2 \text{ and } \theta_x = \theta_3 \tag{21}$$

Where θ is the phase angle between current and voltage and is given by

$$\theta = \frac{X_1}{R_1} \tag{22}$$

The condition for balancing of resistance in figure 1.6 is achieved by adjusting R_1 and R_3 at the same time adjusting the variable capacitor. The bridge is balanced when there is no signal detected by the oscilloscope.

The same type of procedure is followed if a Wayne-Kerr universal bridge is used in the circuit. In this case the balance is obtained by using a photo-electric eye which opens completely when the bridge is fully balanced.

Fig. 1.8: Showing the Picture of Wayne-Kerr universal bridge B-221

With the Wayne-Kerr bridge, the balancing is started with the sensitivity (knob to the left) turned to the lowest value. Then the conductance range is selected, that causes the widest opening of the eye in the course detector. Then, progressively increasing the sensitivity and the alternative changing of the capacitance and the resistance the final balanced is achieved. In the Wayne-Kerr bridge the conductivity is read off directly.

The Preparation of Solutions

The solvents employed should be of low ionic conductance. In aqueous solutions deionized water should be used.[1]

Conductance Ratio

As previously stated the relation between the equivalent conductance of a solution in any concentration to that of an equivalent conductance of a solution in infinitely dilute solution is termed as the ratio of conductance which is stated in the equation 3 and is denoted by α

Dispersion of Conductance at High Frequency

In the high frequency conductometry an electrochemical cell in which a solution to be analyzed between external, Parallel metal sheet electrodes is

[1] In any case the conductance of the solvent must be kept under 5×10^{-6} mhos (5×10 micro-mohs). If this cannot be achieved then the conductivity of the solvent must be subtracted from the conductance of the solution.

called capacitive cell or codensor type cell. Since the solution is insulated from the metal plates by the walls of the container, it can be used only at high frequencies. The high frequency method was suggested first by Blake. In this type of cell, the electrochemical reactions are not present to interefere with the conductance measurement since the electrodes are not in direct contact with the electrolyte. Reilley *et al.* have made an extensive study of the theory of high frequency titrations and their applications. Ermakov *et al.* have used this type of cell to study the structural properties of solutions. Forman etal . have used a capacitive cell in an attempt to verify experimentally the Debye-Falkenhagen effect. It is interesting to abserve that high frequency conductometry is appearing in more applied science and Technology in recent years. High-frequency measurement of impedance of solutions, where the signal depends on electrical conductivity of the solution and the measuring electrodes need not be in direct contact with the solution has also been applied to Capillary Zone Electrophoresis (CZE) detection under the name "contactless conductivity detection". The original contactless systems used for conductivity detection in flowing liquids, e.g., were mechanically and electronically complicated. Recently, a new simplified constructions of contactless detectors, have been published. This high frequency conductometry with such a long history has poorly understood or misrepresented some people claimed this system represent Debye-Falkenhagen effect. Let's see what Debye-Falkenhagen effect is, and does high frequency conductometry describe Debye-Falkenhagen or not ? The Debye-Falkenhagen theory for the dispersion of electrolyte conductance at high frequency was formulated in 1928. The Debye-Falkenhagen effect, or dispersion of conductance, is the variation of conductance with frequency at high frequencies due to existence of ionic atmosphere with a finite time of relaxation . It is a microscopic phenomena due to interaction of high frequency electric field with ionic atmosphere. The essential postulated of the Debye-Huckel theory is that every ion may be considered to be surrounded by an ionic atmosphere of opposite sign. In the vicinity of any given ion there is a predominance of ions of opposite charge (these are called counter ions). The situation is dynamic rather than static, and on the average more counter ions than like-ions pass by any given ion, and they come and go in all directions. This time averaged, spherical haze of opposite charge is called the ionic atmosphere of the ion. As long as the ionic atmosphere is " stationary ", that is to say, it is not exposed to an applied electrical field or to a shearing force tending to cause movement of the ion with respect to the solvent, it has spherical symmetry when an ionic atmosphere is exposed to an applied electrical field, its symmetry will be disturbed. If a particular kind of ion moves to the right for example, each ion will constantly have to build up its ionic atmosphere to the right while the charge density to the left gradually decays. The rate at which the atmosphere to the right forms and that to the left dies away is expressed in terms of a quantity called the time of relaxation of ionic atmosphere. If the oscillation frequency of an applied field is higher than the reciprocal of the relaxation time, the ion will be virtually satationary and the ionic atmosphere will be symmetrical. Therefore, the retarding force due to relaxation or the asymmetry effect will disappear, or entirely, as the frequency of the oscillations of the current is increased. At sufficiently high frequencies above the reciprocal of relaxation time, the conductance of the solution should be greater than that observed with low frequency. Debye-Falkenhagen have shown that this relaxation time, θ, is given by

$$\theta = \frac{8.85 * 10^{-14}\,(F/cm) * D_0}{Z\Lambda_0^*\,(\Omega^{-1}.cm^2.mole^{-1}) * c(mol/liter) * 10^{-3}} \tag{1}$$

D_0= dielectric constant of mater
A_0^*=equivalent conductivity of the solution
C= concentration of the solution
Z= # of valence

$$\omega = 2\pi f = 1/\theta = \frac{Z\Lambda_0^*}{8.85 * 10^{-11} * D_0} \tag{2}$$

$$f = \frac{Z\Lambda_0^* C}{8.85 * 10^{-11} * D_0 * 2\pi} \tag{3}$$

$$f\lambda = v(\text{speed of light}) \rightarrow \lambda = v/f \tag{4}$$

Substituting (3) in (4) we obtain

$$\lambda = \frac{8.85 * 10^{-11} * D_0 * 2\pi * v}{Z\Lambda_0^* * C} \tag{5}$$

λ*C*Z=constant

$$\text{Where constant} = \frac{8.85 * 10^{-11} * D_0 * 2\pi * v}{\Lambda_0^*} \tag{6}$$

Forman and Crisp in 1946 used a capacitive cell and performed some experiments on several binary electrolytes.The method they employed was to determine the temperature rise of a solution held in a quartz calorimeter within the condenser field of a high frequency oscillator. It was found impossible to make reliable measurements on one particular solution concentration with several different frequencies, owing to variations in the power output of the oscillator when the frequency of oscillation was varied. Therefore, the frequency and power output of the oscillator were held constant and the concentrations of the solution were varied. The temperature rise for constant time of power absorption at a constant input voltage was determined and a family of curves was obtained. The frequency corresponding to the maximum power loss was a function of the concentration of the solution and the valence number of binary electrolyte ions. A convenient empirical relation was evaluated to be

$$\lambda^*C^*Z=\text{constant} \quad (7)$$

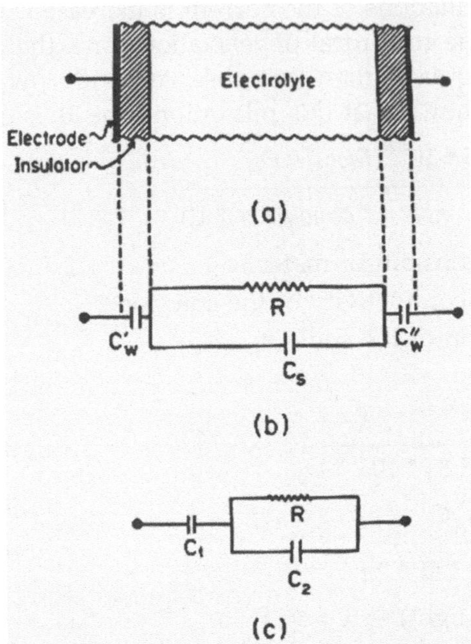

Fig. 1.9: (a) Different layers of a capacitive cell.
(b) Circuit diagram of capacitive cell.
(c)he simplified circuit diagram of the cell.

Which was analogous to eq.(6). Therefore, they concluded that this was an experimental proof of the Debye-Falkenhagen effect. In 1954 Reilley studied this type of cell . He proposed a circuit model for the capacitive cell and from that circuit model for the capacitive cell and from that circuit model he derived an equation analogous to eq.(5). This derivation of Reilley is done Macroscapically. Let's not forget even though the, macroscopically, result of derivation from circuit model is identical to the result of the derivation by ionic atmosphere, microscopically, this result is the equation (7) which is famous to Debye-Falkenhagen effect. Reilley believed that this was a fortuitous concidence, and the experimental proof of Forman etal for the Debye-Falkenhagen effect was under considerable doubt. In 1962 Ermakov and Zagorets measured conductance of several binary electrolytes. In their measurements, they kept the frequency constant and the concentration of the solution was varied. They found maximum conductance at a specific concentration. The relation between concentration and frequency was similar to eq.(6). They concluded that the position of maximum is determined by the relaxation phenomena in solutions. Ermakov's conclusion is in contradiction to Reilley's conclusion. Now the question that needs to be addressed is who is right. In an experimental attempt to verify the Debye-Falkenhagen effect, a capacitor cell was used. Using this cell detailed theoretical and experimental investigation of Debye-Falkenhagen effect an Spectrum Analyzer was studied by us. Consequently, the overall circuit response of this type of cell, which was studied incompletely or misunderstood, was clarified. It was concluded that the Debye-Falkenhagen is a microscopic phenomenon arising from ionic atmosphere relaxation and what is observed in capacitive cell is a macroscopic phenomenon and Reilley's belief is correct that it is fortuitous coincidence that the renspose of capacitive cell is similar to Debye-Falkenhagen relation.

In this section we derive that conductance of a capacitive cell and the tools of trade were described in a paper about application of circuits in chemistry, it is published in 2012 Asian Journal of chemistry. Figure 1.9. (a) demonstrates the layers of a capacitive type of cell. Figure 1.9 (b) shows the circuit corresponding capacitive type of cell. Figure 1.9(c) is the simplified circuit diagram of the cell. The total impedance of the circuit is

$$Z = \frac{1}{j\omega c_1} + \frac{1}{\frac{1}{R} + j\omega c_2} \tag{8}$$

Where ω is the angular frequency of the field. After the necessary transformation, the admittance which is the inverse of the impedance can be obtained

$$Y = \frac{1}{Z} = \frac{(1/R)\omega^2 c_1^2}{(1/R)^2 + \omega^2 (c_1 + c_2)^2} + j\,\frac{\frac{\omega c_1}{R^2} + \omega^3(c_1 c_2^2 + c_2 c_1^2)}{\frac{1}{R^2} + \omega^2 (c_2 + c_1)^2} \tag{9}$$

$$Y=G+jB \tag{10}$$

Where Y is the total admittance of the circuit, G is the conductance term which is the real part of the admittance. The term 1/R in eq. (9) can be substituted by k which is the conductance of the solution, then the total circuit conductance is given by

$$G = \frac{k\omega^2 c_1^2}{k^2 + \omega^2 (c^2 + c^1)} \tag{11}$$

For the cell was used by us in ref.17 $c_1 << c_2$ and $c_2 = 1$ PF, c_1 0.1 PF and k varies between $10^{-3}\ \Omega^{-1}$ to $10^{-6}\ \Omega^{-1}$ and ω varies between 0.5 MHz to 25MHz.

The conductance of the cell G eq.(11) as a function of ω and k is plotted three dimensionally in figure 1.10 for the first time.

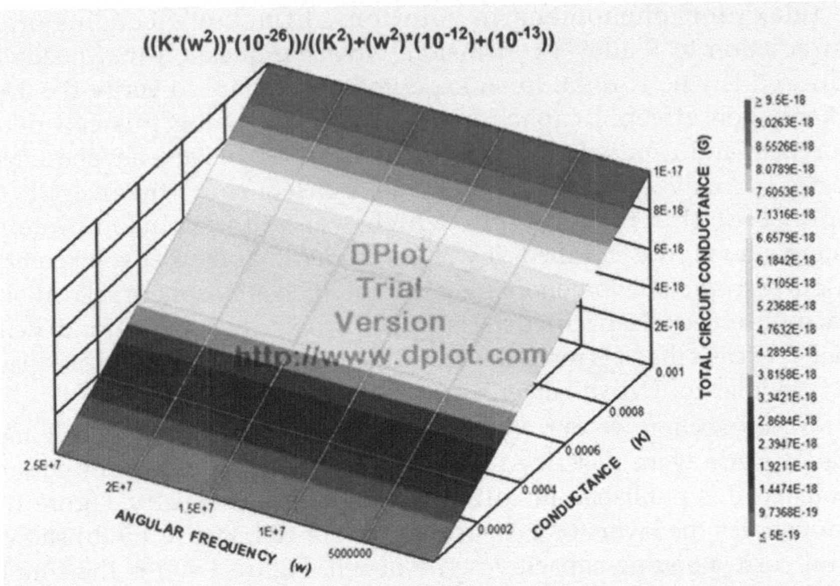

Fig. 1.10: Three dimensional plot of total circuit conductance of the capacitive cell, G, as a function of conductance of electrolyte, k, and angular frequency of the electric signal, ω

Conductance with High Potential Gradient

When Applied potential is of the order of 20 Kv per cm then an ion will move at a speed of 1m/sec and so it will travel several times the thickness of the effective ionic atmosphere in the time of the relaxation. As a result, the moving ion is virtually free from an oppositely charged ion atmosphere, since there is never time for it to be built up to any extent. In these circumstances both asymmetry and electrophoretic effects will be greatly diminished and at sufficiently high voltages should disappear. Under the later conditions the equivalent conductance at any appreciable concentration should be greater that the value at low voltages. The increase in conductance of an electrolyte at high potential gradients was observed by Wien before any theoretical interpretation has been given, and it is consequently known as a *Wien Effect.*

IONIC MOBILITIES

Free electrons and ions in gases

The behaviour of free electrons and ions in pure gases or their admixtures has been studied for most of the 20th century. The properties are important in proportional counters, ionization chambers, drift chambers and in the prediction of the electrical breakdown of gases. In this section it is assumed that the density of charged particles is sufficiently low that the probability of collisions between them are small compared to collisions with atoms or molecules.

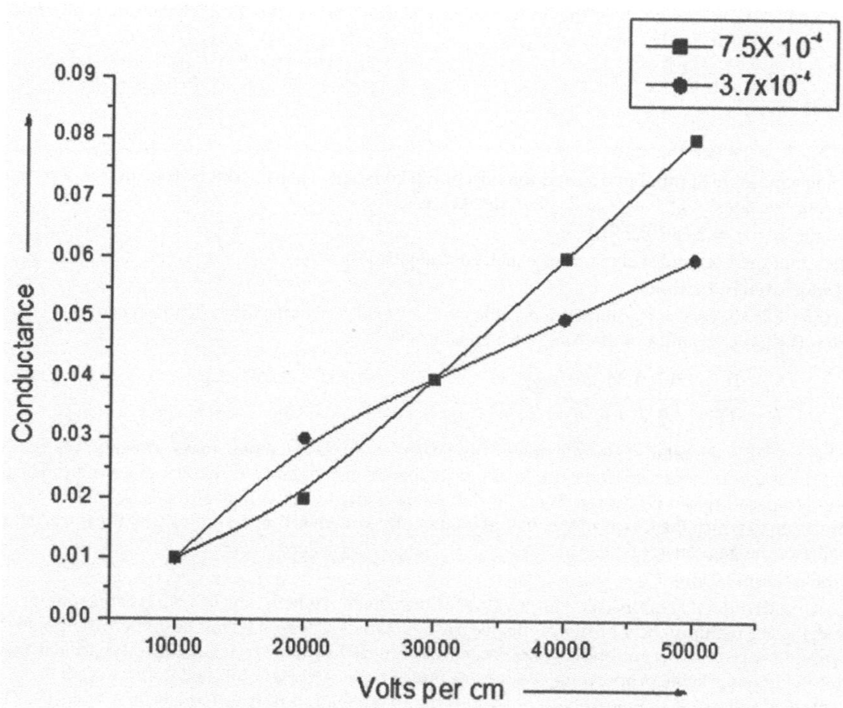

Fig. 1.11: Showing the Wien Effect for the Potassium ferrocyanide at two different concetrations

Ionic mobility

The ionic mobility (μ) is defined as the velocity attained by an ion moving through a gas under unit electric field. A suitable unit is therefore $m^2\ s^{-1}\ volt^{-1}$. In general the mobility is a function of E/N and T, where E is the field strength and N, the Loschmidt constant[2], is the number of molecules m^{-3} at s.t.p. (see Ellis 1978), T is the Temperature. The unit of E/N is the Townsend (Td), 1 Td = 10^{-21} V m^2. Most early work was done using E/p where p is the gas pressure. For measurements around room temperature the effect of T is small but should be taken into account in calculating N.

---

[2] The **Loschmidt constant** or **Loschmidt's number** (symbol: n_0) is the number of particles (atoms or molecules) of an ideal gas in a given volume (the number density). It is usually quoted at standard temperature and pressure, the 2010 CODATA recommended value[1] is 2.686 7805(24)×10^{25} per cubic metre at 0 °C and 1 atm and the 2006 CODATA recommended value[2] was 2.686 7774(47)×10^{25} per cubic metre at 0 °C and 1 atm. It is named after the Austrian physicist Johann Josef Loschmidt, who was the first to estimate the physical size of molecules in 1865.[3] The term "**Loschmidt constant**" is also sometimes used to refer to the Avogadro constant, particularly in German texts.

The Loschmidt constant is given by the relationship:

$$n_0 = \frac{P_0}{k_B T_0}$$

where p_0 is the pressure, k_B is the Boltzmann constant and T_0 is the thermodynamic temperature. It is related to the Avogadro constant, N_A, by:

$$n_0 = \frac{p_0 N_A}{RT_0}$$

where R is the gas constant.

Being a measure of number density, the Loschmidt constant is used to define the amagat, a practical unit of number density for gases and other substances:

1 amagat = n_0 = 2.6867805×10^{25} m^{-3},

such that the Loschmidt constant is exactly 1 amagat.

Modern determinations

In the CODATA set of recommended values for physical constants, the Loschmidt constant is calculated from the gas constant and the Avogadro constant:[4]

$$n_0 = \frac{N_A}{R}\frac{P_0}{T_0} = \frac{A_r(e)\, M_u\, c\alpha^2}{2R_\infty hR}\frac{P_0}{T_0}$$

where $A_r(e)$ is the relative atomic mass of the electron, M_u is the molar mass constant, c is the speed of light, α is the fine structure constant, R_∞ is the Rydberg constant and h is the Planck constant. The pressure and temperature can be chosen freely, and must be quoted with values of the Loschmidt constant. The precision to which the Loschmidt constant is currently known is limited entirely by the uncertainty in the value of the gas constant.

First determinations

Loschmidt did not actually calculate a value for the constant which now bears his name, but it is a simple and logical manipulation of his published results. James Clerk Maxwell described the paper in these terms in a public lecture eight years later: Loschmidt has deduced from the dynamical theory the following remarkable proportion:– As the volume of a gas is to the combined volume of all the molecules contained in it, so is the mean path of a molecule to one-eighth of the diameter of a molecule.To derive this "remarkable proportion", Loschmidt started from Maxwell's own definition of the mean free path:

$$e = \frac{3}{4n_0\,\pi d^2}$$

where n_0 has the same sense as the Loschmidt constant, that is the number of molecules per unit volume, and d is the effective diameter of the molecules (assumed to be spherical). This rearranges to

$$\frac{1}{n_0} = \frac{16}{3}\frac{\pi e d^2}{4}$$

where $1/n_0$ is the volume occupied by each molecule in the gas phase and $\pi e d^2/4$ is the volume of the cylinder made by the molecule in its trajectory between two collisions. However, the true volume of each molecule is given by $\pi d^3/6$, and so $n_0 \pi d^3/6$ is the volume occupied by all the molecules not counting the empty space between them. Loschmidt equated this volume with the volume of the liquified gas. Dividing both sides of the equation by $n_0 \pi d^3/6$ has the effect of introducing a factor of $V_{\text{liquid}}/V_{\text{gas}}$, which Loschmidt called the "condensation coefficient" and which is experimentally measurable. The equation reduces to

$$d = 8\,\frac{V_1}{V_g}\,e$$

relating the diameter of a gas molecule to measurable phenomena.The number density, the constant which now bears Loschmidt's name, can be found by simply substituting the diameter of the molecule into the definition of the mean free path and rearranging:

$$n_0 = \left(\frac{V_g}{V_1}\right)^2 \frac{3}{256\pi e^3}$$

Instead of taking this step, Loschmidt decided to estimate the mean diameter of the molecules in air. This was no minor undertaking, as the condensation coefficient was unknown and had to be estimated–it would be another twelve years before Pictet and Cailletet would liquify nitrogen for the first time. The mean free path was also uncertain. Nevertheless, Loschmidt arrived at a diameter of about one nanometre, of the correct order of magnitude. Loschmidt's estimated data for air give a value of $n_0 = 1.81 \times 10^{24}$ m^{-3}. Eight years later, Maxwell was citing a figure of "about 19 million million million" per cm^3, or 1.9×10^{25} m^{-3}.

The mobility is constant at low values of E/N, the departure from constancy occurring when the ions attain drift velocities comparable with the agitation velocity of the gas molecule. Mobility can be critically dependent on gas purity, especially with the noble gases, because polar impurity molecules tend to cluster around the ion and so reduce its mobility. Many, but not all, early measurements were rendered quite useless by inattention to impurities. The mobility hardly varies with the charge of the ion, a doubly charged ion having practically the same mobility as a singly charged ion of either sign. The reduced mobility μ_0 $m^2 s^{-1} V^{-1}$ is the value at a gas number density of 2.69×10^{25} m^{-3}. The mobility has been shown to vary as (gas number density)$^{-1}$ for pressures from 10 to $6 \times 10^6 Nm^{-2}$. The mobility of positive ions in gas mixtures is given by Blanc's law (Blanc, 1908) $\mu = 1/\Sigma_i f_i/\mu_i$ where f_i is the fractional composition of the ith gas. All values in the table below are for μ_0. A dash indicates that either the particular ion does not exist or has not been examined. Where the mobility is not independent of E/N it is usual to take the mobility corresponding to the limit $E = 0$. Modern techniques have shown that the number of ion species produced is much greater and more complex than was thought earlier. (See McDaniel (1964).) For example xenon ions Xe^{n+} have been identified for $n = 1$ to 13.

Ionic mobilities for ions in their parent gas

$\mu_0/(10^{-4}$ $m^2 s^{-1}$ volt$^{-1})$ at a gas number density of 2.69×10^{25} m^{-3}

Ionic species	H_2	He	N_2	O_2	Ne	Ar	Kr	Xe	CO	CH_4
Atomic positive ion ...	16.0	10.2	3.3	—	4.2	1.53	0.9	0.6	—	—
Molecular positive ion ...	11.3 $(H_+)^3$	20.3	1.8	2.2	6.5	2.3	1.2	0.8	1.6	3.5
Molecular negative ion ...	—	—	—	3.3	—	—	—	—	—	—

Ionic mobilities for ions in various gases

$\mu/(10^{-4}$ $m^2 s^{-1}$ volt$^{-1})$

Ion	Gas								
	He	Ne	Ar	Kr	Xe	H_2	N_2	CO	CO_2	H_2O *vapour*
Li^+	25.6	12	4.99	4.0	3.04	13.3	4.21	2.63		0.725
Na^+	23.4	8.70	3.23	2.34	1.80	15.0	3.40	2.44	1.59	0.715
K^+	22.7	8.0	2.81	1.98	1.44	14	2.7	2.32	1.42	0.705
Rb^+	21.2	7.18	2.40	1.59	1.10	13.4	2.39	2.08	1.20	0.700
Cs^+	19.1	6.50	2.23	1.42	0.99	13.4	2.25	1.98	1.10	0.695

MIGRATION OF IONS

Independent Migration of Ions

A study of equivalent conductance at infinite dilution of a number of electrolytes having an ion in common will bring to light certain regularities as shown in the table, below.

Electrolyte	Equivalent Conductance	Difference between Cations
KCl - NaCl	136.0 - 108.9	21.1
KNO_3 - $NaNO_3$	126.3 - 105.2	21.1
K_2SO_4 - Na_2SO_4	133.6 - 111.9	21.1

For example, are for corresponding sodium and potassium salts at 18 °C. The difference between the conductance of a potassium and a sodium salt of same anion is seen to be independent of the nature.

Similar results have been obtained for other pairs of salts with an anion or cation in common, both in aqueous and non-aqueous solution.

Observations of this kind were first made by Kohlrausch by comparing equivalent conductance of the electrolyte, irrespective of the nature of the other ion with which it is associated in the solution. The value of the equivalent conductance in the infinite dilution may thus be regarded as made up of the sum of the two independent factors one characteristics of each ion; this result is known as Kohlrausch's Law of Independent migration of ions. The Law cam be mathematically expressed below in the equation

$$\Lambda_0 = \lambda^0_+ + \lambda^0_-$$

Where λ^0_+ and λ^0_- are known as the ion conductance of cation, and anion, respectively, at infinite dilution. The ion conductance is a definite constant for each ion, in a given solvent its value, depending only on the temperature.

It will be seen later that the ion conductance at infinite dilution are related to the speeds with which the ions move under the influence of an applied potential gradient.

Although it is possible to derive high values from the equivalent conductances of a number of electrolytes by a method of trial and error a much more satisfactory procedure is based on the use of accurate transference number of data; these transference numbers are determined by the relative speeds of the ions present in the electrolyte and hence are related to the relative ion conductances at infinite dilute solutions. The determination of transference number has been discussed.

Relationship between generalised relative ionic mobility and limiting equivalent conductivity

First of all, it should be noted that the relative mobility of an ion, u, required for calculating liquid junction potentials (as listed in the above tables of mobilities and required in *JPCalc* calculations) represents the generalised (or absolute) mobility of an ion relative to K^+. For example, if u_X, is the relative mobility for ion X, with respect to K^+, it will be given by:

$$u_X = u^*_X / u^*_K$$

where u^*_X and u^*_K represent the absolute values of the generalised mobilities of ions X and K^+ respectively. The units of the relative mobility for ion X, u_X, are (of course) dimensionless.

The following discussion indicates how the generalised mobilities of ions are in turn related to their limiting equivalent conductivities.

Since the velocity of an ion in solution, v, is related to the generalised (absolute) mobility, u*, and the generalised force, F_x, acting on it, then:

$$v = u^* F_x$$

The force may be in Newtons/mole or Newtons, depending on whether it is the force acting on a mole of ions or on a single ion (and whichever is chosen will affect the units of u*). The above generalised mobility is what is required for electrodiffusion flux equations, and would normally be that required for a force acting on a mole of ions.

In contrast, electrochemists, when measuring conductivity, use another definition of mobility, which may be defined as u′, the electrical mobility, sometimes also called the conventional mobility (Bockris & Reddy, 1973; pp. 369-373), since they measure the mobility as the velocity/ electric field, E (e.g., in volts/m) as:

$$v = u' E$$

Since the actual force is zFE, we also have v = u*zFE, where z is the magnitude of the valency and F is the Faraday. Hence,

$$u^* = u'/zF$$

We wish to know the relationship between generalised (absolute) mobility and the limiting equivalent conductivity, L^0 (the conductivity of an electrolyte solution per equivalent, in the limit as the concentration goes to zero). Now L^0 makes allowance for the additional charge of polyvalent ions, so that

$$u' = L^0 /F$$

[cp. Eqs. 4.156 - 4.160 in Bockris & Reddy, 1973 (p.373) for equivalent conductivity (L) and molar conductivity (L_m), where $L = L_m/z$; N.B. error in sign of the anion subscript in Eq. 4.16)]. Hence, from the two equations above, the generalised mobility, u*, and L^0 will be related by:

$$u^* = L^0/(zF^2)$$

[cf. the equation for the generalized mobility, u, for a single ion (e.g., Eq. A4 in Sugiharto *et al.*, 2008), rather than for a mole of ions, u*, which is given by $u = NL^0/(zF^2)$, where N is Avagadro's number]. Hence, the relative mobility of ion X of valency z is given by:

$$u_X = [L^0_X/z]/L^0_K$$

since, for K^+, z = 1 and both limiting equivalent conductivities were measured at the same temperature.

For a monovalent ion Y, its relative mobility will simply be given by:

$$u_Y = L^0_Y / L^0_K$$

where L^0_Y is the limiting equivalent conductivity of Y at the same temperature as for L^0_K, normally 25 °C.

For reference, L^0_K = 73.50 S.cm^2.equiv^{-1} at 25 °C (Robinson & Stokes, 1965).

Molar Conductivity

Molar conductivity is defined as the conductivity of an electrolyte solution divided by the molar concentration of the electrolyte, and so measures the efficiency with which a given electrolyte conducts electricity in solution. Its units are siemens per meter per molarity, or siemens meter-squared per mole. The usual symbol is a capital lambda, Λ, or Λ_m.

Description

From its definition, the molar conductivity is given by:

$$\Lambda_m = \frac{\kappa}{c}$$

where:

- κ is the measured conductivity
- c is the electrolyte concentration.

Two cases should be distinguished: strong electrolytes and weak electrolytes.

For strong electrolytes, such as salts, strong acids and strong bases, the molar conductivity depends only *weakly* on concentration. Based on experimental data Friedrich Kohlrausch (around the year 1900) proposed the non-linear law for strong electrolytes:

$$\Lambda_m = \Lambda^o_m - K\sqrt{c}$$

where

- Λ^o_m is the molar conductivity at infinite dilution (or *limiting molar conductivity*)
- K is the Kohlrausch coefficient, which depends mainly on the stoichiometry of the specific salt in solution.

This law is valid for low electrolyte concentrations only; it fits into the Debye-Hückel-Onsager equation:

For weak electrolytes (i.e. incompletely dissociated electrolytes), however, the molar conductivity *strongly* depends on concentration: The more dilute a solution, the greater its *molar* conductivity, due to increased ionic dissociation. (This, for example, is the case of SDS-coated proteins in the stacking gel of an SDS-PAGE.) The limiting molar conductivity can be decomposed into contributions from the different ions (Kohlrausch's law of independent migration of ions):

$$\Lambda^o_m = \Sigma_i \nu_i \lambda_i$$

where:

- λ_i is the molar ionic conductivity of ion *i*.
- ν_i is the number of ions *i* in the formula unit of the electrolyte (e.g. 2 and 1 for Na^+ and SO_4^{2-} in Na_2SO_4)

Applications

Ostwald's law of dilution, which gives the dissociation constant of a weak electrolyte as a function of concentration, can be written in terms of molar conductivity. Thus, the pKa values of acids can be calculated by measuring the molar conductivity and extrapolating into zero concentration. Namely, $pK_a = p(K/(1 \text{ mol dm}^{-3}))$ at the zero-concentration limit, where K is the dissociation constant from Ostwald's law.

CONDUCTIVITY APPLICATION

Conductivity measurement responds to all ionic contaminants in a sample, whether they are minerals or dissolved gases such as carbon dioxide (in the form of carbonic acid, bicarbonate or carbonate). Contaminants come from many sources. They can be deionizer regenerant chemicals or other materials leaching from inadequately rinsed or fouled resins, air (including CO) not completely removed by deaerators, carry-over from drum boilers or leaks from condensers or other heat exchangers. Conductivity also responds to the treatment chemicals intentionally added. Specific (direct) conductivity measurement in high pressure boiler cycles is typically dominated by treatment chemicals such as ammonia, phosphates, amines, etc. at ppm concentrations which should be well above the ppb concentrations of any contaminants. Therefore, specific conductivity, often with corroboration by pH, is generally used to monitor and control treatment chemical concentrations.

Cation (acid) conductivity is the technique of continuously conditioning the sample by passing it through a hydrogen form cation exchange cartridge. It enhances the sensitivity to contaminants by two means:

- Ammonia or amines that are intentionally present at ppm levels are removed. This eliminates their high conductivity. The lower ppb concentrations and conductivity of contaminants can then be "seen" by the measurement.
- Contaminant corrosive salts are converted to their respective acids which are typically three times as conductive as the original salt because of the highly conductive hydrogen ion. This simplicity and detection sensitivity have made cation conductivity the most widely used measure of contamination in the cycle. The upper left of figure 1.12 illustrates the specific conductivity sample containing the ammonia and traces of sodium chloride and bicarbonate as typical contaminants. It has a relatively high conductivity due to the amount of ammonia present, represented by the left bar of figure 1.13. The conductivity due to sodium

chloride (or other contaminants) is almost insignificant. The sample passes through the cation exchanger and the resin "R" retains the ammonia, sodium and any other cations, but always with an excess of resin in the hydrogen form near the outlet. The exiting sample consists of very dilute hydrochloric, carbonic (and other) acids and yields the cation conductivity value represented by the middle bar in figure 1.13. A comparison of the two bars shows the enhanced sensitivity for contaminant detection noted above. Although cation conductivity is widely applied, there has been little standardization of the cation exchange cartridge and this can add many variables to the measurement. In particular, the sample flow velocity through the cartridge must be high enough to promote turbulent flow and good exchange. If the exchange is not complete, the measurement can be ambiguous. Reasonable guidelines for the technique have been defined in an ASTM standard.

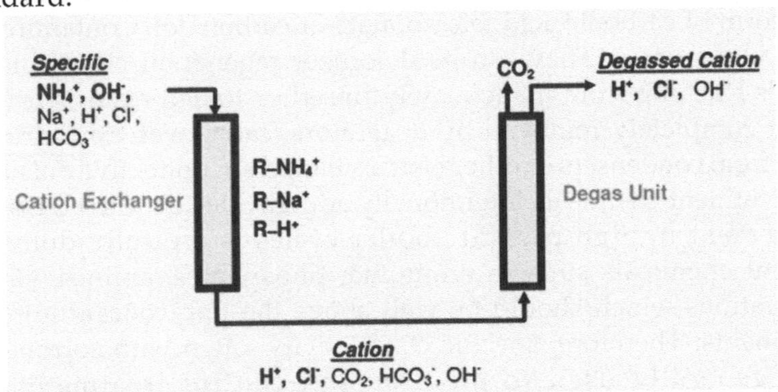

Fig. 1.12: Specific, Cation and Degassed Cation Conductivity Measurements

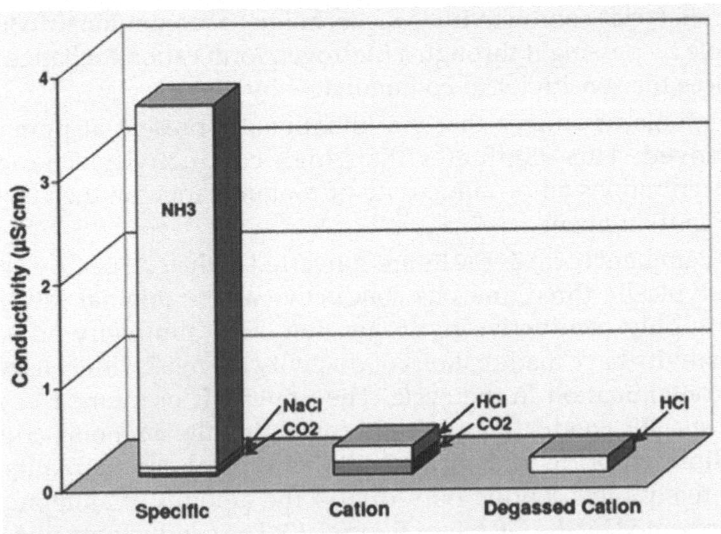

Fig. 1.13: Typical Specific, Cation and Degassed Cation Conductivity Response

Degassed cation conductivity is useful in plants where carbon dioxide is present in the sample and cation conductivity limits are especially low. A degas unit allows measurement of cation conductivity with the carbon dioxide removed as shown on the right side of figure 1.12. Carbon dioxide is acknowledged to be far less corrosive than other contaminants. Degassing can be done with a "reboiler" which heats the sample to boiling to drive off the carbon dioxide, with a sparging scheme which flows pure nitrogen gas across a thin film of the sample or with a membrane contactor that pulls the carbon dioxide through a membrane. Recent studies have been made on the performance of "reboilers" that showed good results. One evaluation compared performance of reboiler, nitrogen sparger, and membrane systems for carbon dioxide removal and they all performed reasonably well. Where a reboiler is used and the sample is measured near 100 °C, extremely accurate temperature compensation is required. Some systems re-cool the sample to near 25 °C for this reason. Although not a precise measurement, degassed cation conductivity does serve a very useful purpose.

Temperature Compensation

Temperature Compensation is required because conductivity is greatly influenced by temperature. All dissolved ions become more mobile and conductive at higher temperatures largely because water becomes less viscous. The increase is at a rate of approximately 2% of conductivity value per °C for most ions. In addition, in pure waters the increasing ionization of the water itself with temperature is significant—there are more hydrogen and hydroxide ions to conduct at higher temperatures. The combination of these two effects can produce temperature coefficients as high as 5 to 7% of conductivity value per °C. Because of this, guidelines and specifications reference conductivity values to 25 °C which dictates sample temperature control and/or compensation. The relationship is shown in figure 1.14, for neutral salt contaminants exemplified by sodium chloride. Conductivity increases with increasing amounts of sodium chloride. However, the temperature coefficient (slope) of the curves increases with decreasing sodium chloride concentration. Also, it can be seen that at conductivity values above 5 µS/cm, the ionization of the water is insignificant and all curves above that are parallel at about 2% per °C. Below that, the non-linearity with both concentration and temperature requires specialized temperature compensation. It should be noted that very few laboratory instruments have more than rudimentary 2% per °C temperature compensation that is unsuitable for low conductivity samples.

High purity water compensation has traditionally been recognized as consisting of two separate components: the properties of the pure water and the properties of the impurities in the water. This is appropriate for neutral salt impurities since the ionization of water changes only with temperature, not with dilute salt concentration. Similarly, the mobility of salt ions varies with temperature, independent of the ionization of water.

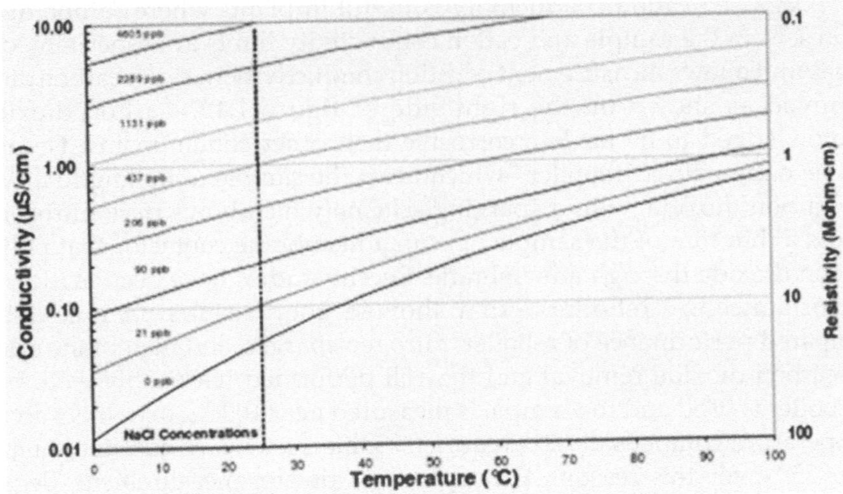

Fig. 1.14: Temperature Effects on Pure Water with Neutral Salt Contamination

A quick visualization of these effects is given by equations 1 and 2 which take place independently of each other in very dilute solutions. The combination of these independent effects was quantified decades ago by General Electric for use with nuclear boiling water reactor (BWR) measurements where no treatment chemicals were added. It must be noted that this compensation is appropriate only for BWR samples and for polished makeup water where low levels of neutral salts are the anticipated contaminants.

Conventional pure water sample

$$H_2O \leftrightarrow H^+ + OH^- \quad (1)$$

$$NaCl \rightarrow Na^+ + Cl^- \quad (2)$$

Of greatest importance is the temperature compensation accuracy of cation conductivity which has become more critical with the wide acceptance of equilibrium phosphate and oxygenated treatment chemistries. The benefits of both of these treatments depend heavily on maintaining very low cation conductivity levels. The challenge of pure water temperature compensation is to provide conductivity readout referenced to 25 °C regardless of the actual sample temperature. This can eliminate the cost of expensive and occasionally unreliable secondary sample cooling equipment and can preserve the measurement if a chiller fails.

Cation conductivity sample

$$H_2O \leftrightarrow H^+ + OH^- \quad (3)$$

$$HCl \rightarrow H^+ + Cl^- \quad (4)$$

A cation conductivity sample behaves differently from makeup water. It has had ammonia and/or amines removed and any salts converted to acids as noted previously. The ionization of acids and water cannot be neatly separated for compensation since they have the hydrogen ion in common. See equations 3 and 4. The additional hydrogen ions from the acid suppress the hydroxide ion of water. This interaction between water and acid ionization and its variation with temperature require an entirely different approach to temperature compensation. The relationship for compensation is much more complex and has pushed the limits of mathematical modeling for a number of years. The standard is to be able to compensate trace hydrochloric acid in pure water across the ranges of concentration and temperature to obtain the value at 25 °C. Hydrochloric acid is representative of cation conductivity samples because the hydrogen ion has the dominant concentration and the dominant ionic conductance. The anion is of secondary importance. Thus sulfuric, formic, acetic, carbonic and other acids would have essentially the same conductivity temperature characteristics. The first cation conductivity temperature compensation was developed using the best curve matching that could be developed at that time. In the intervening years, a number of other attempts have been made at providing this compensation but most have failed to achieve reasonable accuracy. A very close curve match to hydrochloric acid in pure water across the full ranges of temperature and concentration was finally developed at Thornton. A comparison of the compensation of several instrument algorithms, with hydrochloric acid data as the reference, is given in figure 1.15. A vast improvement was achieved, indicated by the results with Instrument E. It is apparent that temperature compensation is by far the greatest source of error in cation conductivity measurement with most instruments installed in U.S. power plants today. Temperature compensation algorithms have also been developed for specific conductivity samples dominated by ammonia or amines, and various instruments were evaluated. Similar wide variations in performance were again observed.

While temperature compensation with accurate algorithms can eliminate substantial errors in the measurement, it should be stressed that sample temperature is still important. Since the sample first passes through a cation exchange cartridge, the consistent performance of that exchange is critical. The flow rate and temperature ranges of the sample and the dimensions of the cartridge, as well as the type of resin can all influence cation conductivity results. Note that the cation conductivity temperature compensation algorithm is also appropriate for degassed cation conductivity since carbonic is just one more of the acids that may be present and all have similar temperature effects.

pH determination from Conductivity

The correlation of pH and conductivity of ammonia has been used for decades to compare cycle chemistry measurements. For a given ammonia concentration in water there is a definite pH and conductivity value which can be calculated from dissociation and conductance data. Because conductivity measurement is typically more reliable than high purity pH measurement, specific conductivity is often used as the primary variable to control ammonia feed although pH is also measured. There are two reasons for conductivity's higher reliability and accuracy:

1. Conductivity is linear with concentration whereas pH is logarithmic. pH therefore has less resolution. For example, a change of only 0.3 pH represents a two-fold (100%) change in both concentration and conductivity in cycle chemistry ranges.
2. pH reference electrode junction potential is notoriously less stable in low conductivity samples and that instability is frequently greater than ± 0.1 pH, depending on the electrode system used.

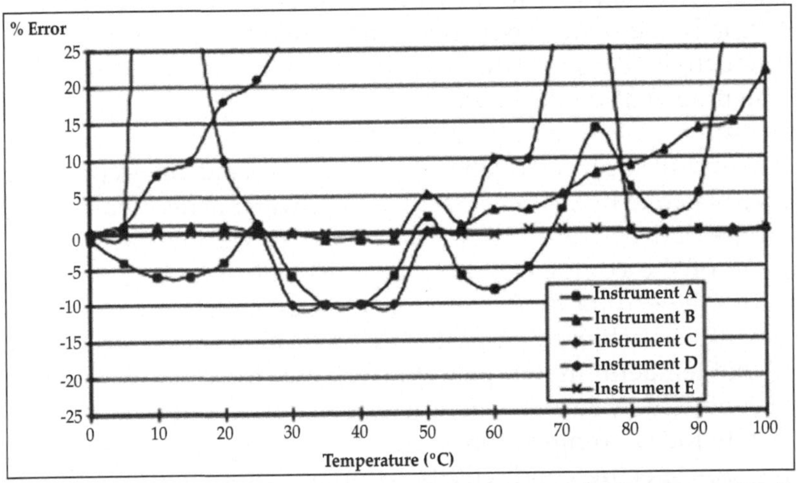

Fig. 1.15: Cation Conductivity Temperature Compensation Performance at 0.1 μS/cm

Inherent in the simple correlation above is the assumption that there is nothing else present but ammonia and water. Any traces of carbon dioxide and/or mineral contaminants must be negligible. Under many operating conditions, this is a reasonable assumption. However, as these trace contaminants grow in concentration during plant startup, unusual conditions, or upsets, their effects must be accommodated. Refinement of the conductivity and pH correlation has been accomplished in various ways by several organizations and was discussed previously. Specific conductivity is the primary influence while cation conductivity is used to trim for the presence of small amounts of mineral and/or carbon dioxide contamination. These algorithms still assume that the primary specific conductivity (and pH) influence is ammonia or amines and that the contaminants have lower concentrations. Generally, the pH must be within 7.5-10.5 and specific conductivity must be greater than cation conductivity, especially at low conductivity levels. Specific conductivity is dominated by hydroxide and ammonium (or amine cation) which are at the highest concentrations.

Hydroxide ion conductivity is 3 times that of other ions (except hydrogen, which is suppressed at the high sample pH). Cation conductivity is dominated by the hydrogen ion which is about 7 times as conductive as other ions (except hydroxide, which has a suppressed concentration at the low pH in the sample at this point) so it makes little difference just what the mix of anions is among chlorides, bicarbonates, sulphates, or others. pH calculation algorithms provide very accurate determinations when the sample composition complies with the conditions above. This excellent performance is acknowledged by its use in plants around the world, especially in Europe. However, it is also important to be aware of the errors that can be produced when operation goes well outside normal operating conditions. To eliminate this risk, multi-channel, multi-parameter instrumentation can measure specific and cation conductivities, compute pH from them, and simultaneously measure from a pH electrode as shown in figure 1.16. This kind of instrumentation covers both situations: it provides highly accurate calculated pH measurement under normal conditions and can give a warning based on a pH electrode measurement when conditions become abnormal.

The multi-parameter instrument can also display and alarm on the difference between the calculated and the measured pH values. This kind of diagnostic can identify the need for pH electrode maintenance or calibration, or warn of conditions outside the range for accurate pH calculation as well as conditions exceeding cycle chemistry guidelines. The availability of both calculated and electrode pH measurements allows more accurate calibration of the electrode measurement when operation is within the conditions for accurate computation of pH. The electrode system should previously have been calibrated at two points using buffer solutions to set up the span response. The final one-point trim calibration eliminates variations in electrode diaphragm/junction potential in buffer solutions and can easily be done more frequently. It greatly enhances the accuracy, reliability and diagnostic capability of the electrode measurement, as well as saving considerable time.

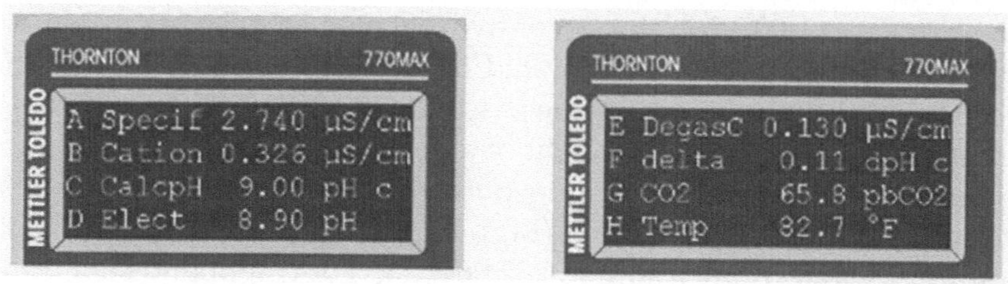

Fig. 1.16: Two pages of the display of a multi-parameter instrument configured with sensors for Specific, Cation and Degassed Cation Conductivity plus a direct pH electrode

There are many different applications of conductivity in electrochemistry which needs to get find out by the research people.

2

Laws of Electrochemistry

INTRODUCTION

This chapter discusses about the Laws of electrochemistry and their explanation.

Statement of Laws

Several versions of the laws can be found in textbooks and the scientific pieces of literature. The most common statements resemble the following:

- **Faraday's 1st Law of Electrolysis** - "The mass of a substance altered at an electrode during electrolysis is directly proportional to the quantity of electricity transferred at that electrode. Quantity of electricity refers to the quantity of electrical charge, typically measured in coulomb."
- **Faraday's 2nd Law of Electrolysis** - "For a given quantity of D.C electricity (electric charge), the mass of an elemental material altered at an electrode is directly proportional to the element's equivalent weight". The equivalent weight of a substance is equal to its molar mass divided by the change in oxidation state it undergoes upon electrolysis (often equal to its charge or valence). This will be explained further in the next paragraph.

For an element the equivalent weight is the quantity that combines with or replaces 1.00797 grams (g) of hydrogen or 7.9997 g of oxygen; or, the weight of an element that is liberated in an electrolysis (chemical reaction caused by an electric current) by the passage of $9.64853399(24) \times 10^4$ coulombs of electricity. The equivalent weight of an element is its gram atomic weight divided by its valence (combining power). Some equivalent weights are: silver (Ag), 107.868 g; magnesium (Mg), 24.312/2 g; aluminum (Al), 26.9815/3 g; sulfur (S, in forming a sulfide), 32.064/2 g. For compounds that function as oxidizing or reducing agents (compounds that act as acceptors or donors of electrons), the equivalent weight is the gram molecular weight divided by the number of electrons lost or gained by each molecule; e.g., potassium permanganate ($KMnO_4$) in acid solution, 158.038/5 g; potassium dichromate ($K_2Cr_2O_7$), 294.192/6 g; and sodium thiosulfate ($Na_2S_2O_3 \cdot 5H_2O$), 248.1828/1 g.

For all oxidizing and reducing agents (elements or compounds) the equivalent weight is the weight of the substance that is associated with the loss or gain of 6.023×10^{23} electrons. The equivalent weight of an acid or base for neutralization reactions or of any other compound that acts by double decomposition is the quantity of the compound that will furnish or react with or be equivalent to 1.00797 g of hydrogen ion or 17.0074 g of hydroxide ion; e.g., hydrochloric acid (HCl), 36.461 g; sulfuric acid (H_2SO_4), 98.078/2 g; sodium hydroxide (NaOH), 40 g; sodium carbonate (Na_2CO_3), 105.9892/ 2 g. The equivalent weight of a substance may vary with the type of reaction it undergoes. Thus, potassium permanganate reacting by double decomposition has an equivalent weight equal to its gram molecular weight, 158.038/1 g; as an oxidizing agent under different circumstances it may be reduced to the manganate ion (MnO_4^{2-}), to manganese dioxide (MnO_2), or to the manganous ion (Mn^{2+}), with the equivalent weights of 158.038/1 g, 158.038/3 g, and 158.038/5 g, respectively. The number of equivalent weights of any substance dissolved in one litre of solution is called the normality of that solution.

Mathematical Form

Faraday's laws can be summarized by

$$m = \left(\frac{Q}{F}\right)\left(\frac{M}{z}\right)$$

where:

- m is the mass of the substance liberated at an electrode in grams
- Q is the total electric charge passed through the substance
- $F = 96485$ C mol^{-1} is the Faraday constant
- M is the molar mass of the substance
- z is the valency number of ions of the substance (electrons transferred per ion).

Note that M/z is the same as the equivalent weight of the substance altered.

For Faraday's first law, M, F, and z are constants, so that the larger the value of Q the larger m will be.

For Faraday's second law, Q, F, and z are constants, so that the larger the value of M/z (equivalent weight) the larger m will be.

In the simple case of constant-current electrolysis, $Q = It$ leading to

$$m = \left(\frac{It}{F}\right)\left(\frac{M}{z}\right)$$

and then to

$$n = \left(\frac{It}{F}\right)\left(\frac{1}{z}\right)$$

where:

- n is the amount of substance ("number of moles") liberated: $n = m/M$
- t is the total time the constant current was applied.

In the more complicated case of a variable electrical current, the total charge Q is the electric current $I(\tau)$ integrated over time τ:

$$Q = \int_0^t I(\tau)\, d\tau$$

Here t is the *total* electrolysis time.

Experimental explanation of Faradays Law

The electrochemical cell with zinc and copper electrodes had an overall potential difference that was positive (+1.10 volts), so the spontaneous chemical reactions produced an electric current. Such a cell is called a *voltaic cell*. In contrast, *electrolytic cells* use an externally generated electrical current to produce a chemical reaction that would not otherwise take place.

An instance of such electrolysis is the decomposition of water to elemental hydrogen and oxygen. The pertinent half reactions are given in table 2.1.

Table 2.1: Electrolysis of Water

Half-Reaction	Type	Electrode	Potential
$4\,H_2O\,(l) + 4\,e^- \rightarrow 2\,H_2\,(g) + 4\,OH^-\,(aq)$	Reduction	Cathode	-0.83 volt
$2\,H_2O\,(l) \rightarrow O_2\,(g) + 4\,H^+\,(aq) + 4\,e^-$	Oxidation	Anode	-0.40 volt

The overall reaction for the electrolysis of water is given by adding the two half reactions to obtain $2\,H_2O\,(l) \rightarrow 2\,H_2\,(g) + O_2\,(g)$ with an overall potential of –1.23 volts. With a negative potential, it requires an externally imposed electrical current to decompose water by the reaction shown. Figure 1 shows two platinum electrodes in water containing a little salt or acid so that the solution can conduct electricity.

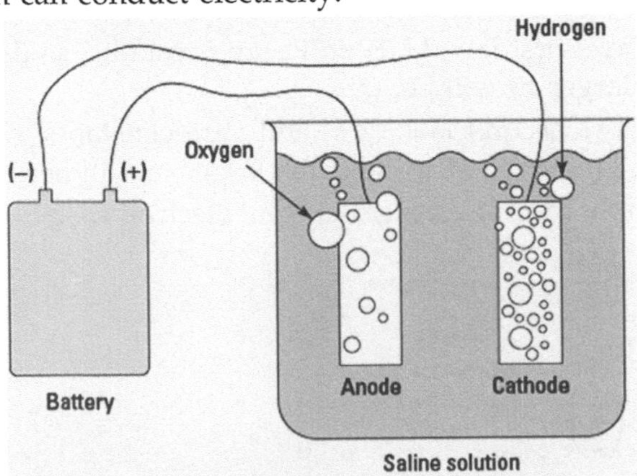

Fig. 2.1: Showing the Electrolysis of Water

The reduction at the cathode yields H_2 gas, and the oxidation at the anode yields O_2 gas. Notice that the figure shows that the volume of hydrogen is twice the volume of oxygen—look at the bubbles. The molar coefficients in the decomposition reaction imply 2 volumes of H_2 gas for each 1 volume of O_2 gas.

Electrolysis is used to decompose many compounds into their constituent elements. You have seen this process with water. Another example is the electrolysis of molten sodium chloride to yield molten sodium metal and chlorine gas: $2NaCl(l) \rightarrow 2\,Na(l) + Cl_2\,(g)$

Chemists throughout the nineteenth century discovered new elements from the electrolytic decomposition of many compounds.

The quantitative laws of electrochemistry were discovered by Michael Faraday of England. His 1834 paper on electrolysis introduced many of the terms that you have seen throughout this book, including *ion, cation, anion, electrode, cathode, anode,* and *electrolyte*. He found that the mass of a substance produced by a redox reaction at an electrode is proportional to the quantity of electrical charge that has passed through the electrochemical cell. For elements with different oxidation numbers, the same quantity of electricity produces fewer moles of the element with the higher oxidation number.

The basic unit of electrical charge used by chemists is appropriately called a faraday, which is defined as the charge on one mole of electrons (6×10^{23} electrons). Incidentally, note that chemists have extended the original definition of the mole as a unit of mass to a corresponding number (Avogadro's number) of particles. Use the electrolysis of molten sodium chloride to see the relationship between faradays of electricity and moles of decomposition products.

The reduction half reaction is

$Na^+\,(l) + e^- \rightarrow Na\,(l)$

so to produce 1 mole of sodium metal requires 1 mole of electrons, so 1 faraday of charge must pass through the cell.

The oxidation half reaction is

$2\,Cl^-\,(l) \rightarrow Cl_2\,(g) + 2\,e^-$

and to produce 1 mole of chlorine gas, 2 faradays of electric charge must pass through the apparatus. Notice how the number of electrons in redox reactions determines the quantity of electricity needed for the reaction.

These half reactions sum to the overall reaction in the electrolytic cell:

$2\,Na^+\,(l) + 2\,Cl^-\,(l) \rightarrow 2\,Na\,(l) + Cl_2\,(g)$

The passage of 2 faradays of charge yields 2 moles of sodium metal and 1 mole of chlorine gas.

The first of Faraday's laws states that the mass of substance produced is proportional to the quantity of electricity. To apply this law to the NaCl example, where 1 mole of Cl_2 was produced by 2 faradays, means that to produce 10 moles of Cl_2 requires the passage of 20 faradays through the apparatus.

The second of Faraday's laws states that a given quantity of electricity produces fewer moles of substances with higher oxidation numbers. Compare the reduction of sodium and calcium ions:

$Na^+ + e^- \rightarrow Na$ (1 mole of electrons)

$Ca^{2+} + 2e^- \rightarrow$ (2 moles of electrons)

It requires twice as much electricity to produce 1 mole of calcium metal as 1 mole of sodium metal.

The electrolytic decomposition of sodium chloride and calcium oxide appear similar:

$2\,NaCl\,(l) \rightarrow 2\,Na\,(l) + Cl_2\,(g)$

$2\,CaO\,(l) \rightarrow 2\,Ca\,(l) + O_2\,(g)$

but the NaCl decomposition requires the transfer of only half as many electrons as does the CaO decomposition. For the NaCl electrolysis, it was previously calculated that the passage of 20 faradays of electric charge produced 20 moles of sodium metal and 10 moles of chlorine gas. The same amount of electric charge passing through the CaO cell yields only 10 moles of calcium metal and 5 moles of oxygen gas.

The reduction half reaction with balanced coefficients:

$2\,Ca^{2+}\,(l) + 2\,e^- \rightarrow Ca\,(l)$

The oxidation half reaction with balanced coefficients:

$2\,O^{2-}\,(l) \rightarrow O_2\,(g) + 2\,e^-$

ARRHENIUS EQUATION

The Arrhenius equation is a formula for the temperature dependence of reaction rates. The equation was proposed by Svante Arrhenius in 1889, based on the work of Dutch chemist Jacobus Henricus van 't Hoff who had noted in 1884 that Van 't Hoff's equation for the temperature dependence of equilibrium constants suggests such a formula for the rates of both forward and reverse reactions. Arrhenius provided a physical justification and interpretation for the formula. Currently, it is best seen as an empirical relationship. It can be used to model the temperature variation of diffusion coefficients, population of crystal vacancies, creep rates, and many other thermally-induced processes/reactions. The Eyring equation, developed in 1935, also expresses the relationship between rate and energy.

A historically useful generalization supported by Arrhenius' equation is that, for many common chemical reactions at room temperature, the reaction rate doubles for every 10 degree Celsius increase in temperature.

Equation

Arrhenius' equation gives the dependence of the rate constant *k* of a chemical reaction on the absolute temperature *T* (in kelvin), where *A* is the pre-exponential factor (or simply the *prefactor*), E_a is the activation energy, and *R* is the universal gas constant:

$$k = Ae^{-Ea/(RT)}$$

Alternatively, the equation may be expressed as

$$k = Ae^{-Ea/(kBT)}$$

The only difference is the energy units of E_a: the former form uses energy per mole, which is common in chemistry, while the latter form uses energy per molecule directly, which is common in physics. The different units are accounted for in using either *R* = gas constant or the Boltzmann constant k_B as the multiplier of temperature *T*.

The units of the pre-exponential factor *A* are identical to those of the rate constant and will vary depending on the order of the reaction. If the reaction is first order it has the units s^{-1}, and for that reason it is often called the *frequency factor* or *attempt frequency* of the reaction. Most simply, *k* is the number of collisions that result in a reaction per second, *A* is the total number of collisions (leading to a reaction or not) per second and $e^{-Ea/(RT)}$ is the probability that any given collision will result in a reaction. It can be seen that either increasing the temperature or decreasing the activation energy (for example through the use of catalysts) will result in an increase in rate of reaction.Given the small temperature range kinetic studies occur in, it is reasonable to approximate the activation energy as being independent of the temperature. Similarly, under a wide range of practical conditions, the weak temperature dependence of the pre-exponential factor is negligible compared to the temperature dependence of the exp $(-E_a/RT)$ factor; except in the case of "barrierless" diffusion-limited reactions, in which case the pre-exponential factor is dominant and is directly observable.

Arrhenius Equation

Taking the natural logarithm of Arrhenius' equation yields:

$$\text{In}\,(k) = \frac{-E_a}{R}\frac{1}{T} + \text{In}\,(A)$$

This has the same form as an equation for a straight line:

$$y = mx + c$$

So, when a reaction has a rate constant that obeys Arrhenius' equation, a plot of ln(*k*) versus T^{-1} gives a straight line, whose gradient and intercept can be used to determine E_a and *A* . This procedure has become so common in experimental chemical kinetics that practitioners have taken to using it to *define* the activation energy for a reaction. That is the activation energy is defined to be (-*R*) times the slope of a plot of ln(*k*) vs. (1/*T*)

$$E_a = -R\left[\frac{\partial \ln k}{\partial (1/T)}\right]_P$$

Modified Arrhenius' equation

The modified Arrhenius' equation makes explicit the temperature dependence of the pre-exponential factor. The modified equation is usually of the form

$k = A\,(T/T_0)^n e\,{-Ea/(RT)}$

where T_0 is a reference temperature and allows n to be a unitless power. Clearly the original Arrhenius expression above corresponds to $n = 0$. Fitted rate constants typically lie in the range $-1<n<1$. Theoretical analyses yield various predictions for n. It has been pointed out that *"it is not feasible to establish, on the basis of temperature studies of the rate constant, whether the predicted* $T^{1/2}$ *dependence of the pre-exponential factor is observed experimentally."* However, if additional evidence is available, from theory and/or from experiment (such as density dependence), there is no obstacle to incisive tests of the Arrhenius law.

Another common modification is the stretched exponential form:

$$k = A \exp\left[-\left(\frac{E_a}{RT}\right)^{\beta}\right]$$

where β is a unitless number of order 1. This is typically regarded as a fudge factor to make the model fit the data, but can have theoretical meaning, for example showing the presence of a range of activation energies or in special cases like the Mott variable range hopping.

Theoretical interpretation of the equation

Arrhenius' Concept of Activation Energy

Arrhenius argued that for reactants to transform into products, they must first acquire a minimum amount of energy, called the activation energy E_a. At an absolute temperature T, the fraction of molecules that have a kinetic energy greater than E_a can be calculated from statistical mechanics. The concept of *activation energy* explains the exponential nature of the relationship, and in one way or another, it is present in all kinetic theories.The calculations for reaction rate constants involve an energy averaging over a Maxwell–Boltzmann distribution with E_a as lower bound and so are often of the type of incomplete gamma functions, which turn out to be proportional to $e^{\frac{-E_a}{RT}}$.

Collision Theory

One example comes from the "collision theory" of chemical reactions, developed by Max Trautz and William Lewis in the years 1916-18. In this theory, molecules are supposed to react if they collide with a relative kinetic energy along their lines-of-center that exceeds E_a. This leads to an expression very similar to the Arrhenius equation.

Transition state Theory

Another Arrhenius-like expression appears in the "transition state theory" of chemical reactions, formulated by Wigner, Eyring, Polanyi and Evans in the 1930s. This takes various forms, but one of the most common is

$$k = \frac{k_B T}{h} e^{-\frac{\Delta G^{\ddagger}}{RT}}$$

where ΔG^{++} is the Gibbs energy of activation, k_B is Boltzmann's constant, and h is Planck's constant.

At first sight this looks like an exponential multiplied by a factor that is *linear* in temperature. However, one must remember that free energy is itself a temperature dependent quantity. The free energy of activation is the difference of an enthalpy term and an entropy term multiplied by the absolute temperature. When all of the details are worked out one ends up with an expression that again takes the form of an Arrhenius exponential multiplied by a slowly varying function of T. The precise form of the temperature dependence depends upon the reaction, and can be calculated using formulas from statistical mechanics involving the partition functions of the reactants and of the activated complex. Limitations of the idea of Arrhenius activation energy both the Arrhenius activation energy and the rate constant k are experimentally determined, and represent macroscopic reaction-specific parameters that are not simply related to threshold energies and the success of individual collisions at the molecular level. Consider a particular collision (an elementary reaction) between molecules A and B. The collision angle, the relative translational energy, the internal (particularly vibrational) energy will all determine the chance that the collision will produce a product molecule AB. Macroscopic measurements of E and k are the result of many individual collisions with differing collision parameters. To probe reaction rates at molecular level, experiments are conducted under near-collisional conditions and this subject is often called molecular reaction dynamics.

LAW OF DILUTION

Wilhelm Ostwald's dilution law is a relationship between the dissociation constant K_d and the degree of dissociation α of a weak electrolyte. The law takes the form

$$K_d = \frac{[A^+]\,[B^-]}{[AB]} = \frac{\alpha^2}{1-\alpha}.c_0$$

Where the square brackets denote concentration, and c_0 is the total concentration of electrolyte.

Concerning conductivity, this results in the following relation:

$$K_c = \frac{\Lambda_c^2}{(\Lambda_0 - \Lambda_c)\,\Lambda_0}.c$$

Derivation

Consider a binary electrolyte AB which dissociates reversibly into A^+ and B^- ions. Ostwald noted that the law of mass action can be applied to such systems as dissociating electrolytes. The equilibrium state is represented by the equation:

$$AB \rightleftharpoons A^+ + B^-$$

If α is the fraction of dissociated electrolyte, then αc_0 is the concentration of each ionic species. $(1 - \alpha)$ must, therefore be the fraction of *undissociated* electrolyte, and $(1 - \alpha)c_0$ the concentration of same. The dissociation constant may therefore be given as

$$K_d = \frac{[A^+]\,[B^-]}{[AB]} = \frac{[\alpha c_0]\,[\alpha c_0]}{(1-\alpha)c_0} = \frac{\alpha^2}{(1-\alpha)}.c_0$$

For very weak electrolytes $\alpha << 1$, implying that $(1 - \alpha) \approx 1$.

$$K_d = \frac{\alpha^2}{1-\alpha}\cdot c_0 \approx \alpha^2 c_0$$

This gives the following results;

$$\alpha = \sqrt{\frac{K_d}{c_0}}$$

Thus, degree of dissociation of a weak electrolyte is proportional to the inverse square root of the concentration, or the square root of the dilution. The concentration of any one ionic species is given by the root of the product of the dissociation constant and the concentration of the electrolyte.

$$[A^+] = [B^-] = \alpha c_0 = \sqrt{K_d c_0})$$

Limitations

The law holds good only for weak electrolytes and fails completely in the case of strong electrolytes. The value of 'α' is determined by conductivity measurements by applying the formula $\Lambda/\Lambda\infty$. The value of 'α' determined at various dilutions of an electrolyte when substituted in Eq. (i) gives a constant value of K only in the case of weak electrolytes like CH3COOH, NH4OH, etc. the cause of failure of Ostwald's dilution law in the case of strong electrolytes is due to the following factors"

(*i*) The law is based on the fact that only a portion of the electrolyte is dissociated into ions at ordinary dilution and completely at infinite dilution. Strong electrolytes are almost completely ionized at all dilutions and $\Lambda/\Lambda\infty$ does not give accurate value of 'α'.

(ii) When concentration of the ions is very high, the presence of charges on the ions appreciably effects the equilibrium. Hence, law of mass action its simple form cannot be strictly applied in the case of strong electrolytes.

- K_c: constant of dissociation
- Λ_c: equivalent conductivity
- Λ_o: boundary conductivity
- c: concentration of electrolyte.

BORN EQUATION

The Born equation is a means of estimating the Gibbs free energy of solvation of a gaseous ion. It is an electrostatic model that treats the solvent as a continuous dielectric medium (it is thus one member of a class of methods known as continuum solvation methods). It was derived by Max Born.

$$\Delta G = -\frac{N_A z^2 e^2}{8\pi\varepsilon_0 r_0}\left(1 - \frac{1}{\varepsilon_r}\right)$$

where:

- N_A = Avogadro constant
- z = charge of ion
- e = elementary charge, 1.6022×10^{-19} C
- ε_0 = permittivity of free space
- r_0 = effective radius of ion
- ε_r = dielectric constant of the solvent

Born–Landé equation

The Born–Landé equation is a means of calculating the lattice energy of a crystalline ionic compound. In 1918 Max Born and Alfred Landé proposed that the lattice energy could be derived from the electrostatic potential of the ionic lattice and a repulsive potential energy term.

$$E = -\frac{N_A M_Z + z - e^2}{4\pi\varepsilon_0 r_0}\left(1 - \frac{1}{n}\right)$$

where:

- N_A = Avogadro constant;
- M = Madelung constant, relating to the geometry of the crystal;
- z^+ = charge number of cation
- z^- = charge number of anion
- e = elementary charge, 1.6022×10^{-19} C
- ε_0 = permittivity of free space
  $4\pi\varepsilon_0 = 1.112\times10^{-10}$ $C^2/(J\cdot m)$
- r_0 = distance to closest ion

- n = Born exponent, typically a number between 5 and 12, determined experimentally by measuring the compressibility of the solid, or derived theoretically

Derivation

The ionic lattice is modeled as an assembly of hard elastic spheres which are compressed together by the mutual attraction of the electrostatic charges on the ions. They achieve the observed equilibrium distance apart due to a balancing short range repulsion.

Electrostatic Potential

The electrostatic potential energy, E_{pair}, between a pair of ions of equal and opposite charge is:

$$E_{pair} = \frac{z^2c^2}{4\pi\varepsilon_0 r}$$

where

z = magnitude of charge on one ion

e = elementary charge, 1.6022×10^{-19} C

ε_0 = permittivity of free space

$4\pi\varepsilon_0 = 1.112\times10^{-10}$ C²/(J m)

r = distance separating the ion centers

For a simple lattice consisting ions with equal and opposite charge in a 1:1 ratio, interactions between one ion and all other lattice ions need to be summed to calculate E_M, sometimes called the Madelung or lattice energy:

$$E_M = \frac{z^2e^2M}{4\pi\varepsilon_0 r}$$

where

M = Madelung constant, which is related to the geometry of the crystal

r = closest distance between two ions of opposite charge

Repulsive term

Born and Lande suggested that a repulsive interaction between the lattice ions would be proportional to $1/r^n$ so that the repulsive energy term, E_R, would be expressed:

$$E_R = \frac{B}{r^n}$$

where

B = constant scaling the strength of the repulsive interaction

r = closest distance between two ions of opposite charge

n = Born exponent, a number between 5 and 12 expressing the steepness of the repulsive barrier

Total energy

The total intensive potential energy of an ion in the lattice can therefore be expressed as the sum of the Madelung and repulsive potentials:

$$E(r) = -\frac{z^2e^2M}{4\pi\varepsilon_0 r} + \frac{B}{r^n}$$

Minimizing this energy with respect to r yields the equilibrium separation T_0 in terms of the unknown constant B:

$$\frac{dE}{dr} = \frac{z^2e^2M}{4\pi\varepsilon_0 r^2} - \frac{nB}{r^n+1}$$

$$0 = \frac{z^2e^2M}{4\pi\varepsilon_0 r_0^2} - \frac{nB}{r_0^{n+1}}$$

$$r_0 = \left(\frac{4\pi\varepsilon_0 nB}{z^2e^2M}\right)^{\frac{1}{n-1}}$$

$$B = \frac{z^2e^2M}{4\pi\varepsilon_0 n} r_0^{n-1}$$

Evaluating the minimum intensive potential energy and substituting the expression for B in terms of r_0 yields the Born–Landé equation:

$$E(r_0) = -\frac{Mz^2e^2}{4\pi\varepsilon_0 r_0}\left(1 - \frac{1}{n}\right)$$

Calculated lattice energies

The Born–Landé equation gives a reasonable fit to the lattice energy

Compound	Calculated Lattice Energy	Experimental Lattice Energy
NaCl	–756 kJ/mol	–787 kJ/mol
LiF	–1007 kJ/mol	–1046 kJ/mol
$CaCl_2$	–2170 kJ/mol	–2255 kJ/mol

Born Exponent

The Born exponent is typically between 5 and 12. Approximate experimental values are listed below:

Ion configuration	He	Ne	Ar, Cu+	Kr, Ag+	Xe, Au+
n	5	7	9	10	12

Born–Mayer equation

The Born–Mayer equation is an equation that is used to calculate the lattice energy of a crystalline ionic compound. It is a refinement of the Born–Landé equation by using an improved repulsion term.

$$E = -\frac{N_A M_Z + Z - e^2}{4\pi\, \varepsilon_0 r_0}\left(1 - \frac{\rho}{r_0}\right)$$

where:

- N_A = Avogadro constant;
- M = Madelung constant, relating to the geometry of the crystal;
- z^+ = charge number of cation
- z^- = charge number of anion
- e = elementary charge, 1.6022×10^{-19} C
- $\mathring{a}_0$ = permittivity of free space
  $4\pi\varepsilon_0 = 1.112\times10^{-10}\ C^2/(J\cdot m)$
- r_0 = distance to closest ion
- p = a constant dependant on the compressibility of the crystal; 30 pm works well for all alkali metal halides

For more than 300 years, substances that behaved like vinegar have been classified as acids, while those that have properties like the ash from a wood fire have been called alkalies or bases. The name "acid" comes from the Latin *acidus*, which means "sour," and refers to the sharp odor and sour taste of many acids. Vinegar tastes sour because it is a dilute solution of acetic acid in water; lemon juice is sour because it contains citric acid; milk turns sour when it spoils because of the formation of lactic acid; and the sour odor of rotten meat can be attributed to carboxylic acids such as butyric acid formed when fat spoils.

Today, when chemists use the words "acid" or "base" they refer to a model developed independently by Brønsted, Lowry, and Bjerrum. Since the most explicit statement of this theory was contained in the writings of Brønsted, it is most commonly known as the "Brønsted acid-base" theory.

Brønsted Acid-Base Theory

The Brønsted–Lowry theory is an acid–base reaction theory which was proposed independently by Johannes Nicolaus Brønsted and Thomas Martin Lowry in 1923. The fundamental concept of this theory is that when an acid and a base react with each other, the acid forms its conjugate base, and the base forms its conjugate acid by exchange of a proton (the hydrogen cation, or H^+). This theory is a generalization of the Arrhenius theory.

Definitions of Acids and bases

In the Arrhenius theory acids are defined as substances which dissociate in aqueous solution to give H+ (hydrogen ions). Bases are defined as substances which dissociate in aqueous solution to give OH– (hydroxide ions).

In 1923 physical chemists Johannes Nicolaus Brønsted in Denmark and Thomas Martin Lowry in England independently proposed the theory that carries their names. In the Brønsted–Lowry theory acids and bases are defined by the way they react with each other, which allows for greater generality. The definition is expressed in terms of an equilibrium expression

acid + base ⇌ conjugate base + conjugate acid.

With an acid, HA, the equation can be written symbolically as:

$HA + B \rightleftharpoons A- + HB^+$

The equilibrium sign,⇌, is used because the reaction can occur in both forward and backward directions. The acid, HA, can lose a proton to become its conjugate base, A-. The base, B, can accept a proton to become its conjugate acid, HB+. Most acid-base reactions are fast so that the components of the reaction are usually in dynamic equilibrium with each other.

Aqueous Solutions

Consider the following acid–base reaction, (also illustrated at top right)

$CH_3COOH + H_2O \rightleftharpoons CH_3OOO^- + H_3O^+$

Acetic acid, CH_3COOH, is an acid because it donates a proton to water (H_2O) and becomes its conjugate base, the acetate ion (CH_3COO–). H_2O is a base because it accepts a proton from CH_3COOH and becomes its conjugate acid, the hydronium ion, (H_3O^+).

The reverse of an acid-base reaction is also an acid-base reaction, between the conjugate acid of the base in the first reaction and the conjugate base of the acid. In the above example, acetate is the base of the reverse reaction and hydronium ion is the acid.

$H_3O^+ + CH_3COO^- \rightleftharpoons CH_3COOH + H_2O$

The power of the Brønsted–Lowry theory is that, in contrast to Arrhenius theory, it does not require an acid to dissociate

Amphoteric substances

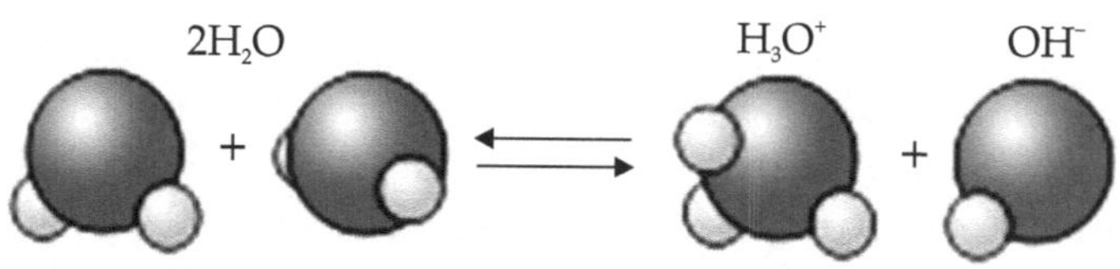

Fig. 2.2: The amphoteric nature of water

The essence of Brønsted–Lowry theory is that an acid only exists as such in relation to a base, and vice versa. Water is amphoteric as it can act as an acid or as a base. In the image shown at the right one molecule of H_2O acts as a base and gains H+ to become H_3O+while the other acts as an acid and loses H+ to become OH–.

Another example is furnished by substances like aluminium hydroxide, $Al(OH)_3$.

$Al(OH)_3 + OH- \rightleftharpoons Al(OH)^-_4$, acting as an acid

$3H^+ + Al(OH)_3 \rightleftharpoons 3H_2O + Al_3+(aq)$, acting as a base

Non-aqueous solutions

The hydrogen ion, or hydronium ion, is a Brønsted–Lowry acid in aqueous solutions, and the hydroxide ion is a base, by virtue of the self-dissociation reaction

$H_2O + H_2O \rightleftharpoons H_3O+ + OH-$

An analogous reaction occurs in liquid ammonia

$NH_3 + NH_3 \rightleftharpoons NH^{4+} + NH_2^-$

Thus, the ammonium ion, NH_4^+, plays the same role in liquid ammonia as does the hydronium ion in water and the amide ion, NH_2^-, is analogous to the hydroxide ion. Ammonium salts behave as acids, and amides behave as bases.

Some non-aqueous solvents can behave as bases, that is, proton acceptors, in relation to Brønsted–Lowry acids.

$AH + S \rightleftharpoons A- + SH+$

where S stands for a solvent molecule. The most important such solvents are dimethyl sulphoxide, DMSO, and acetonitrile, CH_3CN, as these solvents has been widely used to measure the acid dissociation constants of organic molecules. Because DMSO is a stronger proton acceptor than H_2O the acid becomes a stronger acid in this solvent than in water. Indeed, many molecules behave as acids in non-aqueous solution that do not do so in aqueous solution. An extreme case occurs with carbon acids, where a proton is extracted from a C-H bond.

On the other hand, a strongly acidic solvent will increase basicity. For example acetic acid behaves as a base in liquid hydrogen chloride.

$HCl + CH_3C(O)(OH) \rightleftharpoons Cl- + CH_3C(OH)_2^+$

Comparison with Lewis acid–base theory

In the same year that Brønsted and Lowry published their theory, G. N. Lewis proposed an alternative theory of acid–base reactions. The Lewis theory is based on electronic structure. A Lewis base is defined as a compound that can donate an electron pair to a Lewis acid, a compound that can accept an electron pair. Lewis's proposal gives an explanation to the Brønsted-Lowry classification in terms of electronic structure.

$A\text{-}H + B: \rightleftharpoons A:- + B\text{-}H+$

In this representation both the base, B, and the conjugate base, A–, are shown carrying a lone pair of electrons and the proton, which is a Lewis acid, is transferred between them.

Lewis later wrote in "To restrict the group of acids to those substances that contain hydrogen interferes as seriously with the systematic understanding of chemistry as would the restriction of the term oxidizing agent to substances containing oxygen." In Lewis theory an acid, A, and a base, B:, form an adduct, AB, in which the electron pair is used to form a dative covalent bond between A and B. This is illustrated with the formation of the adduct $H_3N\text{-}BF_3$ from ammonia and boron trifluoride, a reaction that cannot occur in aqueous solution because boron trifluoride reacts violently with water in a hydrolysis reaction.

$BF_3 + 3H_2O \rightleftharpoons B(OH)_3 + 3HF$

$HF \rightleftharpoons H+ + F-$

These reactions illustrate that BF3 is an acid in both Lewis and Brønsted-Lowry classifications and emphasizes the consistency between both theories.

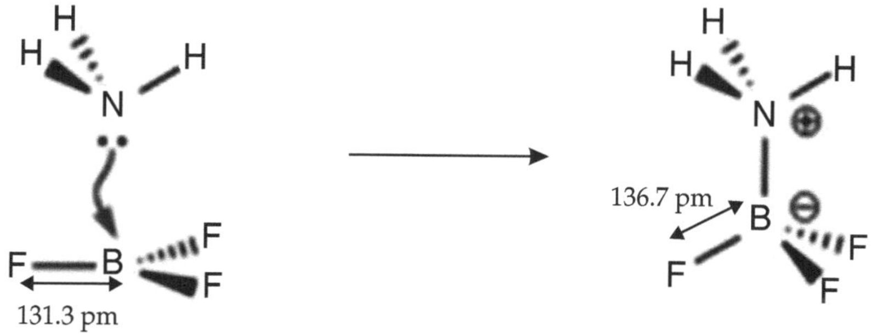

Fig. 2.3: Adduct of ammonia and boron trifluoride

Boric acid is recognized as a Lewis acid by virtue of the reaction

$B(OH)_3 + H_2O \rightleftharpoons B(OH)_4^- + H^+$

In this case the acid does not dissociate, it is the base, H_2O that dissociates. A solution of $B(OH)_3$ is acidic because hydrogen ions are liberated in this reaction.

There is strong evidence that dilute aqueous solutions of ammonia contain negligible amounts of the ammonium ion

$H_2O + NH_3 \neq OH^- + NH_4^+$

and that, when dissolved in water, ammonia functions as a Lewis base.

Comparison with the Lux-Flood theory

The reactions between certain oxides in non-aqueous media cannot be explained on the basis of Brønsted–Lowry theory. For example the reaction

$2MgO + SiO_2 \rightarrow Mg_2SiO_4$

does not fall within the scope of the Brønsted–Lowry definition of acids and bases. On the other hand MgO is basic and SiO_2 is acidic in the Brønsted–Lowry sense, referring to mixtures in water.

$2H^+ + MgO(s) \rightarrow Mg^{2+}(aq) + 2H_2O$

$SiO_2(s) + 2H_2O \rightarrow SiO_4^{4-} + 4H^+ \rightarrow Si(OH)4(aq))$

Lux-Flood theory also classifies magnesium oxide as a base in non-aqueous circumstances. This classification is important in geochemistry. Minerals such as olivine, $(Mg,Fe)SiO_4$ are classed as ultramafic; olivine is a compound of a very basic oxide, MgO, with an acidic oxide, silica, SiO_2.

Brønsted argued that all acid-base reactions involve the transfer of an H^+ ion, or proton. Water reacts with itself, for example, by transferring an H^+ ion from one molecule to another to form an H_3O^+ ion and an OH^- ion.

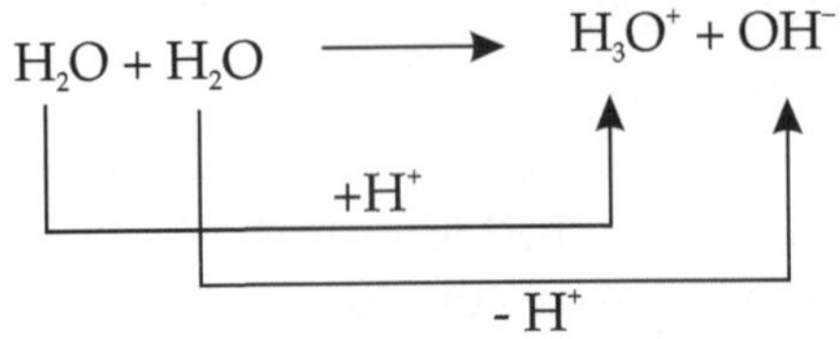

According to this theory, an acid is a "proton donor" and a base is a "proton acceptor."

Acids are often divided into categories such as "strong" and "weak." One measure of the strength of an acid is the acid-dissociation equilibrium constant, K_a, for that acid.

$$K_a = \frac{[H_3O]\,[A^-]}{[HA]}$$

When K_a is relatively large, we have a strong acid.

$$HCl: K_a = 1 \times 10^3$$

When it is small, we have a weak acid.

$$CH_3CO_2H: Ka = 1.8 \times 10^{-5}$$

When it is very small, we have a very weak acid.

$$H_2O: Ka = 1.8 \times 10^{-16}$$

In 1909, S.P.L. Sørenson suggested that the enormous range of concentrations of the H_3O^+ and OH^- ions in aqueous solutions could be compressed into a more manageable set of data by taking advantage of logarithmic mathematics and calculating the pH or pOH of the solution.

$$pH = - \log [H_3O^+]$$
$$pOH = - \log [OH^-]$$

The "p" in pH and pOH is an operator that indicates that the negative of the logarithm should be calculated for any quantity to which it is attached. Thus, pK_a is the negative of the logarithm of the acid-dissociation equilibrium constant.

$$pK_a = - \log K_a$$

The only disadvantage of using pK_a as a measure of the relative strengths of acids is the fact that large numbers now describe weak acids, and small (negative) numbers describe strong acids.

$$HCl: \quad pK_a = -3$$
$$CH_3CO_2H: \quad pK_a = 4.7$$
$$H_2O: \quad pK_a = 15.7$$

An important features of the Brønsted theory is the relationship it creates between acids and bases. Every Brønsted acid has a conjugate base, and vice versa.

$$HCl + H_2O \longrightarrow H_3O^+ + Cl^-$$

Acid + Base → *Acid + Base*

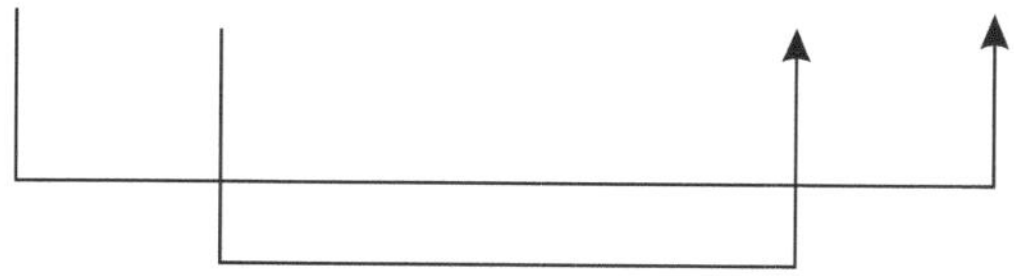

$$NH_3 + H_2O \longrightarrow NH_4^+ + OH^-$$

Acid + Base → *Acid + Base*

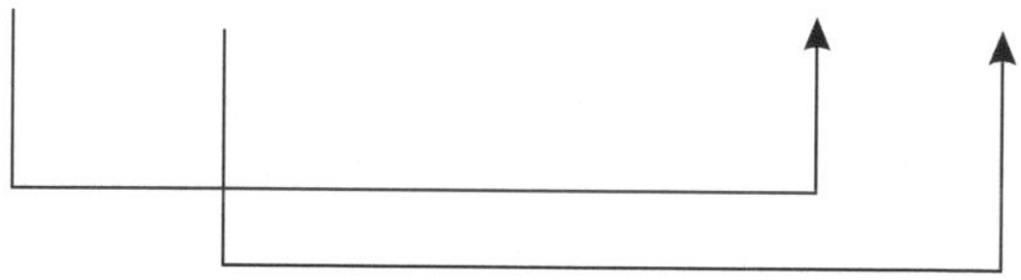

Just as the magnitude of K_a is a measure of the strength of an acid, the value of K_b reflects the strength of its conjugate base. Consider what happens when we multiply the K_a expression for a generic acid (HA) by the K_b expression for its conjugate base (A^-).

$$\frac{[H_3O^+]\,[A^-]}{[HA]} \times \frac{[HA]\,[OH^-]}{[A^-]} = [H_3O^+]\,[OH^-]$$

If we now replace each term in this equation by the appropriate equilibrium constant, we get the following equation.

$$K_aK_b = K_w = 1 \times 10^{-14}$$

Because the product of K_a times K_b is a relatively small number, either the acid or its conjugate base can be "strong." But if one is strong, the other must be weak. Thus, a strong acid must have a weak conjugate base.

$$HCl + H_2O \longrightarrow H_3O^+ + Cl^-$$

Strong acid → *Weak base*

A strong base, on the other hand, must have a weak conjugate acid.

$$NH_4^+ + OH^- \longrightarrow NH_3 + H_2O$$

Strong base → *Weak base*

Brønsted Acids and Bases in Non-aqueous Solutions

Water has a limiting effect on the strength of acids and bases. All strong acids behave the same in water — 1 *M* solutions of the strong acids all behave as 1 *M* solutions of the H_3O^+ ion — and very weak acids cannot act as acids in water. Acid-base reactions don't have to occur in water, however. When other solvents are used, the full range of acid-base strength shown in the following table can be observed.

Debye–Hückel theory

The Debye–Hückel theory was proposed by Peter Debye and Erich Hückel as a theoretical explanation for departures from ideality in solutions of electrolytes and plasmas. It is a linearized Poisson–Boltzmann model, which assumes an extremely simplified model of the electrolyte solution but nevertheless gave accurate predictions of mean activity coefficients for ions in dilute solution. The Debye–Hückel equation provides a starting point for modern treatments of non-ideality of electrolyte solutions.

Overview

In the chemistry of electrolyte solutions, an ideal solution is a solution whose colligative properties are proportional to the concentration of the solute. Real solutions show departures from this kind of ideality at all but the very lowest concentrations (see, for example, Raoult's law). In order to accommodate these effects in the thermodynamics of solutions, the concept of activity was introduced: the properties are then proportional to the activities of the ions. Activity, a, is proportional to concentration, c. The proportionality constant is known as an activity coefficient, γ.

$$a = \gamma c$$

In an ideal electrolyte solution the activity coefficients of all the ions are equal to one. Non-ideality arises principally (but not exclusively) because ions of opposite charge attract each other due to electrostatic forces, while ions of the same charge repel each other. In consequence ions are not randomly distributed throughout the solution, as they would be in an ideal solution.

Activity coefficients of single ions cannot be measured experimentally because an electrolyte solution must contain both positively charged ions and negatively charged ions. Instead, a mean activity coefficient, $\gamma\pm$ is defined. For example, with the electrolyte NaCl

$$\gamma\pm = (\gamma_{Na} + \gamma Cl^-)^{1/2}$$

In general, the mean activity coefficient of a fully dissociated electrolyte of formula AnBm is given by

$$\gamma\pm = (\gamma_A{}^n \gamma B^m)^{1/(n+m)}$$

Activity coefficients are themselves functions of concentration as the amount of inter-ionic interaction increases as the concentration of the electrolyte increases. Debye and Hückel developed a theory with which single ion activity coefficients could be calculated. By calculating the mean activity coefficients from them the theory could be tested against experimental data. It was found to give excellent agreement for "dilute" solutions.

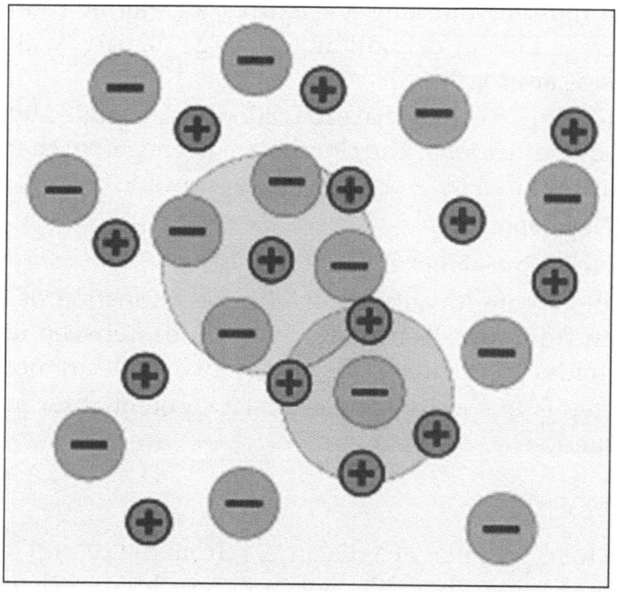

Fig. 2.4: An idealized representation of a solution of a 1:1 electrolyte

A description of Debye–Hückel theory includes a very detailed discussion of the assumptions and their limitations as well as the mathematical development and applications.

A snapshot of a 2-dimensional section of an idealized electrolyte solution is shown in the adjacent picture. The ions are shown as spheres with unit electrical charge. The solvent (pale blue) is shown as a uniform medium, without structure. On average, each ion is surrounded more closely by ions of opposite charge than by ions of like charge. These concepts were developed into a quantitative theory involving ions of charge z1e+ and z2e", where z can be any integer. The principal assumption is that departure from ideality is due to electrostatic interactions between ions, mediated by Coulomb's law: the force of interaction between two electric charges, separated by a distance, r in a medium of relative permittivity εr is given by

$$\text{force} = \frac{z_1 z_2 e_2}{4\pi\varepsilon_0\varepsilon_r r^2}$$

It is also assumed that

The solute is completely dissociated; it is a strong electrolyte.

Ions are spherical and are not polarized by the surrounding electric field. Solvation of ions is ignored except insofar as it determines the effective sizes of the ions.

The solvent plays no role other than providing a medium of constant relative permittivity (dielectric constant).

There is no electrostriction.

Individual ions surrounding a "central" ion can be represented by a statistically averaged cloud of continuous charge density, with a minimum distance of closest approach.

The last assumption means that each cation is surrounded by a spherically symmetric cloud of other ions. The cloud has a net negative charge. Similarly each anion is surrounded by a cloud with net positive charge.

Mathematical Development

Main article: Debye–Hückel equation

The deviation from ideality is taken to be a function of the potential energy resulting from the electrostatic interactions between ions and their surrounding clouds. To calculate this energy two steps are needed.

The first step is to specify the electrostatic potential for ion j by means of Poisson's equation

$$\Delta^2\psi_j(r) = -\frac{1}{\varepsilon_0\varepsilon_r}\rho_j(r)$$

ψ(r) is the total potential at a distance, r, from the central ion and ρ(r) is the averaged charge density of the surrounding cloud at that distance. To apply this formula it is essential that the cloud has spherical symmetry, that is, the charge density is a function only of distance from the central ion as this allows the Poisson equation to be cast in terms of spherical coordinates with no angular dependence.

The second step is to calculate the charge density by means of a Maxwell–Boltzmann distribution.

$$n_i^j = n_i \exp\left(\frac{-z_i e\psi_j(r)}{kT}\right)$$

This distribution also depends on the potential ψ(r) and this introduces a serious difficulty in terms of the superposition principle. Nevertheless, the two equations can be combined to produce the Poisson–Boltzmann equation.

$$\nabla^2\psi_j(r) = -\frac{1}{\varepsilon_0\varepsilon_r}\sum_i \left\{n_i(z_i e)\exp\left(\frac{-z_i e\psi_j(r)}{kT}\right)\right\}$$

Solution of this equation is far from straightforward. It can be solved by successive approximations using modern electronic computers, but these were not available to Debye and Hückel. Instead they expanded the exponential as a truncated Taylor series to first order. The zeroth order term vanishes because the solution is on average electrically neutral (so that Δ ni zi = 0), which leaves us with only the first order term. This results in the truncated Poisson–Boltzmann equation,

$$\nabla^2\psi_j(r) = \kappa^2\psi_j(r) \text{ with } \kappa^2 = \frac{e^2}{\varepsilon_0\varepsilon_r kT}\sum_i n_i z_1^2$$

which is a type of differential equation (the Helmholtz equation) which has an analytical solution. This equation applies to 1:1, 2:2 and 3:3 electrolytes; for unsymmetrical electrolytes another term in ψ2 must be included. Incidentally, the truncated expansion may also remove the difficulty with the superposition principle. For a symmetrical electrolyte, this reduces to the modified spherical Bessel equation

$$(\partial_r^2 + \frac{2}{r}\partial_r - \kappa^2)\psi_j = 0 \text{ with solutions } \psi_j(r) = A'\frac{e^{-\kappa r}}{r} + A''\frac{e^{\kappa r}}{r}$$

The coefficients A′ and A are fixed by the boundary conditions. As r → ∞, ψ should not diverge, so A″ = 0. At r = a0, which is the distance of closest approach of ions, the force exerted by the charge at r=0 should be balanced by the force of other ions, imposing ∂ψj(a0) = -zj e/(4πε0 εr a02), from which A′ can be calculated. Finally

$$\psi_j(r) = \frac{z_j e}{4\pi\varepsilon_0\varepsilon_r}\frac{\varepsilon^{\kappa a0}}{1+\kappa a_0}\frac{e^{-\kappa r}}{r}$$

and the potential energy uj of the ion at r=0 is

$$u_j = z_j e\,(\psi_j(a_0) - \frac{z_j e}{4\pi\varepsilon_0\varepsilon_r}\frac{1}{a_0} = \frac{z_j^2 e^2}{4\pi\varepsilon_0\varepsilon_r}\frac{\kappa}{1+\kappa a_0}$$

From this it is possible to get the mean activity coefficient, given as

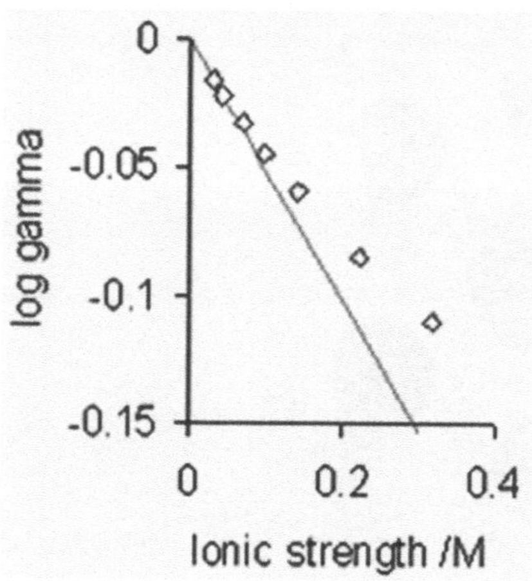

Experimental logγ± values for KBr at 25°C (points) and Debye–Hückel limiting law (coloured line)

$$\log_{10} \gamma \pm = - A z_j^2 \frac{\sqrt{I}}{I + B a_0 \sqrt{I}}$$

$$A = \frac{e^2 B}{2.303 \times 8\pi\varepsilon_0\varepsilon_r kT}$$

$$B = \left(\frac{2e^2 N}{\varepsilon_0\varepsilon_r kT}\right)^{1/2}$$

I is the ionic strength and a0 is a parameter which represent the distance of closest approach of ions. For aqueous solutions at 25 °C A = 0.51 mol–1/2dm3/2 and B = 3.29 nm–1mol–1/2dm3/2

The most significant aspect of these algebraic manipulations is the prediction that the mean activity coefficient is a function of ionic strength. Of course the ionic strength of a 1:1 electrolyte is equal to its concentration, but that is not true for other types of electrolyte. Generally, activity coefficients are discussed in terms of ionic strength rather than the electrolyte concentration. For very low values of the ionic strength the value of the denominator in the expression above becomes nearly equal to one. In this situation the mean activity coefficient is proportional to the square root of the ionic strength. This is known as the Debye–Hückel limiting law.

Limitations and extensions

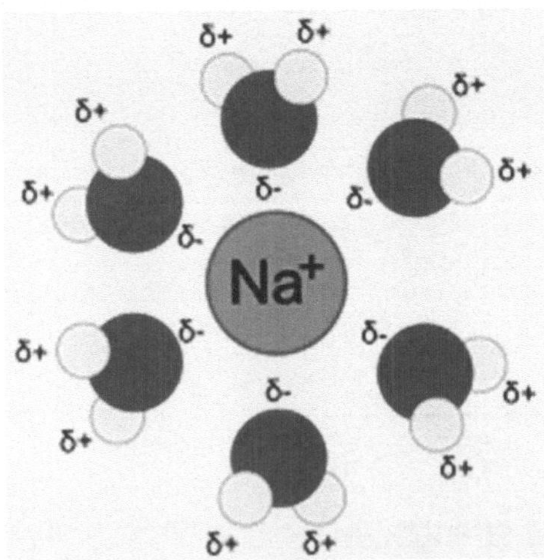

The first solvation shell of asodium ion dissolved in water. The oxygen atoms are arranged at the vertices of an octahedron with the sodium ion at its centre The equation for logγ± gives satisfactory agreement with experimental measurements for low electrolyte concentrations, typically less than 10–3 mol dm–3. Deviations from the theory occur at higher concentrations and with electrolytes that produce ions of higher charges, particularly unsymmetrical electrolytes. Essentially these deviations occur because the model is hopelesslyoversimplified, so there is little to be gained making small adjustments to the model. The individual assumptions can be challenged in turn.

Complete dissociation. Ion-association may take place, particularly with ions of higher charge. This was followed up in detail by Niels Bjerrum. The Bjerrum length is the separation at which the electrostatic interaction between two ions is comparable in magnitude to kT.

Weak electrolytes. A weak electrolyte is one that is not fully dissociated. As such it has a dissociation constant. The dissociation constant can be used to calculate the extent of dissociation and hence, make the necessary correction needed to calculate activity coefficients.

Ions are spherical, not point charges and are not polarized. Many ions such as the nitrate ion, NO_3^-, are manifestly not spherical. Polyatomic ions are also polarizable.

Role of the solvent. The solvent is not a structureless medium but is made up of molecules. The water molecules in aqueous solution are both dipolar and polarizable. Both cations and anions have a strong primary solvation shell and a weaker secondary solvation shell. Ion-solvent interactions are ignored in Debye–Hückel theory.

Moreover, we assume that the ionic radius is negligible, but at higher concentrations, the ionic radius becomes comparable to the radius of the ionic cloud. Most extensions to Debye–Hückel theory are empirical in nature. They usually allow the Debye–Hückel equation to be followed at low concentration and add further terms in some power of the ionic strength to fit experimental observations. The main extensions are the Davies equation, Pitzer equations and Specific ion interaction theory.

Conductivity

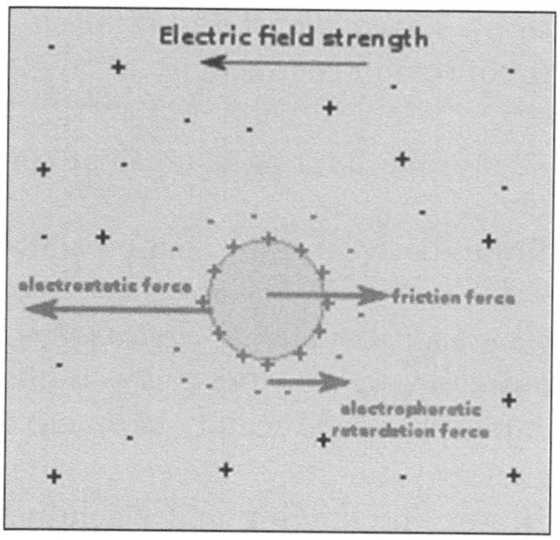

Fig. 2.5: Forces affecting a charged ion or cloud moving in an electric field

The treatment given so far is for a system not subject to an external electric field. When conductivity is measured the system is subject to an oscillating external field due to the application of an AC voltage to electrodes immersed in the solution. Debye and Hückel modified their theory in 1926 and their theory was further modified by Lars Onsager in 1927. All the postulates of the original theory were retained. In addition it was assumed that the electric field causes the charge cloud to be distorted away from spherical symmetry. After taking this into account, together with the specific requirements of moving ions, such as viscosity and electrophoretic effects, Onsager was able to derive a theoretical expression to account for the empirical relation known as Kohlrausch's Law, for the molar conductivity, Λm.

$$\Lambda_m = \Lambda^0_m - K\sqrt{c}$$

Λ^0_m is known as the limiting molar conductivity, K is an empirical constant and c is the electrolyte concentration Limiting here means "at the limit of the infinite dilution"). Onsager's expression is

$$\Lambda_m = \Lambda^0_m - (A + B\Lambda^0_m)\sqrt{c}$$

where A and B are constants that depend only on known quantities such as temperature, the charges on the ions and the dielectric constant and viscosity of the solvent. This is known as the Debye-Hückel-Onsager equation. However, this equation only applies to very dilute solutions and has been largely superseded by other equations due to Fuoss and Onsager, 1932 and 1957 and later.

In 1874, Kohlrausch formulated the law of independent migration of ions based on the experimental data of conductivities of various electrolytes. This law can be stated as follows:

At infinite dilution, the dissociation of the electrolyte is complete and hence each ion makes definite contribution to the equivalent conductivity of the electrolyte irrespective of the nature of other ions associated with it.

Therefore the limiting equivalent conductivity of an electrolyte is the algebraic sum of limiting equivalent conductivities of its constituent ions.

i.e., The limiting equivalent conductivity of an electrolyte, $\Lambda_o^{\text{electrolyte}}$

$$\Lambda_o^{\text{electrolyte}} = \lambda^+_0 + \lambda^-_0$$

Where λ^+_0 and λ^-_0 are the limiting equivalent conductivities of cation and anion respectively.

However the Kohlrausch law can also be stated in terms of molar conductivities as:

The limiting molar conductivity of an electrolyte is the sum of individual contributions of limiting molar conductivities of its constituent ions.

i.e., The molar equivalent conductivity of an electrolyte, $\mu_o^{\text{electrolyte}}$

$$\mu_o^{\text{electrolyte}} = \eta_0\mu^+_0 + \mu^-_0$$

Where μ_o^+ and μ_o^- are the limiting molar conductivities of cation and anion respectively.

And n_+ and n_- are the stoichiometric numbers of positive and negative ions formed during the dissociation of electrolyte.

Experimental basis and Theoretical Explanation of Kohlrausch Law

Kohlrausch observed that at infinite dilutions, the difference between the conductivities of sodium and potassium salts is constant irrespective of the associated anions, as tabulated below.

Salt pair	Conductivity (mho cm^2 equiv)	Difference
NaCl	108.90	21.20
KCl	130.10	
$NaNO_3$	105.33	21.17
KNO_3	126.50	
NaBr	111.10	21.20
KBr	132.30	

Kohlrausch argued that the constant difference in the conductivities of above pairs can be ascribed to the fact that the mobility of sodium and potassium ions at infinite dilution is not influenced by the nature of counter ions. The ions at such a low concentration migrate in the electric field as they are independent i.e., they show same ionic conductance irrespective of the nature of counter ion.

Applications of Kohlrausch Law

1. **Calculation of limiting conductivities of weak electrolytes:** The Kohlrausch law can be used to calculate the limiting conductivities of weak electrolytes.

E.g., The calculation of limiting equivalent conductance of acetic acid, a weak electrolyte is illustrated below.

According to Kohlrausch law, the limiting equivalent conductance values of CH_3COOH, CH_3COONa, HCl and NaCl can be written as follows:

$$\Lambda_0^{CH_3COOH} = \lambda_0^{CH_3COO-} + \lambda_0^{H+}$$

$$\Lambda_0^{CH_3COONa} = \lambda_0^{CH_3COO-} + \lambda_0^{Na+}$$

$$\Lambda_0^{HCl} = \lambda_0^{H+} + \lambda_0^{Cl-}$$

$$\Lambda_0^{NaCl} = \lambda_0^{Na+} + \lambda_0^{Cl-}$$

Therefore

$$\Lambda_0^{CH_3COOH} = \Lambda_0^{CH_3COONa} + \Lambda_0^{HCl} - \Lambda_0^{Nacl}$$

2. **Determination of degree of ionization (a) of weak electrolyte:** The degree of ionization of a weak electrolyte at a particular concentration is equal to the ratio of actual number of ions formed due to partial ionization to the expected number of ions formed upon complete dissociation.

Since the conductance is proportional to the number of ions in the solution, the degree of ionization is equal to the conductance ratio as given below.

$$\alpha = \frac{\text{Actual No. of Ions formed}}{\text{Expected No of particles formed due to complete dissociation}}$$

$$\alpha = \frac{\Lambda_c}{\Lambda_0} = \frac{\Lambda_c}{\lambda^+_0 + \lambda^-_0}$$

Where

Λ_c= equivalent conductivity at given concentration.

Λ_o= limiting equivalent conductivity.

λ_o^+ = limiting equivalent conductivity of cation.

λ_o^- = limiting equivalent conductivity of anion.

Tafel Equation

The Tafel equation is an equation in electrochemical kinetics relating the rate of an electrochemical reaction to the over potential. The Tafel equation was first deduced experimentally and was later shown to have a theoretical justification. The equation is named after Swiss chemist Julius Tafel.

On a single electrode the Tafel equation can be stated as

$$\Delta V = A \times \text{In}\left(\frac{i}{i_0}\right)$$

where

- ΔV is the over-potential, V (note that the graph uses η for this quantity)
- A is the so-called "Tafel slope", V
- i is the current density, A/m^2 and
- i_0 is the so-called "exchange current density", A/m^2.

Overview of the terms

The exchange current is the current at equilibrium, i.e. the rate at which oxidized and reduced species transfer electrons with the electrode. In other words, the exchange current density is the rate of reaction at the reversible potential (when the over-potential is zero by definition). At the reversible potential, the reaction is in equilibrium meaning that the forward and reverse reactions progress at the same rates. This rate is the exchange current density.

The Tafel slope is measured experimentally. It, however, can be shown theoretically that when the dominant reaction mechanism involves the transfer of a single electron that

$$\frac{kT}{e} < A$$

where A is defined as

$$A = \frac{kT}{e\alpha}$$

where

- k is Boltzmann's constant
- T is the absolute temperature
- e is the electron charge, and
- α is the so-called "charge transfer coefficient", the value of which must be between 0 and 1.

An alternative form

The Tafel equation can be also written as:

$$i = nFk\exp\left(\pm \alpha F\frac{\Delta V}{RT}\right)$$

where

- the plus sign under the exponent refers to an anodic reaction, and a minus sign to a cathodic reaction
- k is the rate constant for the electrode reaction,
- R is the universal gas constant,
- F is the Faraday constant.

Applicability

Where an electrochemical reaction occurs in two half reactions on separate electrodes, the Tafel equation is applied to each electrode separately.

The Tafel equation assumes that the reverse reaction rate is negligible compared to the forward reaction rate.

The Tafel equation is applicable to the region where the values of polarization are high. At low values of polarization, the dependence of current on polarization is usually linear (not logarithmic):

$$i = i_0\frac{nF}{RT}\Delta E$$

This linear region is called *polarization resistance* due to its formal similarity to the Ohm's law.

Nernst Equation

In electrochemistry, the Nernst equation is an equation that relates the reduction potential of a half-cell (or the total voltage, i.e. the electromotive force, of the full cell) at any point in time to the standard electrode potential, temperature, activity, and reaction quotient of the underlying reactions and species used. When the reaction quotient is equal to the equilibrium constant of the reaction for a given temperature, i.e. when the concentration of species are at their equilibrium values, the Nernst equation gives the equilibrium voltage of the half-cell (or the full cell), which is zero; at equilibrium, Q=K, ΔG=0, and therefore, E=0. It is named after the German physical chemist who first formulated it, Walther Nernst. The Nernst equation gives a formula that relates the numerical values of the concentration gradient to the electric gradient that balances it. For example, if a concentration gradient is established by dissolving KCl in half of a divided vessel that is full of H_2O, and then a membrane permeable to K^+ ions is introduced between the two halves, then after a relaxation period, an equilibrium situation arises where the chemical concentration gradient, which at first causes ions to move from the region of high concentration to the region of low concentration, is exactly balanced by an electrical gradient that opposes the movement of charge.

Expression

The two (ultimately equivalent) equations for these two cases (half-cell, full cell) are as follows:

$$E_{red} = E^{e}_{red} + \frac{RT}{zF} \ln \frac{a_{Ox}}{a_{Red}} \quad \text{(half-cell reduction potential for Ox + } ze^- = \text{Red)}$$

$$E_{cell} = E^{e}_{cell} - \frac{RT}{zF} \ln Q_r \quad \text{(total cell potential)}$$

where

- E_{red} is the half-cell reduction potential at the temperature of interest
- E^{o}_{red} is the *standard* half-cell reduction potential
- E_{cell} is the cell potential (electromotive force) at the temperature of interest
- E^{o}_{cell} is the *standard* cell potential
- R is the universal gas constant: $R = 8.314\ 472(15)$ J K^{-1} mol^{-1}
- T is the absolute temperature
- a is the chemical activity for the relevant species, where a_{Red} is the reducing agent and a_{Ox} is the oxidizing agent. $a_X = \gamma_X c_X$, where γ_X is the activity coefficient of species X. (Since activity coefficients tend to unity at low concentrations, activities in the Nernst equation are frequently replaced by simple concentrations.)
- F is the Faraday constant, the number of coulombs per mole of electrons: $F = 9.648\ 533\ 99(24) \times 10^4$ C mol^{-1}
- z is the number of moles of electrons transferred in the cell reaction or half-reaction
- Q_r is the reaction quotient.

At room temperature (25 °C), RT/F may be treated like a constant and replaced by 25.693 mV for cells.

The Nernst equation is frequently expressed in terms of base 10 logarithms (*i.e.*, common logarithms) rather than natural logarithms, in which case it is written, *for a cell at 25 °C*:

$$E = E^0 + \frac{0.05916\ \text{V}}{z} \log_{10} \frac{a_{Ox}}{a_{Red}}$$

The Nernst equation is used in physiology for finding the electric potential of a cell membrane with respect to one type of ion.

Nernst Potential

The Nernst equation has a physiological application when used to calculate the potential of an ion of charge z across a membrane. This potential is determined using the concentration of the ion both inside and outside the cell:

$$E = \frac{RT}{zF} \ln \frac{[\text{ion outside cell}]}{[\text{ion inside cell}]} = 2.3026 \frac{RT}{zF} \log_{10} \frac{[\text{ion outside cell}]}{[\text{ion inside cell}]}$$

When the membrane is in thermodynamic equilibrium (i.e., no net flux of ions), the membrane potential must be equal to the Nernst potential. However, in physiology, due to active ion pumps, the inside and outside of a cell are not in equilibrium. In this case, the resting potential can be determined from the Goldman equation:

$$E_m = \frac{RT}{F} \ln \left(\frac{\sum_i^N P_{M_i^+} [M_i^+]_{out} + \sum_j^M P_{A_j^-} [A_j^-]_{in}}{\sum_i^N P_{M_i^+} [M_i^+]_{in} + \sum_j^M P_{A_j^-} [A_j^-]_{out}} \right)$$

- E_m = The membrane potential (in volts, equivalent to joules per coulomb)
- P_{ion} = the permeability for that ion (in meters per second)
- $[ion]_{out}$ = the extracellular concentration of that ion (in moles per cubic meter, to match the other SI units, though the units strictly don't matter, as the ion concentration terms become a dimensionless ratio)
- $[ion]_{in}$ = the intracellular concentration of that ion (in moles per cubic meter)
- R = The ideal gas constant (joules per kelvin per mole)
- T = The temperature in kelvin
- F = Faraday's constant (coulombs per mole)

The potential across the cell membrane that exactly opposes net diffusion of a particular ion through the membrane is called the Nernst potential for that ion. As seen above, the magnitude of the Nernst potential is determined by the ratio of the concentrations of that specific ion on the two sides of the membrane. The greater this ratio the greater the tendency for the ion to diffuse in one direction, and therefore the greater the Nernst potential required to prevent the diffusion.

A similar expression exists that includes r (the absolute value of the transport ratio). This takes transporters with unequal exchanges into account. See: Sodium-Potassium Pump where the transport ratio would be 2/3. The other variables are the same as above. The following example includes two ions: Potassium (K^+) and sodium (Na^+). Chloride is assumed to be in equilibrium.

$$V_m = \frac{RT}{F}\ln\left(\frac{rP_k[K]_o + P_{Na}[Na]_o}{rP_k[K]_i + P_{Na}[Na]_i}\right)$$

When Chloride (Cl^-) is taken into account, its part is flipped to account for the negative charge.

$$V_m = \frac{RT}{F}\ln\left(\frac{P_k[K]_o + P_{Na}[Na]_o + P_{Cl}[Cl]_i}{P_k[K]_i + P_{Na}[Na]_i + P_{Cl}[Cl]_o}\right)$$

Derivation

Using Boltzmann factors

For simplicity, we will consider a solution of redox-active molecules that undergo a one-electron reversible reaction

$$Ox + e^- \rightleftharpoons Red$$

and that have a standard potential of zero. The chemical potential μ_c of this solution is the difference between the energy barriers for taking electrons from and for giving electrons to the working electrode that is setting the solution's electrochemical potential.

The ratio of oxidized to reduced molecules, [Ox]/[Red], is equivalent to the probability of being oxidized (giving electrons) over the probability of being reduced (taking electrons), which we can write in terms of the Boltzmann factor for these processes:

$$\frac{[Red]}{[Ox]} = \frac{\exp(-[\text{barrier for losing an electron}]/kT)}{\exp(-[\text{barrier for gaining an electron}]/kT)} = \exp(\mu c/kT)$$

Taking the natural logarithm of both sides gives

$$\mu_c = kT\ln\frac{[Red]}{[Ox]}$$

If $\mu_c \neq 0$ at [Ox]/[Red] = 1, we need to add in this additional constant:

$$\mu_c = \mu_c^0 + kT\ln\frac{[Red]}{[Ox]}$$

Dividing the equation by e to convert from chemical potentials to electrode potentials, and remembering that $k/e = R/F$, we obtain the Nernst equation for the one-electron process $Ox + e^- \rightarrow Red$:

$$E = E^0 + \frac{kT}{e}\ln\frac{[Red]}{[Ox]}$$

$$= E^0 - \frac{RT}{F}\ln\frac{[Ox]}{[Red]}$$

Using Thermodynamics (Chemical Potential)

Quantities here are given per molecule, not per mole, and so Boltzmann constant k and the electron charge e are used instead of the gas constant R and Faraday's constant F. To convert to the molar quantities given in most chemistry textbooks, it is simply necessary to multiply by Avogadro's number: $R = k N_A$ and eN_A.

The entropy of a molecule is defined as

$$S \stackrel{\text{def}}{=} k \ln \Omega,$$

where Ω is the number of states available to the molecule. The number of states must vary linearly with the volume V of the system, which is inversely proportional to the concentration c, so we can also write the entropy as

$$S = k \text{ In (constant} \times V) = -k \text{ In (constant} \times c)$$

The change in entropy from some state 1 to another state 2 is therefore

$$\Delta S = S_2 - S_1 = -k \ln \frac{c_2}{c_1},$$

so that the entropy of state 2 is

$$S_2 = S_1 - k \ln \frac{c_2}{c_1},$$

If state 1 is at standard conditions, in which c_1 is unity (e.g., 1 atm or 1 M), it will merely cancel the units of c_2. We can, therefore, write the entropy of an arbitrary molecule A as

$$S(A) = S^0 (A) - k \ln[A]$$

where S^0 is the entropy at standard conditions and $[A]$ denotes the concentration of A. The change in entropy for a reaction

$$aA + bB \rightarrow yY + zZ$$

is then given by

$$\Delta S_{rxn} = [yS(Y) + zS(Z)] - [aS(A) + bS(B)] = \Delta S^0_{rxn} - k \ln \frac{[Y]^y[Z]^z}{[A]^a[B]^b}$$

We define the ratio in the last term as the reaction quotient:

$$Q = \frac{\Pi j a_j^{v_j}}{\Pi j a_i^{v_i}} \approx \frac{[Z]^z\,[Y]^y}{[A]^a\,[B]^b}$$

where the numerator is a product of reaction product activities, a_j, each raised to the power of a stoichiometric coefficient, ν_j, and the denominator is a similar product of reactant activities. All activities refer to a time t. Under certain circumstances (see chemical equilibrium) each activity term such as $a_j^{\nu_j}$ may be replaced by a concentration term, $[A]$. In an electrochemical cell, the cell potential E is the chemical potential available from redox reactions ($E = \mu_c/e$). E is related to the Gibbs energy change ΔG only by a constant: $\Delta G = -nF E$, where n is the number of electrons transferred and F is the

Faraday constant. There is a negative sign because a spontaneous reaction has a negative free energy ΔG and a positive potential E. The Gibbs energy is related to the entropy by $G = H - TS$, where H is the enthalpy and T is the temperature of the system. Using these relations, we can now write the change in Gibbs energy,

$$\Delta G = \Delta H - T\Delta S = \Delta G^0 + kT \ln Q.$$

and the cell potential,

$$E = E^0 - \frac{kT}{ne} \ln Q$$

This is the more general form of the Nernst equation. For the redox reaction $\mathrm{Ox} + ne^- \rightarrow \mathrm{Red}$, $Q = \frac{[\mathrm{Red}]}{[\mathrm{Ox}]}$, and we have:

$$E = E^0 - \frac{kT}{ne} \ln \frac{[\mathrm{Red}]}{[\mathrm{Ox}]}$$

$$= E^0 - \frac{RT}{nF} \ln \frac{[\mathrm{Red}]}{[\mathrm{Ox}]}$$

$$= E^0 - \frac{RT}{nF} \ln Q.$$

The cell potential at standard conditions E^0 is often replaced by the formal potential $E^{0'}$, which includes some small corrections to the logarithm and is the potential that is actually measured in an electrochemical cell.

Relation to equilibrium

At equilibrium, $E = 0$ and $Q = K$. Therefore

$$0 = E^0 - \frac{RT}{nF} \ln K$$

$$\ln K = \frac{nFE^0}{RT}$$

Or at standard temperature,

$$\log_{10} K = \frac{nE^0}{59.2 \text{ mV}} \quad \text{at } T = 298 \text{ K}.$$

We have thus related the standard electrode potential and the equilibrium constant of a redox reaction.

Limitations

In dilute solutions, the Nernst equation can be expressed directly in terms of concentrations (since activity coefficients are close to unity). But at higher concentrations, the true activities of the ions must be used. This complicates the use of the Nernst equation, since estimation of non-ideal activities of ions generally requires experimental measurements. The Nernst equation also only applies when there is no net current flow through the electrode. The activity of ions at the electrode surface changes when there is current flow, and there are additional over potential and resistive loss terms which contribute to the measured potential. At very low concentrations of the potential-determining ions, the potential predicted by Nernst equation approaches toward $\pm\infty$. This is physically meaningless because, under such conditions, the exchange current density becomes very low, and there is no thermodynamic equilibrium necessary for Nernst equation to hold. The electrode is called to be unpoised in such case. Other effects tend to take control of the electrochemical behavior of the system.

Time Dependence of the Potential

The expression of time dependence has been established by Karaoglanoff.

Significance to related Scientific Domains

The equation has been involved in the scientific controversy involving cold fusion. The discoverers of cold fusion, Fleischmann and Pons, calculated that a palladium cathode immersed in a heavy water electrolysis cell could achieve up to 10^{27} atmospheres of pressure on the surface of the cathode, enough pressure to cause spontaneous nuclear fusion. In reality, only 10,000-20,000 atmospheres were achieved. John R. Huizenga claimed their original calculation was affected by a misinterpretation of Nernst equation. He cited a paper about Pd-Zr alloys.

Nernst Plank Equation

The time dependent form of the Nernst–Planck equation is a conservation of mass equation used to describe the motion of a charged chemical species in a fluid medium. It describes the flux of ions under the influence of both an ionic concentration gradient ∇c and an electric field $E = -\nabla\phi - \frac{\partial A}{\partial t}$. It extends Fick's law of diffusion for the case where the diffusing particles are also moved with respect to the fluid by electrostatic forces:

$$\frac{\partial c}{\partial t} = \nabla.\left[D\nabla c - uc + \frac{Dze}{k_B T} c(\nabla\phi + \frac{\partial A}{\partial t})\right]$$

Where

- t is time,
- D is the diffusivity of the chemical species,
- c is the concentration of the species, and u is the velocity of the fluid,
- z is the valence of ionic species,
- e is the elementary charge,
- k_R is the Boltzmann constant
- T is the temperature.
- u is relative velocity of the observer to the ionic system

If the diffusing particles are themselves charged they influence the electric field on moving. Hence the Nernst–Planck equation is applied in describing the ion-exchange kinetics in soils.

In the context of Neuroscience, this equation is best known in its steady-state form, where there is a balance of diffusion and drift. Setting time derivatives to zero, and noting that the term $J = -uc$ represents a current flux J

$$\nabla.\left[D\nabla c + J + \frac{Dze}{k_B T} c(\nabla\phi)\right] = 0$$

Integrating the divergence over an arbitrary surface, one obtains the steady state Nernst-Planck equation

$$J = -\left[D\nabla c + \frac{Dze}{k_B T} c(\nabla\phi)\right]$$

Finally, in units of $\frac{Coulombs}{M^2}$ and the gas constant R, one obtains the more familiar form (e.g.

$$J = -zFD\left[\nabla c + \frac{Fzc}{RT}(\nabla\phi)\right]$$

The Tafle Equation

The Tafel equation is an equation in electrochemical kinetics relating the rate of an electrochemical reaction to the over potential. The Tafel equation was first deduced experimentally and was later shown to have a theoretical justification. The equation is named after Swiss chemist Julius Tafel.

On a single electrode the Tafel equation can be stated as

$$\Delta V = A \times \ln\left(\frac{i}{i_0}\right)$$

where

- ΔV is the overpotential, V (note that the graph uses ç for this quantity)
- A is the so-called "Tafel slope", V
- i is the current density, A/m^2 and
- i_0 is the so-called "exchange current density", A/m^2.

Overview of the Terms

The exchange current is the current at equilibrium, i.e. the rate at which oxidized and reduced species transfer electrons with the electrode. In other words, the exchange current density is the rate of reaction at the reversible potential (when the over potential is zero by definition). At the reversible potential, the reaction is in equilibrium meaning that the forward and reverse reactions progress at the same rates. This rate is the exchange current density.

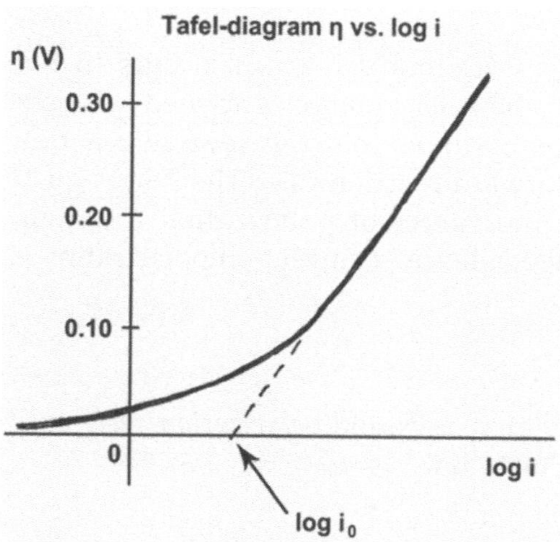

Fig. 2.6: Showing Tafel plot for an anodic process

The Tafel slope is measured experimentally. It, however, can be shown theoretically that when the dominant reaction mechanism involves the transfer of a single electron that

$$\frac{kT}{e} < A$$

where A is defined as

$$A = \frac{kT}{c\alpha}$$

where

- k is Boltzmann's constant,
- T is the absolute temperature,
- e is the electron charge, and
- α is the so-called "charge transfer coefficient", the value of which must be between 0 and 1.

An alternative form

The Tafel equation can be also written as:

$$i = nFk\,\exp\left(\pm\alpha F\frac{\Delta V}{RT}\right)$$

where

- the plus sign under the exponent refers to an anodic reaction, and a minus sign to a cathodic reaction,
- k is the rate constant for the electrode reaction,
- R is the universal gas constant,
- F is the Faraday constant.

Applicability

Where an electrochemical reaction occurs in two half reactions on separate electrodes, the Tafel equation is applied to each electrode separately. The Tafel equation assumes that the reverse reaction rate is negligible compared to the forward reaction rate. The Tafel equation is applicable to the region where the values of polarization are high. At low values of polarization, the dependence of current on polarization is usually linear (not logarithmic):

$$i = i_0 \frac{nF}{RT} \Delta E$$

This linear region is called *polarization resistance* due to its formal similarity to the Ohm's law.

3

Electrochemical Kinetics

INTRODUCTION

On the basis of the nature of the reactants and products, three main types of electrode processes may be identified: (a) ionic redox reactions, (b) gaseous redox reactions, and (c) phase change reactions.

In an *ionic redox electrode process* (Figure 3.1a), both the reactant and product are water-soluble ionic species, although they have different charges. In *gaseous redox reactions* (Figure 3.1b), a reactant or a product is a gas. Examples are the oxygen, hydrogen, and the chlorine electrodes. In a typical gaseous redox process, a hydrated ion or a water molecule reacts, through adsorbed intermediates, on the electrode surface; dissolved gas molecules are produced initially, and these subsequently combine to form gas bubbles.

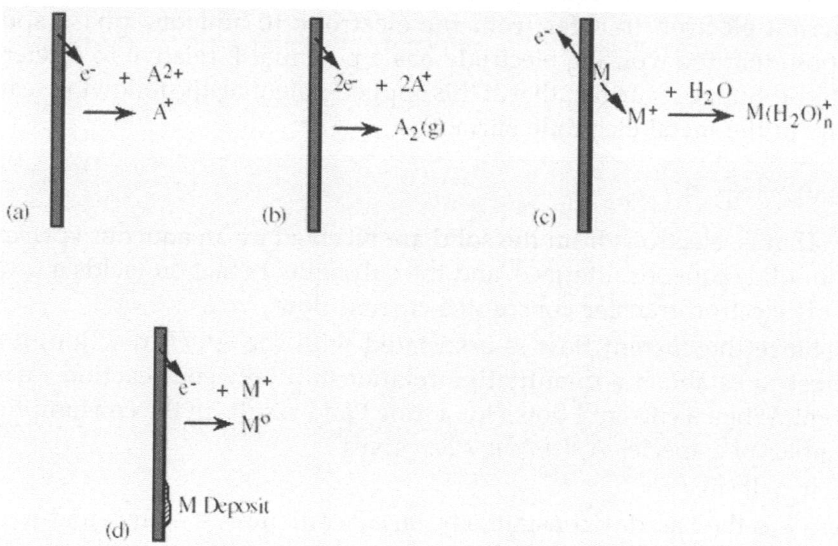

Fig. 3.1: Types of electrode processes: (a) ionic redox reactions (b) gaseous redox reactions, (c) electrodissolution, (d) electrodeposition, (e) surface film reactions

Phase change electrode processes may involve phase formation or dissolution. In the case of *electrodissolution* (Figure 3.1c), a surface metal ion detaches and enters the aqueous phase as a hydrated ion; the associated electron is donated to the electrode. In *electrodeposition*, a hydrated metal ion receives electrons from the electrode and the resulting electroneutral metal becomes incorporated into the crystal structure of the metallic deposit. The metal ion released during a dissolution process may combine with an aqueous species to give an insoluble product, i.e., a *surface film* (Figure 3.1e). In a related process, a previously formed surface film may be made to undergo dissolution.

We shall limit the discussion in this Chapter to electron-transfer reactions in which the electrode is inert, i.e., cases where the electrode serves only as a source or sink for electrons, without undergoing any chemical transformation itself. Also, we will not consider here those cases where there is surface deposition. This means that the focus in this Chapter is primarily on ionic redox electrodes and gaseous electrode processes. Dissolution processes are discussed in Chapter 2.

ELECTRON TRANSFER AT METAL ELECTRODES

Electron Transfer and Reaction Rate

The potential of an electrode is a measure of the energy of the constituent electrons. As the electrode potential moves in the negative direction, the electrons rise to increasingly high energy levels. At sufficiently negative potentials, the energy levels occupied by the electrons become high enough to permit electron transfer from the electrode to aqueous phase species. Suppose that the working electrode has a potential E relative to a reference electrode. Suppose further, that at this applied potential, the following reaction occurs at the metal electrode surface:

$$A^{z+} + \underset{k_r}{\overset{k_f}{\leftrightarrow}} B \tag{3.1}$$

That is, electrons from the solid are received by an aqueous species A^{z+} at the solid/aqueous interface, and the subsequent reaction yields a product B. This electron transfer constitutes current flow.

Since the current flow is associated with the A^{z+}/B reaction, it is of interest to establish a quantitative relationship between reaction rate and current. When a current I flows for a time t and results in the consumption of nA moles of a species A, *Faraday's law* gives

$$n_A = It/nF \tag{3.2}$$

where F is the Faraday constant, i.e., 96487 coulombs/g equiv., and n moles of electrons are involved in the reaction of 1 g mol of A; n has units of g equiv./g mol.

Let us recall the definition of reaction rate on a unit surface basis.

$$r_A = (1/S)dn_A/dt \quad (3.3)$$

For constant current, Equation 3.2 can be differentiated with respect to time to give,

$$r_A = (1/S)dn_A/dt = I/nFS \quad (3.4)$$

$$= i/nF \quad (3.5)$$

where iA is the *current density*, defined as

$$i = I/S \quad (3.6)$$

For the reaction occurring on a metal electrode surface (Equation 3.1), let kf and kr respectively be the rate constants for the forward and reverse reactions. Then the net reaction rate is given by

$$r_A = (1/S)dn_A/dt= -k_fCA + k_rCB \quad (3.7)$$

Using Equation 3.6 in Equation 3.5 gives

$$i = -nFk_f\,CA + nFk_rCB \quad (3.8)$$

Inspection of Equations 3.1 and 3.8 reveals that the forward reaction (which consumes electrons) contributes a negative current, whereas the reverse reaction (which releases electrons) contributes a positive current. A convention shall be used such that a *positive current* is said to flow when positive charge flows from electrode to solution, i.e., electron generation (anodic reaction) occurs and electrons flow from solution to electrode. Thus, the forward reaction of Equation 3.1 is associated with a *negative current* density since it involves the transfer of A^{z+} (a positively charged species) from the solution to the electrode, and electrons from the electrode to the solution, i.e., electrons are consumed (cathodic reaction). On the other hand, the reverse reaction which transfers a positively charged species to the aqueous phase, and electrons from the solution to the electrode, gives rise to a positive current.

Activation Energy for Electron Transfer

The activation energy of a *chemical* reaction can be taken as a constant at a given temperature. In contrast, the activation energy of an *electrochemical* reaction is greatly influenced by the electrode potential. Recalling the electrode reaction described by Equation 3.1, it would be expected that, since A^{z+} is charged, its reaction would be affected by the potential difference between the metal electrode (ϕM) and the aqueous solution (ϕ_{Aq}). As the value of (ϕ_M - ϕ_{Aq} = •ϕ) becomes less positive, the attraction of A^{z+} to the electrode surface would be enhanced and therefore the rate of the forward reaction would rise (i.e., k_f would increase). Furthermore, it would be harder to reject A^{z+} from the electrode surface and therefore the reverse reaction would slow down (i.e., k_r would decrease). This dependence of the rate constants on the potential difference can be expressed quantitatively in terms of an Arrhenius-type equation, with an activation energy which is proportional to (ϕM - ϕAq):

$$k_f = k_{f,o} \exp[-(1 - \alpha)nF(\phi M - \phi_{Aq})/RT] \tag{3.9a}$$

$$k_r = k_{r,o} \exp[\alpha nF(\phi M - \phi A_q)/RT] \tag{3.9b}$$

where F is the Faraday constant, a is termed the *transfer coefficient* and gives the fraction of the potential difference that influences the forward reaction, i.e., $(1 - \alpha)(\phi M - \phi_{Aq})$, as well as the fraction that affects the reverse reaction, i.e., $\alpha(\phi M - \phi Aq)$.

We can gain some insight into the origin of the α parameter by considering the free energy changes associated with the electron transfer process. When a potential is applied to the electrode, the energy of an electron in the electrode is altered. As illustrated in figure 3.2, with a positive potential (E>0), the energy is lowered compared with the E=0 condition. In contrast, when a negative potential (E<0) is applied, the energy of the electron is raised.

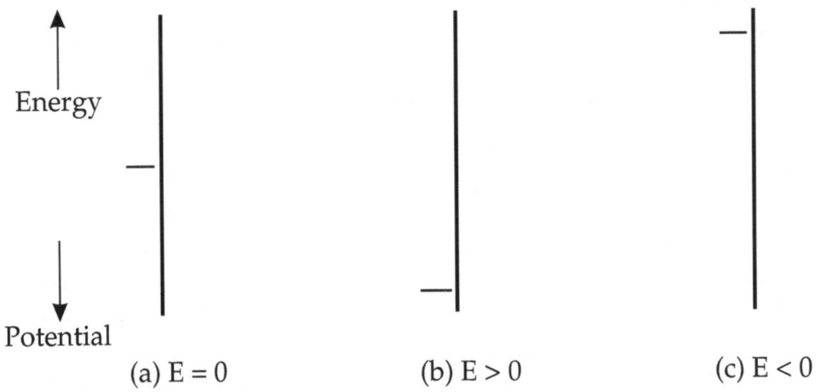

Fig. 3.2: A Relationship between electrode potential and electron energy

We can say that when the electrode potential is zero (E = 0 V), the reactants ($A^{z+} + ne^-$) and the product (B) are associated with free energies which change with distance as shown by the solid curves. It must be noted that the free energy of A^{z+} increases as it approaches the electrode surface since it becomes necessary to (fully or partially) discard the waters of hydration of this species. Correponding to the cathodic (forward) and anodic (reverse) reactions of Equation 3.1 are the activation energies $\Delta G\#_{oc}$ and $\Delta G\#_{oa}$ respectively.

When a positive potential (E) is imposed on the electrode, the energy of the electron is lowered (Figure 3.3) and consequently, the curve representing the ($A^{z+} + ne^-$) configuration moves downwards by the amount nFE, as shown by the dashed curve in Figure 3.3. The resulting cathodic and anodic activation energies are $\Delta G\#_c$ and $\Delta G\#_a$ respectively. It can be seen that application of the positive potential E has the consequence of lowering the anodic activation energy by a certain fraction (anFE) of the overall energy change. It follows from Figure 3.3 that

$\Delta G\#_a = \Delta G\#_{oa} - \alpha nFE$ (3.10a)

Examination of Figure 3.3 further shows that:

$\Delta G\#_c + \alpha nFE = \Delta G\#_{oc} + nFE$ (3.10b)

Thus

$\Delta G\#_c = \Delta G\#_{oc} + (1-\alpha)nFE$ (3.10c)

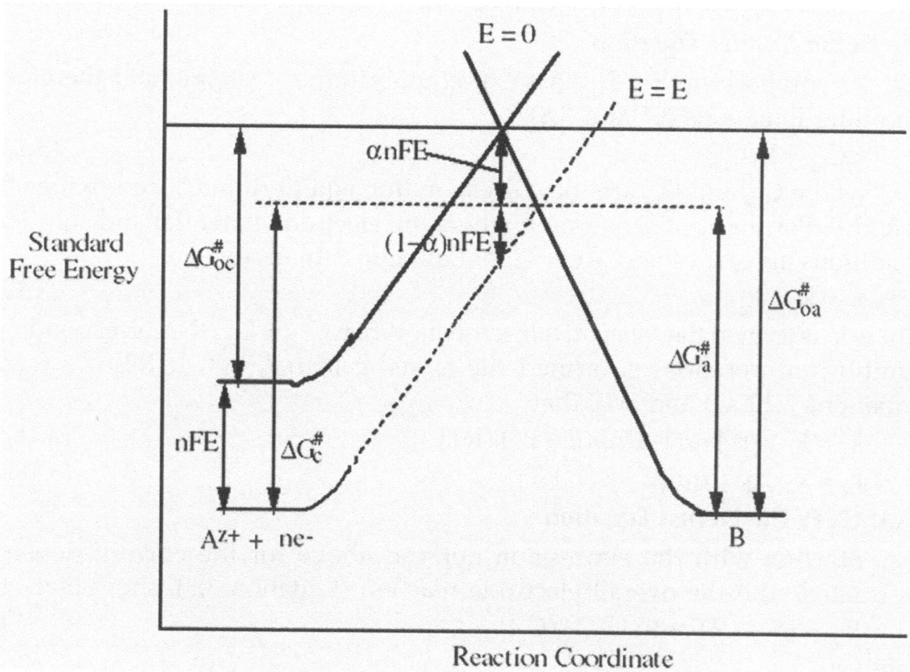

Fig. 3.3: Relationship between electrode potential and the activation energy for electron transfer

We can express the rate constants kf and kr in terms of the following Arrhenius-type equations:

$k_f = k'_{f,o} \exp[-\Delta G^{\#}_c/RT]$ (3.11a)

$k_r = k'_{r,o} \exp[-\Delta G^{\#}_a/RT]$ (3.11b)

It follows from Equations 3.10 a, c and 3.11 a, b, that

$k_f = k'_{f,o} \exp[-(\Delta G^{\#}_{oc} + (1-\alpha)nFE)/RT]$

$= (k'_{f,o} \exp- \Delta G^{\#}_{oc}/RT)\exp[-(1-\alpha)nFE/RT]$ (3.12a)

$= k_{f.o} \exp[-(1-\alpha)nFE/RT]$

$k_r = k'_{r,o} \exp[-(\Delta G^{\#}_{oa} - \alpha nFE)/RT]$

$=(k'_{r,o} \exp - \Delta G^{\#}_{oa}/RT) \exp[\alpha nFE/RT)$

$= k_{r,o} \exp[\alpha nFE/RT]$ (3.12b)

where

$k_{f,o} = k'_{f,o} \exp[-\Delta G^{\#}_{oc}/RT]$ (3.13a)

$$k_{r,o} = k'_{f,o} \exp[-\Delta G^{\#}_{oa}/RT] \tag{3.13b}$$

Based on Equations 3.12a and 3.12b, Equation 3.7 can be rewritten as:

$$r_A = -k_{f,o}C_A\exp[-(1-\alpha)nFE/RT] + k_{r,o}C_B\exp[\alpha nFE/RT] \tag{3.14}$$

Also, in view of Equations 3.8, 3.12a, and 3.12b, the current density can be expressed as:

$$i_A = -nFk_{f,o}C_A\exp[-(1-\alpha)nFE/RT] + nFk_{r,o}C_B\exp[\alpha nFE/RT] \tag{3.15}$$

The Butler-Volmer Equation

At equilibrium, $E = E_{eq}$. Also, at equilibrium, $r_A = 0$, i=0, and therefore (recalling Equations 3.7 and 3.8),

$$k_fC_{Ae} = k_r\, C_{Be} \tag{3.16}$$

where C_{Ae} and C_{Be} are the corresponding equilibrium concentrations of A and B. For the special situation where the electrode potential and solution conditions are such that CAe = CBe, Equation 3.16 gives:

$$k_f = k_r = k_o \tag{3.17}$$

where k_o is termed the *standard rate constant*. When $C\text{-}_{Ae} = C_{Be}$, the corresponding equilibrium potential is termed the *formal potential*, Eθ'. It follows from Equations 3.12 a,b and 3.17 that

$$k_f = k_o \exp[-\alpha(1-\alpha)nF(E - E^{\theta'})/RT] \tag{3.18a}$$

$$k_f = k_o \exp[\alpha nF(E - E^{\theta'})/RT] \tag{3.18b}$$

EXAMPLE: The Nernst Equation

Starting with the expression derived above for the current density associated with the overall electrode reaction (Equation 3.8), show that

$$E_{eq} = E^{\theta'} + (RT/nF)\ln(C_A/C_B) \tag{1}$$

Solution

From Equation 3.8 we know that

$$i = -nFk_fC_A + nFk_rC_B \tag{3.8}$$

Also, at equilibrium, i = 0 and therefore $k_fC_{Ae} = k_rC_{Be}$; also, $E = E_{eq}$. It follows then from Equations 3.18a,b, and 3.8 that

$$C_{Ae}k_o \exp[-(1-\alpha)nf(E_{eq} - E^{\theta'})/RT]=C_{Be}k_o \exp[^{\theta'}nF(E_{eq} - E^{\theta'})/RT] \tag{2}$$

Thus,

$$(C_{Ae}/C_{Be})= \exp[(\alpha + 1 - \alpha)nF(E_{eq} - E^{\theta'})/RT] = \exp[nF(E_{eq} - E^{\theta'})/RT] \tag{3}$$

Rearranging, we get the desired expression:

$$E_{eq} = E^{\theta'} + (RT/nF)\ln(C_{Ae}/C_{Be}) \tag{4}$$

Equation 4 represents the Nernst equation for the A^{z+}/B couple.

Combining Equation 3.8 with Equations 3.18a, b gives:

$$i = nFk_oC_A \exp[-(1-\alpha)nF(E-E^{\theta'})/RT]+nFk_oC_B\exp[\alpha nF(E-E^{\theta'})/RT] \tag{19.19}$$

Equation 3.19 can be rewritten as:

$$i = i\text{-} + i_+ \tag{3.20}$$

where i- is the *cathodic current*, and i+ the *anodic current*:

$i_- = -nFk_oC_A\exp[-(1-\alpha)nF(E-E^{\theta'})/RT]$ (3.21a)

and

$i_+ = nFk_oC_B\exp[\alpha nF(E-E^{\theta'})/RT]$ (3.21b)

At equilibrium, i = 0. Thus, Equation 3.20 gives:

$i_+ = -i_- = i_o = nFk_oC_{Be}\exp[\alpha nF(E_{eq} - E^{\theta'})/RT] =$ (3.22)

$nFk_oC_{Ae}\exp[-(1-\alpha)nF(E_{eq} - E^{\theta'})/RT]$

That is, at equilibrium, the anodic and cathodic currents have the same magnitude, i.e., io, termed the *exchange current density*. It follows from Equation 3.22 that:

$nFk_o C_{Ae} = i_o\exp[(1-\alpha)nF(E_{eq} - E^{\theta'})/RT]$ (3.23a)

$nFk_oC_{Be} = i_o\exp[-\alpha nF(E_{eq} - E^{\theta'})/RT$ (3.23b)

From 3.21a and 3.23a,

$i_- = -(C_A/C_{Ae})i_o\exp[-(1-\alpha)nF(E - E^{\theta'} - E_{eq} + E^{\theta'}/RT]$

$= -(C_A/C_{Ae})i_o\exp[-(1-\alpha)nF(E-E_{eq})/RT]$ (3.24a)

From 3.21b and 3.23b,

$i_+ = (C_B/C_{Be})i_o\exp[\alpha nF(E - E^{\theta'} - E_{eq} + E^{\theta'})/RT]$

$= (C_B/C_{Be})\, i_o\exp[\alpha nF(E - E_{eq})/RT]$ (3.24b)

Using Equations 3.24a and 3.24b in Equation 3.20,

$i = i_o\{(C_B/C_{Be})\exp[\alpha nF(E-E_{eq})/RT] - (C_A/C_{Ae})\exp[-(1-\alpha nf(E-E_{eq})/RT]\}$

$= i_o\{(C_B/C_{Be})\exp[\alpha nF\eta/RT] - (C_A/C_{Ae})\exp[-(1-\alpha)nF\eta/RT]\}$ (3.25a)

where h is termed the *activation overpotential* and is given by:

$n = E - E_{eq}$ (3.25b)

Equation 3.25a is called the *Butler-Volmer equation*. Figures 3.4a and b illustrate respectively, the variation of (i/i_o) and $\log(|i|/i_o)$ with the overpotential η.

The above analysis indicates that if the rate of electron transfer is slow, then in order to obtain significant reaction rates, it is necessary to provide an applied potential that is sufficiently greater than the equilibrium potential.

EXAMPLE: Relationship between the exchange current density and the standard rate constant

Show that when $C_{Ae} = C_{Be} = C_o$,

$i_o = nFk_oC_o$

Solution

Recall the Nernst equation (Ex19.1):

$E_{eq} = E^{\theta'} + (RT/nF)\ln(C_{Ae}/C_{Be})$ (1)

That is,

$\exp[nF(E_{eq} - E^{\theta'})/RT] = C_{Ae}/C_{Be}$ (2)

Multiply Equation 2 by $\exp[-(1-\alpha)]$:

$\{\exp[-(1-\alpha)]\}\exp[nF(E_{eq} - E^{\theta'})/RT] = (C_{Ae}/C_{Be})\exp[-(1-\alpha)] = \exp[-(1-\alpha)]$ (3)

In Equation 3 the condition CAe = CBe has been used.

We know from Equation 3.22 that

$i_o = nFk_oC_{Ae}\exp[-(1-\alpha)nF(E_{eq} - E^{\theta'})/RT]$

Therefore, it follows from Equation 3 that Equation 3.22 can be rewritten as

$i_o = nFk_oC_{Ae} = nFk_oC_o$

where the condition $C_{Ae} = C_o$ has been used.

Recall: from 3.8 and 3.20,

$i- = -nFk_f\,CA$ (3.26)

Compare 3.24a and 3.26:

$-nFk_fC_A = (-C_A/C_{Ae})i_o\exp[-(1-\alpha)nF\eta/RT]$

$k_f = (i_o/nFC_{Ae})\exp[-(1-\alpha)nF\eta/RT]$ (3.27)

Similarly, from 3.8 and 3.20,

$i+ = nFk_r\,C_B$ (3.28)

Compare 3.24b and 3.28:

$nFk_rC_B = (C_B/C_{Be})i_o\exp[\alpha nf\,(E - E_{eq})/RT]$

$k_r = (i_o/nFC_{Be})\exp[\alpha nF(E-E_{eq})/RT]$

$k_r = (i_o/nFC_{Be})\exp(\alpha nF\eta/RT]$ (3.29)

Summary

$k_f = k'_{f,o}\exp[-\Delta G^{\#}_c/RT]$ (3.11a)

$= k_{f,o}\exp[-(1-\alpha)nFE/RT]$ (3.12a)

$= k_o\exp[-(1-\alpha)\,nF(E - E^{\theta'})/RT]$ (3.18a)

$= (i_o/nFC_{Ae})\exp[-(1-\alpha)nF\eta/RT]$ (3.27)

$K_r = k'_{r,o}\exp[-\Delta G^{\#}_a/RT]$ (3.11b)

$=k_{r,o}\exp[\alpha nFE/RT]$ (3.12b)

$= k_o\exp[\alpha nF\,(E - E^{\theta'})/RT]$ (3.18b)

$= (i_o/nFC_{Be})\exp[\alpha nF\eta/RT]$ (3.29)

The Tafel Equations

If |h| >> (RT/F), two simplified relations called the *Tafel equations* arise:

(a) When η is positive, the second term in Equation 3.25a can be neglected, with the result that:

$i = i_o\exp[\alpha nF\eta/RT]$ (3.30a)

or

$\ln i = \ln i_o + \alpha nF\eta/RT$ (3.30b)

That is,

$\ln i = \ln\,(nFC_Bk_{r,o}\exp[\alpha nFE_{eq}/RT]) + \alpha nF\eta/RT$ (3.30c)

(b) When η is negative, the first term in Equation 3.25a can be neglected to give:

$i = -i_o\exp[-(1-\alpha)nF\eta/RT]$ (3.31a)

or

$$\ln |i| = \ln i_o - (1 - \alpha)nF\eta/RT \quad (3.31b)$$

That is,

$$\ln |i| = \ln \{nFC_A k_{f,o} \exp[-(1 - \alpha)nFE_{eq}/RT\} - (1 - \alpha)nF\eta/RT \quad (3.31c)$$

The linear relationship between log (|i|/io) and h implied in Equations 3.30b and 3.31b can be seen in Figure 3.4b for large values of $|\eta|$.

EXAMPLE: The Fe^{3+}/Fe^{2+} electrode

Gerischer, Z. Elektrochem., 54, 366 (1950)

Lewartowicz, J. Chim. Phys. 49, 564 (1952)

Vetter and Manecke, Z. Physik. Chem., 195, 270 (1950)

Lewartowicz, J. Chim. Phys. 49, 573 (1952)

Petrocelli and Paolucci, J. Electrochem. Soc., 98, 291 (1950)

EXAMPLE: The Ce^{4+}/Ce^{3+} electrode

Vetter, Z. Physik. Chem., 196, 260 (1951)

Petrocelli and Paolucci, J. Electrochem. Soc., 98, 291 (1950) or 1951?

Lewartowicz, J. Chim. Phys. 49, 564, 573 (1952)

Mass Transfer Effects

It was pointed out that the motion of an ion in an aqueous electrolyte solution is controlled by: (a) diffusion caused by a concentration gradient, (b) migration due to the presence of an electric field, and (c) a convective or hydrodynamic transport due to bulk fluid motion. In the absence of migration and convection, the rate of transport is determined by the concentration gradient.

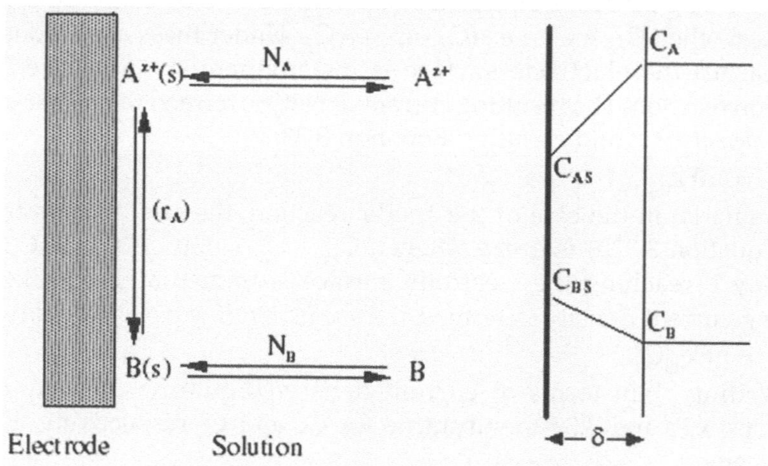

Fig. 3.4: Mass transfer in electrode processes

Recall the A^{Z+}/B reaction at the electrode surface:

$$A^{z+} + \underset{k_r}{\overset{k_f}{\Leftrightarrow}} B \quad (3.1)$$

Referring to Figure 3.5 and considering Equation 3.1:

Flux of A to the surface:

$$N_A = k_{d,A}(C_A - C_{AS}) \quad (3.32a)$$

Flux of B from the surface:

$$N_B = k_{d,B}(C_{BS} - C_B) \quad (3.32b)$$

Rate of consumption of A by the reaction at the electrode:

$$r_A = (1/S)dn_A/dt = -k_fC_{AS} + k_r C_{BS} = i/nF \quad (3.32c)$$

Under steady-state conditions, we must have

$$N_A = r_A = N_B = i/nF \quad (3.33)$$

From Equation 3.32a,

$$C_{AS} = C_A - (N_A/k_{dA}) \quad (3.34)$$

From Equation 3.32b,

$$C_{BS} = C_B + (N_B/k_{dB}) \quad (3.35)$$

Substituting Equations 3.34 and 3.35 into Equation 3.32c,

$$r_A = -k_f[(N_A/k_{dA}) + C_A] + K_r [C_B - (N_B/k_{dB})] \quad (3.36)$$

Recalling Equation 19.33, $N_A = N_B = r_A$, and thus, Equation 3.36 becomes:

$$r_A = -(k_r/k_{dA})r_A - k_fC_A + k_rC_B - (k_r/k_{dB})r_A$$

$$r_A[1+(k_f/k_{dA}) + (k_r/k_{dB})] = k_rC_A + k_rC_B$$

$$r_A = \frac{-k_fC_A + k_rC_B}{1 + (k_f/k_{dA}) + (k_r/k_{dB})} \quad (3.37)$$

It can be seen from Equation 3.32a that the rate of mass transport of A is greatest when $C_{AS} \ll C_A$, i.e., $(C_A - C_{As}) \approx C_A$. Under these conditions, any A that reaches the electrode surface is instantaneously consumed by the reduction reaction. The resulting current density is termed the *cathodic limiting current density*, i_{Lc}, and recalling Equation 3.33:

$$i_{LC} = -nFk_{dA}C_A \quad (3.38)$$

Similarly, in the case of the anodic reaction, the rate of mass transport of B (Equation 3.32b) is greatest when $C_{Bs} \ll C_B$, i.e., $(C_B - C_{BS}) \approx C_B$. In this case, any B reaching the electrode surface is immediately oxidized. The resulting current density is termed the *anodic limiting current density*, i_{La}:

$$i_{La} = nFk_{dB}C_B \quad (19.39)$$

Writing r_A in terms of current density (Equation 3.33), and using Equations 3.38 and 3.39 to substitute for C_A and C_B respectively, Equation 3.37 becomes:

$$(i/nF) = \frac{-k_f(-i_{LC}/nFk_{dA})+k_r(i_{La}/nFk_{dB})}{1+ (k_f/k_{dA}) + (k_r/k_{dB})} \quad (3.40a)$$

$$i = [(k_f/k_{dA})i_{LC} + (k_r/k_{dB})i_{La}]/[1+(k_f/k_{dA})+(k_r/k_{dB}) \quad (19.40b)$$

CASE 1: Only A is present in solution. What happens when only A is present in solution? Under these conditions, $C_B = 0 \rightarrow i_{La} = 0$. It should be noted that both k_f and k_r are potential-dependent. Recalling Equations 3.12a and 3.12b, it can be seen that as the potential (E) becomes more negative, k_f increases while k_r decreases. In the absence of B, the potential must be decreased sufficiently to drive the cathodic reaction. Under these circumstances, $k_f \gg k_r$. Therefore, using the constraints $i_{La} = 0$, and $k_f \gg k_r$, we get from Equation 3.40b:

$$i = (k_f/k_{dA})i_{LC}/[1+k_f/k_{dA}]$$
$$= k_f i_{LC}/[k_{dA} + k_f] \qquad (3.41a)$$

Rearranging,

$$\frac{1}{i} = \frac{k_{dA}}{k_f i_{LC}} + \frac{1}{i_{LC}} \qquad (3.41b)$$

Recalling Equation 3.38, (i.e., $i_{LC} = -\,nFk_{dA}C_A$), Equation 3.41b becomes

$$-1/i = 1/nFk_fC_A + 1/nFk_{dA}C_A \qquad (3.41c)$$

Depending on the relative magnitudes of k_f and k_{dA}, the electrode reaction will be kinetic or transport controlled. When $k_{dA} \gg k_f$, Equation 3.41c becomes:

$$-1/i = 1/nFk_fC_A \qquad (3.41d)$$

or

$$i = -nFk_fC_A \qquad (3.41e)$$

That is, in this case, the reaction is under kinetic control. On the other hand, when $k_{dA} \ll k_f$, Equation 3.41c simplifies to:

$$-1/i = 1/nFk_{dA}C_A \qquad (3.41f)$$

or

$$i = -nFk_{DA}C_A \qquad (3.41g)$$

In this case the reaction is transport controlled.

CASE 2: Only B is present in solution. Here $C_A = 0 \rightarrow i_{LC} = 0$. Also $k_r \gg k_f$ (for reverse of reasons given above for Case 1). Therefore, Equation 3.40b simplifies to:

$$i = (k_r/k_{dB})i_{La}/[1+(k_r/k_{dB})]$$
$$= k_r i_{La}/[k_{dB} + k_r] \qquad (3.42a)$$

or

$$1/i = k_{dB}/k_r i_{La} + 1/i_{La} \qquad (3.42b)$$

Recalling Equation 3.39 (i.e., $i_{La} = nFk_{dB}C_B$), Equation 3.42b may be rearranged as:

$$1/i = 1/nFK_rC_B + 1/nFk_{dB}C_B \qquad (3.42c)$$

When $k_{dB} \gg k_r$, the reaction is under kinetic control:

$$1/i = 1/nFk_rC_B \qquad (3.42d)$$

i.e.,

$$i = nFk_rC_B \tag{3.42e}$$

On the other hand, when $k_{dB} \ll k_r$, the reaction is under transport control and

$$1/i = 1/nFk_{dB}C_B \tag{3.42f}$$

$$i = nFk_{dB}C_B \tag{3.42g}$$

ELECTRICAL DOUBLE LAYER EFFECTS

Redox Electrodes

Multi-step Reactions at Metal Electrodes

An overall chemical reaction will typically consist of two or more steps. Electrochemical reactions are no exception. Thus, for example, on certain metal surfaces, the hydrogen evolution reaction involves a two-step process of the form:

$$H_3O^+ + e^- (M) \rightarrow H (M) + H_2O \tag{3.43a}$$

$$H (M) + H (M) \rightarrow H_2 \tag{3.43b}$$

The dissolution of a divalent metal ion, e.g., Cu, may involve the following steps:

$$Cu \rightarrow Cu^+ + e^- \tag{3.44a}$$

$$Cu+ \rightarrow Cu^{2+} + e^- \tag{3.44b}$$

The Mn^{4+}/Mn^{3+} redox electrode has the following overall reaction:

$$Mn^{3+} = Mn^{4+} + e^- \tag{3.45a}$$

The reaction steps are:

$$2Mn^{3+} \rightarrow Mn^{4+} + Mn^{2+} \tag{3.45b}$$

$$Mn^{2+} \rightarrow Mn^{3+} + e^- \tag{3.45c}$$

In the case of iodine reduction, the overall reaction is:

$$I_3^- + 2e^- = 3I^- \tag{3.46a}$$

The relevant reaction steps are:

$$I_3^- \leftrightarrow I_2 + I^- \tag{3.46b}$$

$$I_2 \leftrightarrow 2I \tag{3.46c}$$

$$I + e^- \rightarrow I^- \tag{3.46d}$$

Consider a general electrochemical reaction in which 2 electrons are transferred from an electrode to a species A, transforming it to C:

$$A + 2e^- = C \tag{3.47}$$

We can derive a rate law for this reaction with the aid of the steady-state assumption or the rapid equilibrium assumption.

Suppose this reaction proceeds via the following single-electron transfer steps:

Steady-state Assumption

$$A + e^- \leftrightarrow (k_1, k_{-1})\ B \quad \text{(Step 1)} \tag{3.48}$$

$B + e^- \leftrightarrow (k2, k\text{-}2)\ C$ (Step 2) (3.49)

Following the procedures developed, we can write:

$$r_A = -k_1C_A + k_{-1}C_B \quad (3.50)$$
$$r_B = k_1C_A - k_{-1}C_B - k_2C_B + k_{-2}C_C \quad (3.51)$$
$$r_C = k_2C_B - k_{-2}C_C \quad (3.52)$$

Applying the steady-state approximation to reactive intermediate B (i.e., $r_B = 0$) gives:

$$C_B = (k_1C_A + k_{-2}C_C)/(k_{-1} + k_2) \quad (3.53)$$

Inserting Equation 3.53 into Equations 3.50 and 3.52,

$$r_A = (-k_1k_2C_A + k_{-1}k_{-2}C_C)/(k_{-1} + k_2) \quad (3.54)$$
$$r_C = (k_1k_2C_A - k_{-1}k_{-2}C_C)/(k_{-1} + k_2) \quad (3.55)$$

Bearing in mind the convention adopted here, i.e., a reaction that releases an electron generates positive current, the net current associated with the overall reaction can be expressed as:

$$i/F = -k_1C_A + k_{-1}C_B - k_2C_B + k_{-2}C_C \quad (3.56)$$

Using Equation 3.53 to substitute for CB in Equation 3.56 gives:

$$i/F = 2(-k_1k_2C_A + k_{-1}k_{-2}C_C)/(k_{-1} + k_2) \quad (3.57)$$

It can be seen by comparing Equations 3.54 and 3.57 that $i/F = 2r_A$. This is consistent with the fact that the overall reaction involves the transfer of two electrons and that when the steady-state approximation is valid, the rates of the successive steps are equal. Recalling Equations 3.12a and 3.12b, the rate constants can be expressed as:

$$k_1 = k_{1,o} \exp[-(1-\alpha_1)FE/RT] \quad (3.58)$$
$$k_{-1} = k_{-1,o} \exp[\alpha_1 FE/RT] \quad (3.59)$$
$$k_2 = k_{2,o} \exp[-(1-\alpha_2)FE/RT] \quad (3.60)$$
$$k_{-2} = k_{-2,o} \exp[\alpha_2 FE/RT] \quad (3.61)$$

It is instructive to consider approximate forms of Equations 3.54, 3.55, and 3.57. For example, when $k_{-2} << k_1$, and $k_2 << k_{-1}$, we get:

$$C_B = k_1k_2C_A/k_{-1} \quad (3.62)$$
$$r_A = -k_1k_2C_A/k_{-1} \quad (3.63)$$
$$r_C = k_1k_2C_A/k_{-1} \quad (3.64)$$
$$i/F = -2k_1k_2C_A/k_{-1} \quad (3.65)$$

Recalling Equations 3.58, 3.59, and 3.60, Equation 3.63 can be rewritten as:

$$r_c = C_A \bullet k_{1,0} \exp[\alpha_1 FE/RT] \bullet k_{2,0} \exp[\alpha_2 FE/RT] \bullet k_{-1,0} \exp[(1-\alpha_1)FE/RT]$$
$$= (k_{1,0}k_{2,0}/k_{-1,0})C_A \exp[(\alpha_1 + \alpha_2 + 1 - \alpha_1)FE/RT]$$
$$r_c = ((k_{1,0}k_{2,0}/k_{-1,0})C_A \exp[(1+\alpha_2)FE/RT] \quad (3.66a)$$
$$= kC_A \exp[\alpha FE/RT] \quad (3.66b)$$

where

$$k = (k_{1,0}k_{2,0}/k_{-1,0}) \quad (3.67)$$
$$\alpha = 1 + \alpha_2 \quad (3.68)$$

Accordingly, the net current density becomes:

$$i = 2kc_A \exp[\alpha FE/RT] \tag{3.69}$$

The parameter $\alpha(=1+\alpha_2)$ is termed an *apparent transfer coefficient.*

Rapid Equilibrium Assumption. Let us now consider the case where the first electron transfer involves a rapid equilibrium:

$$A \overset{K_1}{\Leftrightarrow} B + e^- \quad \text{(fast)} \tag{3.70}$$

$$B \overset{K_2}{\Leftrightarrow} C + e^- \quad \text{(slow)} \tag{3.71}$$

The rapid equilibrium means that the forward and reverse rates of Equation 19.89 are equal in k_1 magnitude:

$$-k_1C_A + k_{-1} + C_B = 0 \tag{3.72}$$

Also

$$r_c = k_2\,C_B \tag{3.73}$$

It follows from Equation 3.72 that

$$C_B = (k_1/K_{-1})C_A \tag{3.74}$$

Inserting Equation 3.74 into Equation 3.73,

$$r_c = (k_1k_2/k_{-1})C_A \tag{3.75}$$

Referring to the stoichiometry of the overall reaction (Equation 3.47), production of 1 mole of C_A is associated with the generation of two moles of electrons. Thus:

$$i/F = 2_{rc} = 2_{k1k2}C_A/k_{-1} \tag{3.76}$$

It can be seen that Equations 3.74, 3.75, and 3.76 are identical to Equations 3.62, 3.64, and 3.65 respectively. Thus, applying the conditions k_{-2}<<k_2 and k_2<<k_{-1} to Equations 3.48 and 3.49 is equivalent to replacing Equation 3.49 by the irreversible reaction of Equation 3.71.

Adsorbed Intermediates and Electron Transfer

In the discussion above, the Butler-Volmer equation was derived on the assumption that the entire metal electrode surface was accessible to the reactants in the aqueous solution. In fact, there are many situations where reaction intermediates adsorb on the electron surface, thereby decreasing the effective surface available for reaction. Referring to Equation 3.1, suppose now that the product B is retained as an adsorbed intermediate on the electrode surface:

$$A^{z+} + ne^- \leftrightarrow B\ (\text{ads}) \tag{3.77}$$

Then recalling Equation 3.14, the corrresponding rate equation can be written as:

$$r_A = -CA(1 - \theta_B)k_{f,o}\exp[-(1 - \alpha)nFE/RT] + \theta_Bk_{r,o}\exp[\alpha nFE/RT] \tag{3.78a}$$

where θ_B is the fraction of the electrode surface that is occupied by the adsorbed intermediate B.

Similarly, recalling Equation 3.15, the current density now becomes:

$$i = -nFCA(1 - \theta_B)k_{f,o}\exp[-(1 - \alpha)nFE/RT] + nF\theta_B k_{r,o}\exp[\alpha nFE/RT] \quad (3.78b)$$

At equilibrium, the exchange current density is given by:

$$i_o = i_+ = nF\theta_{Be}k_{r,o}\exp[\alpha nFE_{eq}/RT] \quad (3.79a)$$

$$= -i_- = nFC_A(1 - \theta_{Be})k_{f,o}\exp[-(1 - \alpha)nFE_{eq}/RT] \quad (3.79b)$$

where qBe is the equilibrium surface coverage of B. Thus, we can rewrite Equation 3.78b as:

$$i = -nFC_A[(1 - \theta_B)/(1 - \theta_{Be})](1 - \theta_{Be})k_{f,o}\exp[-(1 - \alpha)nFE/RT]$$
$$+ nF[\theta_B/\theta_{Be}]\theta_{Be}k_{r,o}\exp[\alpha nFE/RT] \quad (3.80a)$$
$$= -i_o [\theta_B/\theta_{Be}]\exp[-(1 - \alpha)nF(E - E_{eq})/RT]$$
$$+ i_o[(1 - \theta_B)/(1 - \theta_{Be})] \exp[\alpha nF(E - E_{eq})/RT] \quad (3.80b)$$
$$= i_o \{[\theta_B/\theta_{Be}]\exp[\alpha nF\eta/RT] - [(1 - \theta_B)/(1 - \theta_{Be})]\exp [-(1 - \alpha)nF\eta/RT]\} \quad (3.80c)$$

The Langmuir Adsorption Isotherm. Also, it follows from Equations 3.79a and 3.79b that

$$\theta/(1 - \theta) = C_A K\exp[-nFE_{eq}/RT] \quad (3.81)$$

where $K = k_{f,o}/k_{r,o}$. Equation 3.81 represents a Langmuir adsorption isotherm for the intermediate B. The standard free energy of adsorption is given by

$$\Delta G_{ad\theta} = -RT\ln K \quad (3.82)$$

The Temkin Adsorption Isotherm. The Langmuir adsorption isotherm is based on the assumption that the free energy of adsorption is independent of the surface coverage. However, there is experimental evidence indicating that this is not generally the case. The coverage-dependent adsorption has a number of origins, including interactions between adsorbed species, heterogeneity of surface sites, and surface-dipole effects. According to the Temkin treatment, the surface is a composite of Langmuir adsorption sites, each with its own characteristic standard freee energy of adsorption. It is assumed that the standard free energy of adsorption varies linearly with coverage:

$$\Delta G_{ads,\theta} = \theta G_{ads,0} + r\theta \quad (3.83)$$

where r is a proportionality constant and $\Delta G_{ads,0}$ represents the standard free energy of adsorption at zero coverage. It should be noted that since the free energy of adsorption is a negative quantity, Equation 3.83 shows that with r positive, the magnitude of the free energy of adsorption decreases with coverage. It follows from Equation 3.83 that

$$\bullet\Delta G_{ads,\theta}/\bullet\theta = r \quad (3.84)$$

Similarly, in the case of the free energy of desorption, we can write:

$$\Delta G_{des,\theta} = \Delta G_{des,0} + r'\theta \quad (3.85)$$

where $\Delta G_{des'}\theta = -\Delta G_{ads'}\theta$, $\Delta G_{des'}0 = -\Delta G_{ads'}0$, and $r' = -r$.

Associated with the coverage-dependence of the free energy of adsorption is a coverage-dependence of the activation energy of adsorption ($\bullet G^*_{ads'\theta}$). In general, it is assumed that the two are related linearly, i.e.,

$\bullet\Delta G^*_{ads,\theta}/\bullet\theta = \gamma\bullet\Delta G_{ads,\theta}/\bullet\theta = \gamma r$ (3.86)

Similarly, for the activation energy of desorption,

$\bullet\Delta G^*_{des,\theta}/\bullet\theta = \gamma\bullet\Delta G_{des,\theta}/\bullet\theta = \gamma' r' = -(1 - \gamma)r$ (3.87)

where the proportionality constant γ' is related to γ as:

$\gamma' = (1 - \gamma)$ (3.88)

It can be seen from Equation 3.88 that γ has the characteristics of a symmetry factor.

It follows from Equations 3.86 and 3.87 that:

$\Delta G^*_{ads,\theta} = \Delta G^*_{ads,0} + \gamma r\theta$ (3.89)

$\Delta G^*_{des,\theta} = \Delta G^*_{des,0} + \gamma' r'\theta = \Delta G^*_{des,0} - (1 - \gamma)rq$ (3.90)

Returning now to Equation 3.77, we can write the rate equation for the Temkin condition as:

$i = -nFC_A(1 - \theta_B)k'_{f,o}\exp[-(1-\alpha)nFE/RT]\exp[-\Delta G^*_{ads,\theta}/RT]$
$+ nF\theta Bk'_{r,o}\exp[\alpha nFE/RT]\exp[-\Delta G^*_{des,\theta}/RT]$ (3.91)

Using Equations 3.89 and 3.90 respectively to substitute for $\Delta G^*_{ads,\theta}$ and $\Delta G^*_{des,\theta}$ in Equation 3.91 gives:

$i = -nFC_A(1 - \theta_B)k_{f,o}\exp[-(1-\alpha)nFE/RT]\exp[-\gamma r\theta/RT]$
$+ nF\theta_B k_{r,o}\exp[\alpha nFE/RT]\exp[(1 - \gamma)r\theta/RT]$ (3.92)

For intermediate coverages, the contributions of the pre-exponential terms in q are small compared with the corresponding exponential terms. Thus, Equation 3.92 may be simplified to:

$i = -nFC_A k_{f,o}\exp[-(1-\alpha)nFE/RT]\exp[-\gamma r\theta/RT]$
$+ nFk_{r,o}\exp[\alpha nFE/RT]\exp[(1 - \gamma)r\theta/RT]$ (3.93)

At equilibrium, i = 0, and Equation 3.93 reduces to:

$\theta = -nFE_{eq}/RTr + (1/r)\ln KC_A$ (3.94)

For purposes of comparison, the Langmuir adsorption isotherm (Equation 3.81) may be re-expressed in logarithmic form as:

$\ln\theta - \ln(1 - \theta) = -nFE_{eq}/RT + \ln KC_A$ (3.95)

Examination of Equations 3.94 and 3.95 indicates that as C_A is increased, θ increases more rapidly with the Langmuir isotherm compared with the Temkin isotherm; this effect increases with increase in the magnitude of the proportionality constant, r. This situation can be understood physically by recognizing that as the coverage increases, further adsorption becoms less favorable, because of the corresponding decrease in $|\bullet G\theta|$.

The Hydrogen Electrode

It was pointed out that water decomposes under reducing conditions to give molecular hydrogen, and under oxidizing conditions to give molecular oxygen. These reactions frequently serve as the half-reactions for many technologically important electrochemical processes. They may also represent competing reactions which therefore decrease the efficiency of the reactions of interest. Thus, in oxygen-free solutions metals with standard reduction potentials below that of the standard hydrogen electrode will dissolve, with evolution of hydrogen:

$$M + 2H^+ \rightarrow M^{2+} + H_2 \quad (3.96)$$

This reaction can be decoupled into its anodic and cathodic half-reactions as:

$$M \rightarrow M^{2+} + 2e^- \quad (3.97)$$

$$2H^+ + 2e^- \rightarrow H_2 \quad (3.98)$$

The cathodic evolution of hydrogen is also of importance in metal deposition systems where it represents a competing reaction to the metal reduction reaction.

Pathways for the Hydrogen Evolution Reaction. Two main mechanisms are accepted for the hydrogen evolution reaction. These are the *chemical-desorption* mechanism:

$$H_3O^+ + e^- \rightarrow H\ (ad) + H_2O \quad (3.99)$$

$$H\ (ad) + H\ (ad) \rightarrow H_2 \quad (3.100)$$

and the *electrochemical-desorption* mechanism:

$$H_3O^+ + e^- \rightarrow H\ (ad) + H_2O \quad (3.99)$$

$$H\ (ad) + H_3O^+ + e^- \rightarrow H_2 + H_2O \quad (3.101)$$

It can be seen from Equations 3.99-3.101 that in both cases, the first step is the reduction of a hydrated proton to give an adsorbed hydrogen atom. However, the two mechanisms differ in what happens next. In the chemical-desorption mechanism, the adsorbed hydrogen atoms diffuse over the electrode surface. When two such atoms encounter one another, they react chemically to give a hydrogen molecule, which then desorbs (Equation 3.100). In the case of the electrochemical-desorption pathway, additional protons are reduced onto the first layer of adsorbed hydrogen atoms. Atoms from the first and second layers then combine to form hydrogen molecules (Equation 19.101). For either mechanism, the rate-determining step may be the the first step (case a) or the second step (case b).

The chemical-desorption mechanism. Let us first consider case (a), i.e., the situation where the first step (i.e., the discharge step) is rate-determining:

$$H_3O^+ + e- \rightarrow H\ (ad) + H_2O \quad k_1 \quad (3.102)$$

$$H\ (ad) + H\ (ad) \leftrightarrow H_2 \quad k_2, k_{-2} \quad (3.103)$$

The current density associated with the rate-determining step is given by:

$$i_1 = Fk_{1,0}[H_3O+](1 - \theta H)\exp[-(1 - \alpha)FE/RT] \quad (3.104)$$

For relatively low surface concentration of adsorbed atomic hydrogen, $\theta_H \rightarrow 0$ and Equation 3.104 simplifies to:

$$i_1 = Fk_{1,0}[H_3O+]\exp[-(1 - \alpha)FE/RT] \quad (3.105)$$

Now, the entire two-step reaction involves the transfer of two electrons. Thus, the net current is given by:

$$i = 2i_1 = 2Fk_1[H_3O+]\exp[-(1 - \alpha)F\Delta\phi/RT] \quad (3.106)$$

Alternatively, for case (b), where the second step (i.e., chemical desorption) is rate-determining, we have:

$$H_3O^+ + e^- \leftrightarrow H\ (ad) + H_2O\ k_1, k_{-1} \quad (3.107)$$

$$H\ (ad) + H\ (ad) \rightarrow H_2\ k_2 \quad (3.108)$$

Here, the first step (Equation 3.107) is at quasi-equilibrium. Thus:

$$k_{1,0}[H_3O+](1 - \theta H)\exp[-(1 - \alpha)FE/RT] = k_{-1,0}\theta_H\exp[\alpha FE/RT] \quad (3.109)$$

That is,

$$\Delta_H = \{k_1,0[H_3O^+]\exp[-FE/RT]\}/\{k_{-1,0} + k_{1,0}[H_3O+]\exp[-FE/RT]\} \quad (3.110)$$

For low overpotentials, k1,0[H3O+]exp[-FE/RT] << k-1,0, and Equation 3.110 reduces to:

$$\Delta_H = (k_{1,0}/k_{-1,0})[H_3O+]\exp[-FE/RT]\} \quad (3.111)$$

The rate equation for the second step (Equation 3.108) is given by:

$$i_2 = Fk_2\theta H_2 \quad (3.112)$$

Thus, it follows from Equations 3.111 and 3.112 that the net current is:

$$i = 2i_2 = 2Fk_2\theta H^2 = 2Fk_2\,(k_{1,0}/k_{-1,0})^2[H_3O+]^2\exp[-2FE/RT]\} \quad (3.113)$$

The electrochemical-desorption mechanism. For case (a), where the first step is rate-determining, we have:

$$H_3O^+ + e^- \rightarrow H\ (ad) + H_2O\ \ k_1 \quad (3.114)$$

$$H\ (ad) + H_3O^+ + e- \leftrightarrow H^2 + H^2O\ \ k_2, k_{-2} \quad (3.115)$$

It can be seen that Equation 3.114 is the same as Equation 3.102, i.e., it represents the same situation as that treated above for the chemical-desorption mechanism. Thus the same net rate law is obtained (Equation 3.106).

On the other hand, for case (b), where the electrochemical desorption step is rate-determining, the reaction steps can be represented as:

$$H_3O^+ + e^- \leftrightarrow H\ (ad) + H_2O\ \ k_1, k_1 \quad (3.116)$$

$$H\ (ad) + H_3O^+ + e^- \rightarrow H_2 + H_2O\ k_2 \quad (3.117)$$

Here, the first step is the same as in case (b) of the chemical desorption pathway. Hence, we can also use Equations 3.110 and 3.111 to represent qH. For the second step, the relevant rate equation is:

$$i_2 = Fk_2,0\theta_H[H_3O+]\exp[-(1 - \theta)FE/RT]\} \quad (3.118)$$

Combining Equations 3.111 and 3.118 gives:

$$i_2 = Fk_{2,0}\,(k_{1,0}/k_{-1,0})[H_3O+]^2\exp[-(2 - \alpha)FE/RT]\} \quad (3.119)$$

The net current is then given by:

$$i = 2i_2 = 2Fk_{2,0}\,(k_{1,0}/k_{-1,0})[H_3O+]^2\exp[-(2 - \alpha)FE/RT]\} \quad (3.120)$$

A summary of kinetic parameters arising from the above reaction mechanisms is presented in Table 3.1.

Table 3.1: Kinetic parameters for the hydrogen evolution reaction

Mechanism	Rate-limiting step	αc	H_3O^+ R'n order*
Chemical-desorption	Discharge Desorption	(1 - α) 2	1.0 2.0
Electrochemical-desorption	Discharge Desorption	(1 - α) (2 - α)	1.0 2.0

* From (•lni/•ln[H_3O+])E

The Oxygen Electrode

Pathways for Oxygen Reduction. Two overall pathways have been identified for oxygen reduction in aqueous solutions. These are the *four-electron pathway* (Equations 3.121 and 3.122), and the *two-electron pathway* (Equations 3.123 and 3.124):

$$O_2 + 4H^+ + 4e^- \rightarrow 2H_2O \quad \text{(acid solutions)} \qquad (3.121)$$

$$O_2 + 2H_2O + 4e^- \rightarrow 4OH^- \text{ (alkaline solutions)} \qquad (3.122)$$

$$O_2 + 2H^+ + 2e^- \rightarrow H_2O_2 \text{ (acid solutions)} \qquad (3.123)$$

$$O_2 + H_2O + 2e^- \rightarrow HO_2^- + OH^- \text{ (alkaline solutions)} \qquad (3.124)$$

It must be noted that the hydrogen peroxide produced in the two-electron pathway may undergo further reaction:

$$H_2O_2 + 2H+ + 2e^- \rightarrow 2H_2O \text{ (acid solutions)} \qquad (3.125)$$

$$2H_2O_2 \rightarrow 2H_2O + O_2 \text{ (acid solutions)} \qquad (3.126)$$

$$HO_2^- + H_2O + 2e^- \rightarrow 3OH^- \text{ (alkaline solutions)} \qquad (3.127)$$

$$2HO_2^- \rightarrow 2OH^- + O_2 \text{ (alkaline solutions)} \qquad (3.128)$$

Table 3.2: Electrode materials and reaction pathways for oxygen reduction

Reaction Pathway	Electrode Material
Four-electron	Platinum group metals Other metals: Ag Oxides: Pyrochlores (e.g., lead ruthenate)
Two-electron	Graphite Metals: Au, Hg, most oxide-covered metals (e.g., Ni, Co) Oxides: Most transition metal oxides (e.g., NiO, spinels)

(Modified from E. Yeager, J. Mol. Catal., 38, 5 (1986)

The electrochemical reactions of oxygen are influenced by the nature of the metal electrode. On the basis of the pathways noted above, electrode materials may be classified. The manner in which molecular oxygen first binds (i.e., adsorbs on) to the metal atoms on the electrode surface determines whether the overall reduction reaction will follow the four-electron or the two electron pathway. Molecular orbital representations of the possible modes of attachment, that with the Griffith and bridge-type interactions, both oxygens of O_2 form M-O bonds. These arrangements should favor the dissociation of O_2 and therefore, the direct 4-electron process.

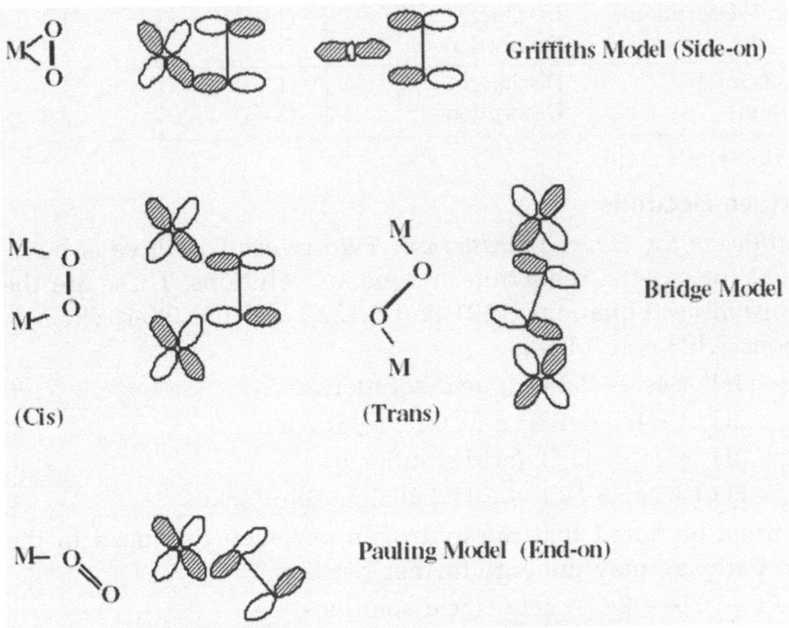

Fig. 3.5: Molecular orbital representations of the types of interactions of molecular oxygen with metal atoms

Oxygen Reduction on Bare Platinum in Acid Solution. The following rate mechanism has been proposed:

$$O_2 + H^+ + e^- \rightarrow HO_2\,(ads) \quad k1 \tag{3.129}$$

$$HO_2\,(ads) + H^+ + e^- \leftrightarrow O\,(ads) + H_2O \; k_2, k_{-2} \tag{3.130}$$

$$O\,(ads) + H^+ + e^- \leftrightarrow OH\,(ads) \quad k_3, k_{-3} \tag{3.131}$$

$$OH\,(ads) + H^+ + e^- \leftrightarrow H_2O \quad k_4, k_{-4} \tag{3.132}$$

The first step (Equation 3.129) is taken to be rate-determining, while the remaining steps are assumed to be at quasi-equilibrium. Thus, assuming Temkin conditions, we can write, in analogy with Equation 3.91.

$$i = -nFC_A(1 - \theta B)k'_{f,o}\exp[-(1-\alpha)nFE/RT]\exp[-\Delta G^*_{ads,\theta}/RT]$$
$$+ nFqBk'r,o\exp[anFE/RT]\exp[-DG^*des,q/RT] \tag{3.91}$$

$$i_1 = Fk'_1[H^+]p_{O2}(1 - \theta)\exp[-(1 - \alpha)FE/RT]\,\exp[-\Delta G^*_{ads,\theta}/RT] \tag{3.133}$$

where

$$\Delta G^*_{ads,\theta} = \Delta G^*ads,0 + \gamma r\theta \tag{3.89}$$

Inserting Equation 3.89 in Equation 3.133 gives:

$$i_1 = Fk_1[H^+]pO_2(1 - \theta)\exp[-(1 - \alpha)FE/RT]\,\exp[-\gamma r\theta/RT] \tag{3.134}$$

The steps which follow the rate-determining step are assumed to be in quasi-equilibrium. Thus, in the case of the last step,

$Fk_4[H^+]\theta \exp[-(1 - \alpha)FE/RT] \exp[(1 - \gamma)r\theta/RT]$
$= Fk_{-4}[H_2O](1 - \theta)\exp[\alpha FE/RT] \exp[-\gamma r\theta/RT]$ (3.135)

Again, neglecting the pre-exponential terms in q, Equation 3.135 reduces to:

$Fk_4[H^+]\exp[-(1 - \alpha)FE/RT] \exp[(1 - \gamma)r\theta/RT]$
$= Fk_{-4}[H_2O]\exp[\alpha FE/RT] \exp[-\gamma r\theta/RT]$ (3.136)

It follows from Equation 3.136 that

$\exp[-r\theta/RT] = K_4[H^+]\exp[-FE/RT]$ (3.137)

Rearranging Equation 3.137 gives the surface coverage as:

$\theta = (F/r)\Delta\phi + (2.3RT/r)pH -(2.3RT/r)\log K_4$ (3.138)

Using Equation 3.137 in Equation 3.134 gives:

$i_1 = Fk_1[H+]pO_2\exp[-(1 - \alpha)FE/RT]\ K_4\gamma[H+]\gamma\exp[-\gamma FE/RT]$ (3.139a)

$i_1 = Fk_1K_4\gamma[H+]^{1+\gamma}pO_2\exp[-(1 - \alpha + \gamma)FE/RT]$ (3.139b)

For α •γ•½, Equation 3.139a becomes:

$i_1 = k[H^+]^{3/2}pO_2\exp[-FE/RT]$ (3.140)

$OH\ (ads) + H^+ + e^- \leftrightarrow H_2O\quad k_4, k_{-4}$ (3.132)

Also, the relationship between θ and potential is approximately linear (see Equation 3.138):

$\alpha = (RT/r)pH + (F/r)V$ (3.141)

Combining Equations 5, 6, and 7, it can be shown that:

$i_1 = Fk_1[H^+]^{3/2}pO_2\exp[-FE/RT]$ (3.142)

With increase in the absolute value of the potential, q becomes negligibly small and Langmuirian behavior prevails, resulting in a change in the Tafel slope to -2RT/F.

The reaction on iridium has been rationalized in terms of the following mechanism:

$O_2 + 2M \leftrightarrow 2MO$ (Step 1) (3.143a)

$MO + H^+ + e^- \rightarrow MOH$ (Step 2) (3.143b)

$MOH + H^+ + e^- \leftrightarrow M + H_2O$ (Step 3) (3.143c)

where Step 2 is rate-determining.

Oxygen Reduction on Bare Platinum in Alkaline Solution. Two pathways have been identified, one of which involves H_2O_2 intermediate. The mechanism for the H_2O_2 intermediate pathway is:

$O_2 + e^- \rightarrow O_2^-\ (ads)\ k_1$ (3.144)

$O_2^-\ (ads) + H_2O \leftrightarrow HO_2^- + OH\ (ads)\ k_2, k_{-2}$ (3.145)

$OH\ (ads)\ e^- \leftrightarrow OH^-\ k_3, k_{-3}$ (3.146)

With step one rate-determining and Temkin adsorption for the peroxide intermediate, we get:

$i_1 = Fk_1pO_2(1 - \theta)\exp[-(1 - \theta)FE/RT] \exp[-(1 - \alpha)f(\theta)]$ (3.147)

where

$f(\theta) = FDf/RT - \ln[H^+]$ (3.148)

For α • 0.5, we get the following rate equation:

$$i_1 = Fk_1[H^+]^{1/2}pO_2exp[-FE/RT] \quad (3.149)$$

When the cathodic potential is relatively high, $\theta \rightarrow 0$ so that surface coverage no longer follows Temkin behavior. Accordingly, the rate becomes:

$$i_1 = Fk_1pO_2exp[-(1 - \alpha)FE/RT] \quad (3.150)$$

A comparison of Equations 3.149 and 3.150 indicates a change in the Tafel slope from -RT/F to -2RT/F as the surface coverage changes from Temkin to Langmuirian behavior.

Oxygen Reduction on Gold in Alkaline Solution. The following mechanism has been proposed by Zurilla et al.:

$$O_2 + e^- \rightarrow O2^- \text{ (ads) } k_1 \quad (3.151)$$

$$2O_2^- \text{ (ads) } + H_2O \leftrightarrow O_2 + HO_2^- + OH^- \;\; k_2, k_{-2} \quad (3.152)$$

The first step is believed to be rate-determining.

Oxygen Reduction on Iron in Neutral Solution. The following mechanism has been proposed by Zurilla et al:

$$O_2 \rightarrow O_2 \text{ (ads) } k_1 \quad (3.153)$$

$$O_2 \text{ (ads) } + H_2O + e^- \leftrightarrow O_2H \text{ (ads) } + OH^- \quad (3.154)$$

$$O_2H \text{ (ads) } + e^- \leftrightarrow O_2H^- \quad (3.155)$$

$$O_2H^- + H_2O \leftrightarrow H_2O_2 + OH^- \quad (3.156)$$

On oxide-covered iron, the surface coverage of adsorbed intermediates (O_2H (ads)) under Temkin conditions is given by

$$\theta = (F/r)E + (2.3RT/r) \log[OH^-] + const \quad (3.157)$$

Thus with adsorption (Equation 3.151) as the rate-determining step, we can write the following rate equation:

$$i_1 = Fk'_1pO_2 \exp[-(1 - \alpha)FE/RT] \exp[-\Delta G^*_{ads'}\theta/RT] \quad (3.158)$$

where

$$\Delta G^*_{ads'}\theta = \Delta G^*_{ads'}0 + \gamma r\theta \quad (3.159)$$

Using Equations 3.157 and 3.159 in 3.158,

$$i_1 = Fk_1pO_2 [OH^-]^{-1}/2exp[-(1 - \alpha + \gamma)FE/RT] \quad (3.160)$$

Since the rate-determining step is a chemical rather than an electrochemical reaction, $(1 - \alpha) = 0$, and assuming $\gamma = 1/2$, Equation 19.192 becomes:

$$i_1 = Fk_1pO_2 [OH^-]^{-1/2}exp[-FE/2RT] \quad (3.161)$$

On bare iron, the first electron transfer was found to be rate-determining:

$$O_2 + e^- \rightarrow O2^- \text{ (ads) } k_1 \quad (3.162)$$

Experimentally it was found that: •E/•log i = -120mV, •log i/•log pO_2 = 1, •log i/•pH = 0.

Oxygen Evolution on Platinum in Acid Solution. The oxygen evolution reaction may be contrasted with the oxygen reduction reaction in that the oxidation reaction occurs on an oxide-coated surface in contrast to the reduction reaction which may involve both oxide and bare surfaces.

$$OH^- \rightarrow OH + e^- \quad (3.163)$$

$$OH + OH^- \rightarrow O^- + H_2O \quad (3.164)$$

$$O^- \rightarrow O + e^- \quad (3.165)$$

$$O + O \rightarrow O_2 \quad (3.166)$$

In the case of acid solutions at low potentials (low current densities),

$$H_2O \rightarrow OH + H^+ + e^- \text{ (slow)} \quad (3.167)$$

$$OH + OH^- \rightarrow O^- + H_2O \quad (3.168)$$

$$O^- \rightarrow O + e^- \quad (3.169)$$

$$O + O \rightarrow O_2 \quad (3.170)$$

At higher potentials, mediation by surface metal ions:

$$M(^{z-1})+ \leftrightarrow M^{z+} + e^- \quad (3.171)$$

$$M^{z+} + H_2O \rightarrow M^{(z-1)+} + OH + H^+ \text{ (slow)} \quad (3.172)$$

$$OH + OH^- \rightarrow O- + H_2O \quad (3.173)$$

$$O^- \rightarrow O + e^- \quad (3.174)$$

$$O + O \rightarrow O_2 \quad (3.175)$$

Alkaline solutions at low potentials (low current densities) (Conway, *Langmuir*, 1990),

$$OH^- \rightarrow OH + e^- \quad (3.176a)$$

$$OH + OH^- \rightarrow O^- + H_2O \quad (3.176b)$$

$$O^- \rightarrow O + e^- \text{ (slow)} \quad (3.177)$$

$$O + O \rightarrow O_2 \quad (3.178)$$

THE HYDROGEN PEROXIDE ELECTRODE

The Chlorine Electrode

Mixed Potentials

Multiple Redox Couples at an Electrode

Up to this point, we have confined our discussion of electrode kinetics to situations where there is only a single overall electron transfer reaction at the electrode. There are many important practical systems, however, where two or more overall electron transfer reactions occur simultaneously at the same electrode. Examples are found in oxidative dissolution and in electroless deposition.

Let us consider the surface of a metallic particle immersed in a solution containing the reactants A and B. Immediately after contact with the two reactants, the metal surface develops two sites, i.e., anodic and cathodic sites at different potentials E1 and E2 respectively. These different potentials are a result of the anodic (Equation 3.179) and cathodic (reverse direction of Equation 3.180) reactions, as shown in figure 3.6. The presence of two different potentials on the same surface represents a non-steady-state situation and in order to achieve a uniform surface potential, electrons will begin to flow through the surface of the metal particle, from the anodic site to the cathodic site.

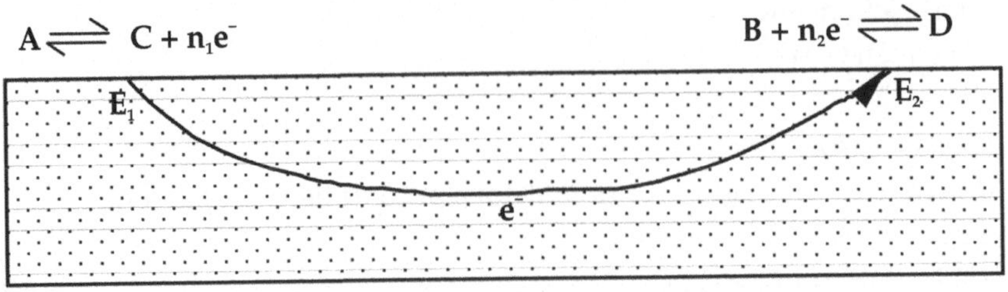

Fig. 3.6: Multiple electrode reactions and electron flow

$$A \underset{k_{-1}}{\overset{k_1}{\rightleftharpoons}} X + n_1e^- \quad (3.179)$$

$$D \underset{k_{-2}}{\overset{k_2}{\rightleftharpoons}} B + n_2e^- \quad (3.180)$$

The current flow reaches a steady-state when the net anodic and net cathodic currents balance each other (i.e., are equal and opposite in sign and therefore the net current is zero). The potential at this stage is termed the *mixed potential*, E_m, as illustrated for various scenarios. The term *rest potential* is often used. This term refers to the open circuit potential irrespective of whether the observed potential is a mixed potential (i.e., due to multiple overall electrode reactions, e.g., Equations 3.179 and 3.180) or a reversible potential (i.e., due to a single overall electrode reaction, e.g., Equation 3.179). The resulting overall reaction is given by:

$$n_2A + n_1B = n_2C + n_1D \quad (3.181)$$

It follows from Equations 3.179 and 3.180 that the corresponding equilibrium potentials are given by:

$$E_{1,eq} = E1^o + (RT/n_1F) \ln (C_C/C_A) \quad (3.182)$$

$$E_{2,eq} = E2^o + (RT/n_2F) \ln (C_B/C_D) \quad (3.183)$$

Surface-Controlled Kinetics

Under conditions where both the overall anodic and the overall cathodic reactions are activation-controlled, The relevant current vs potential situation. Referring to the two redox couples presented above (Equations 3.179 and 3.180), the corresponding reaction rates can be expressed as:

$$r_1 = dC_C/dt = =dC_A/dt = i_1/n_1F = k_1C_A{}^a = k_{-1}C_C{}^c \quad (3.184a)$$

$$r_2 = dC_B/dt = -dC_D/dt = i_2/n_2F = k_2C_D{}^d = k_{-2}C_B{}^b \quad (3.184b)$$

It is assumed here that stirring is sufficiently high such that both the anodic and cathodic reactions are completely activation controlled, i.e., $C_A = C_{As}$, $C_B = C_{Bs}$.

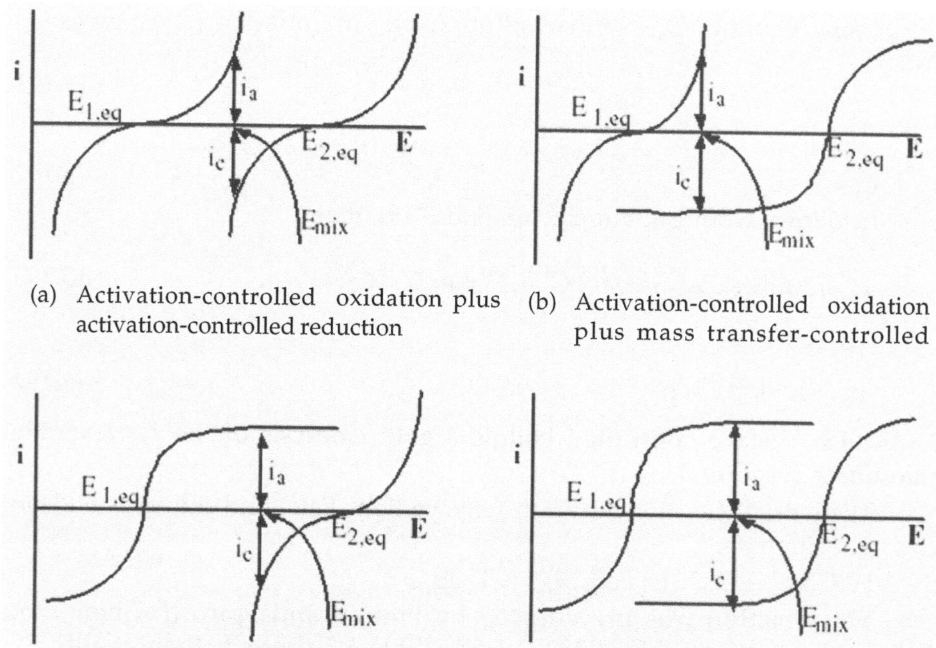

(a) Activation-controlled oxidation plus activation-controlled reduction

(b) Activation-controlled oxidation plus mass transfer-controlled

(c) Mass transfer-controlled oxidation plus activation-controlled reduction

(d) Mass transfer-controlled oxidation plus mass transfer-controlled reduction

Fig. 3.7: Relationship between the steady-state reaction rate and the mixed potential

The stoichiometry of Equation 3.181 implies that at steady-state,

$$(1/n_2)dC_C/dt = -(1/n_1)dC_B/dt \quad (3.185)$$

It follows then from Equations 3.184a, 3.184b, and 3.185 that

$$i_1/n_1n_2F = -i_2/n_1n_2F = r_1/n_2 = -r_2/n_1 = r_{cat} \quad (3.186)$$

Thus,

$$i_1 = -i_2 = i_m = r_1n_1F = -r_2n_2F = n_1n_2Fr_{cat} \quad (3.187)$$

where i_m is the current density at the mixed potential (where $E = E_m$).

When only the anodic component of the net current is significant for the first redox couple (i.e., the A/C couple), we can rewrite Equation 3.184a as:

$$r_1 = i_1/n_1F = k_1C_A^{\ a} = k_{1,0}C_A^{\ \circ} \exp[a_1FE_m/RT] \quad (3.188a)$$

Similarly, when only the cathodic current predominates for the second redox couple (i.e., the D/B couple), Equation 3.184b simplifies to:

$$r_2 = i_2/n_2F = -k_2C_B^{\ b} = -k_{-2,0}C_B^{\ b} \exp[-(1 - a_2)FE_m/RT] \quad (3.188b)$$

Recalling Equations 7 and 8, we can manipulate Equations 3.188a and 3.188b to derive an expression for the mixed potential as:

$$a_1FE_m/RT = -u_1 \ln(n_1k_{1,0}C_A^{\ a}/n_2k_{-2,0}C_B^{\ b}) \quad (3.189)$$

where

$$u_1 = \alpha_1/(1 + \alpha_1 = \alpha_2) \quad (3.190)$$

Using Equation 3.189 to substitute for E_m in Equation 3.188a gives:

$$r_1 = k_{1.0}^{u_2} k_{-2.0}^{u_1} (n_2 n_1)^{u'} C_A^{au_2} C_B^{bu_1} \tag{3.191}$$

where

$$u_2 = 1 - u_1 \tag{3.192}$$

It follows from Equation 3.186 and 3.191 that

$$r_{cat} = r_1/n_2 = (k_{1,0}^{u_2} k_{-2.0}^{u_1} n_{2,0}^{u_2}/n_1^{u_1})\, C_A^{au_2} C_B^{bu_1} = k_{cat} C_A^{au_2} C_B^{bu_1} \tag{3.193}$$

where

$$k_{cat} = k_{1,0}^{u_2}\, k_{-2,0}^{u_1}\, n_2^{u_2}/n_1^{u_1} \tag{3.194}$$

EXAMPLE: Surface-controlled colloidal gold catalysis of the ferricyanide-thiosulfate reaction

The overall reaction between ferricyanide (Feic) and thiosulfate (Thio) can be written as:

$$Fe(CN)_6^{3-} + S_2O_3^{2-} = Fe(CN)_6^{4-} + 1/2 S_4O_6^{2-} \tag{1}$$

This reaction was investigated by Freund and Spiro (J. Chem. Soc. Faraday Trans. 1, 82, 2277-2282 (1986)). Table 3.3 presents their results.

Table 3.3: Effects of reactant concentrations on the initial rates of the gold-sol-catalyzed Feic-Thio reaction

Concentration (10^{-3} mol dm^{-3})				Initial Rate (10^{-9} mol dm^{-3} s^{-1})
Feic	K_2SO_4	Thio	Na_2SO_4	(rexp)
1.0	0.0	10.0	-	47.5
0.8	0.3	10.0	-	39.8
0.6	0.6	10.0	-	38.2
0.4	0.9	10.0	-	27.1
0.2	1.2	10.0	-	19.5
0.1	1.35	10.0	-	14.2
1.0	-	10.0	0.	46.0
1.0	-	7.5	2.5	43.9
1.0	-	5.0	5.0	34.6
1.0	-	2.5	7.5	23.4
1.0	-	1.25	8.75	20.3
1.0	-	0.625	9.38	14.6
1.0	-	0.25	9.75	5.6

According to previous experiments, the electrochemical reaction order of ferricyanide in the cathodic process is unity and the corresponding order for thiosulfate in the anodic reaction is also unity. Show that the results presented in Table 3.3 are consistent with a completely surface-controlled mechanism for the Feic/Thio reaction in the presence of gold sols.

Solution

According to the electrochemical analysis presented.

$$r_{cat} = k_{cat}\, C_A^{au_2}\, C_B^{bu_1} \tag{3.193}$$

Thus, comparing the overall reaction (Equation 1) and Equation 3.193, we note that Feic represents the oxidant (B) and Thio represents the reductant (A). Therefore, we can write:

$$r_{cat} = k_{cat}\,(C_{Thio})^{au_2}\,(F_{eic})^{bu_1} \tag{2}$$

We know from the problem statement that the electrochemical reaction order of ferricyanide in the cathodic process is unity and the corresponding order for thiosulfate in the anodic reaction is also unity. Therefore, Equation 2 becomes:

$$r_{cat} = k_{cat}(C_{Thio})^{u_2}\,(C_{Feic})^{u_1} \tag{3}$$

Figure shows a plot of ln r_{exp} vs ln C_{Feic}. It is seen that a straight line of slope 0.53 is obtained by least squares. A similar diagram is shown for ln rexp vs ln CThio; in this case the slope is 0.42. Therefore, the experimental data can be represented by the following rate law:

$$r_{exp} = k(C_{Thio})^{0.53}(C_{Feic})^{0.42} \tag{4}$$

Now, referring to Equation 3.192, we find that

$$u_1 + u_2 = 0.53 + 0.42 = 0.95 \sim 1 \tag{5}$$

The fact that the sum of the experimentally based kinetic orders is nearly unity, shows that the experimental data conform to the requirement of Equation 3.192, and therefore the kinetic results are consistent with a complete surface controlled electrochemical mechanism.

Mixed-Control Kinetics

If the assumption used above that C = Cs is relaxed, then the bulk and surface concentrations of the reactants and the products can be related with the aid of Fick's first law. Recalling the discussion for the reactants A and B we have:

$$N_A = k_{dA}(C_A - C_{As}) \tag{3.195a}$$

$$N_B = k_{dB}(C_B - C_{Bs}) \tag{3.195b}$$

Under steady-state conditions we must have

$$N_A = r_1 = i_1/n_1F \tag{3.196a}$$

$$N_B = r_2 = i_2/n_2F \tag{3.196b}$$

It follows from Equations 3.195a and 3.196a that

$$C_{As} = (1 - i_1/i_{LA})C_A \tag{3.197}$$

where i_{LA} is the limiting current density attained when $C_{As} = 0$:

$$i_{LA} = n_1Fk_{dA}C_A = k'_{dA}C_A \tag{3.198}$$

Similarly, from Equations 3.195b and 3.196b,

$$C_{Bs} = (1 = i_2/i_{LB})C_B \tag{3.199}$$

where

$$i_{LB} = n_2 F k_{dB} C_B = k'_{dB} C_B \quad (3.200)$$

Referring to Equations 3.188a and 3.188b, we recognize that we must now use surface concentrations. Thus,

$$r_1 = i_1/n_1F = k_1 C_{As}^{\ a} \quad (3.201a)$$

$$r_2 = i_2/n_2F = -k_{-2} C_{Bs}^{\ b} \quad (3.201b)$$

Replacing C_{As} and C_{Bs} with Equations 3.197 and 3.199 gives

$$r_1 = i_1/n_1F = k_1(1 - i_1/i_{LA})^a C_A^{\ a} \quad (3.202a)$$

$$r_2 = i_2/n_2F = -k_{-2}(1 - i_2/i_{LB})^b C_B^{\ b} \quad (3.202b)$$

Again, at the mixed potential, $E - E_m$, and $i_m = i_1 = -i_2$. Therefore, it follows from Equations 3.202a and 3.202b that:

$$\ln i_m = u_2 \ln (n_1k_1) + au_2 \ln (1 - i_m/i_{LA}) + au_2 \ln C_A$$
$$+ u_1 \ln (n_2k_{-2}) + bu_1 \ln (1 - i_m/i_{LB}) + bu_1 \ln C_B \quad (3.203)$$

At infinite stirring speed, $i_L \rightarrow \infty$ and, thus, Equation 3.203 becomes

$$\ln i_{m,\infty} = u_2 \ln (n_1k_1) + au_2 \ln C_A + u_1 \ln (n_2k_{-2}) + bu_1 \ln C_B \quad (3.204)$$

Combining Equations 3.203 and 3.204 gives:

$$\ln (i_m/i_{m,\infty}) = au_2 \ln (1 - i_m/i_{LA}) + bu_1 \ln (1 - i_m/i_{LB}) \quad (3.205)$$

For conditions where the mixed current is smaller than the respective limiting currents, i.e., $i_m << i_{LA}$ and $i_m << i_{LB}$, Equation 3.205 simplifies to:

$$1/i_m = 1/i_{m,\infty} + au_2/i_{LA} + bu_1/i_{LB} \quad (3.206)$$

It can also be shown that when $i_m << i_{LA}$ and $i_m << i_{LB}$, the mixed potential is given:

$$(1 + \alpha_1 - \alpha_2)FE_m/RT = \ln (C_B^{\ b}/C_A^{\ a}) - \ln (n_1k_{1,0}/n_2k_{-2,0}) + (a/i_{LA} - b/i_{LB})i_m \quad (3.207)$$

At infinite stirring speed, $i_L \rightarrow \infty$ and $E_m \rightarrow E_{m,\infty}$ and Equation 3.207 becomes:

$$(1 + \alpha_1 - \alpha_2)FE_{m,\infty}/RT = \ln (C_B^{\ b}/C_A^{\ a}) - \ln (n_1k_{1,0}/n_2k_{-2,0}) \quad (3.208)$$

Substituting Equation 3.208 into Equation 3.207 gives the mixed potential as:

$$E_m = E_{m,\infty} + [RT/F(1 + \alpha_1 - \alpha_2)](a/i_{LA} - b/i_{LB})i_m \quad (3.209)$$

Reaction at a rotating disc surface. The mass transfer coefficient (k_i) for a rotating disc is given by:

$$(k_i d/D_i) = 0.62(d^2\omega/)^{1/2}(\nu/D_i)^{1/3} \quad (3.210)$$

That is,

$$k_i = 0.62\nu^{-1/6} D_i^{2/3} \omega^{1/2} \quad (3.211)$$

Recalling Equations 3.198 and 3.200, we can write the limiting currents as:

$$i_{LA} = n_1 F k_{dA} C_A = n_1 F(0.62\nu^{-1/6} D_A^{\ 2/3}) C_A \omega^{1/2} = \beta_A \omega^{1/2} \quad (3.212a)$$

$$i_{LB} = n_2 F k_{dB} C_B = n_2 F(0.62\nu^{-1/6} D_B^{\ 2/3}) C_B \omega^{1/2} = \beta_B \omega^{1/2} \quad (3.212b)$$

Inserting Equations 3.212a and 3.212b into Equation 3.206 gives:

$$1/i_m = 1/i_{m,\infty} + (au_2/\beta_A + bu_1/\beta_B)\omega^{-1/2} \quad (3.213)$$

Alternatively, in view of Equation 3.187, we can write:

$$1/r_{cat} = n_2/r_1 = -n_1/r_2 = n_1n_2F/i_m = 1/r_{cat,\infty} + n_1n_2F(au_2/\beta_A + bu_1/\beta_B)\omega^{-1/2} \quad (3.214)$$

The corresponding mixed potential is obtained from Equations 13.209, 3.212a, and 3.212b as:

$$E_m = E_{m,\infty} + [RT/F(1 + \alpha_1 - \alpha_2)](a/\beta_A - b/\beta_B)i_m\omega^{-1/2} \quad (3.215a)$$

Alternatively, recalling Equation 3.187,

$$E_m = E_{m,\infty} + [RTn_1n_2/(1 + \alpha_1 - \alpha_2)](a/\beta_A - b/\beta_B)r_{cat}\omega^{-1/2} \quad (3.215b)$$

$$E_m = E_{m,\infty} + (y/x)(1 - i_m/i_{m,\infty}) = E_{m,\infty} + (y/x)(1 - r_{cat}/r_{cat,\infty}) \quad (3.216)$$

where x is the slope of the $1/r_{cat}$ vs. $\omega^{-1/2}$ plot and y is the slope of the E_m vs. $r_{cat}w^{-1/2}$ plot.

Transport-Controlled Kinetics

When the rate of electron transfer is relatively fast while the rate of mass transfer is relatively slow, the overall reaction will essentially proceed at equilibrium at the solid surface. Under these conditions, the following relationship must hold:

$$E_{1s,eq} = E_{2s,eq} = Em \quad (3.217)$$

where the subscript (s) denotes surface conditions.

Parallel to Equations 3.197 and 3.199, the surface concentrations of the products C and D can be expressed as:

$$C_{Cs} = (1 + i_1/i_{LC})C_C \quad (3.218a)$$

$$C_{Ds} = (1 + i_2/i_{LD})C_D \quad (3.218b)$$

where

$$i_{LC} = n_1Fk_{dC}C_C = k'_{dC}C_C \quad (3.219a)$$

$$i_{LD} = n_2Fk_{dD}C_D = k'_{dD}C_D \quad (3.219b)$$

The positive signs in Equations 3.218a and 3.218b (cf negative signs in Equations 3.197 and 3.199) reflect the fact that the surface concentrations of C and D are higher than the respective bulk concentrations. By using the conditions $i_m = i_1 = =i_2$, and Equations 3.197, 3.199, 3.218a, and 3.218b to relate the surface and bulk concentrations, while recalling Equations 3.182 and 3.183, we find:

$$E_{1s,eq} = E_1^\circ + (RT/n_1F)\ln(C_C/C_A) + (RT/n_1F)\ln[(1 + i_m/i_{LC})/(1 - i_m/i_{LA})] \quad (3.220a)$$

$$E_{2s,eq} = E_2^\circ + (RT/n_2F)\ln(C_B/C_D) + (RT/n_2F)\ln[(1 - i_m/i_{LB})/(1 + i_m/i_{LD})] \quad (3.220b)$$

When Equation 3.220a is subtracted from Equation 13.220b, we get upon rearrangement,

$$C_A^{n_2}C_B^{n_1}/C_C^{n_2}C_D^{n_1})\exp[n_1n_2F(E_2^\circ - E_1^\circ)/RT] = K/Q - f(i_m) \quad (3.221)$$

where

$$f(i_m) = (1+i_m/i_{LC})^{n_2}(1+i_m/i_{LD})^{n_1}/(1-i_m/i_{LA})^{n_2}(1-i_m/i_{LB})^{n_1} \quad (3.222)$$

Let ω define a new function $g(i_m)$ as:

$$g(i_m) = (i_{LC})^{n_2}(i_{LD})^{n_1}f(i_m) \quad (3.223)$$

Then from Equations 3.198, 3.200, 3.219a, 3.219b, and 3.223

$$g(i_m) = (k'_{dC})^{n_2} (k'_{dD})^{n_1} C_C^{n_2} C_D^{n_1} f(i_m) \quad (3.224)$$

Using Equation 3.221 to substitute for $f(i_m)$ in Equation 3.224,

$$g(i_m) = (k'_{dc})^{n_2} (k'_{dD})^{n_1} C_A^{n_2} C_B^{n_1} \exp[n_1 n_2 F(E_2^\circ - E_1^\circ)/RT] \quad (3.225)$$

Initial Rate. If the reaction products C and D are absent from the initial reaction mixture, then at the beginning of the reaction the following condition is satisfied:

$$i_m/i_{LC} >> 1, i_m/i_{LD} >> 1 \quad (3.226)$$

Also, for $t \to \infty$,

$$i_m/i_{LA} << 1, i_m/i_{LB} << 1 \quad (3.227)$$

Under these conditions it can be shown that:

$$1/i_m = 1/W + \phi n_2/i_{LA} + \phi n_1/i_{LB} \quad (3.228a)$$

$$1/r_{cat} = n_1 n_2 F/W + \phi n_1 n_2^2/i_{LA} + \phi n_1^2 n_2/i_{LB} \quad (3.228b)$$

and

$$W = (k'_{dC})^{n_2\phi} (k'_{dD})^{n_1\phi} C_A^{n_2\phi} C_B^{n_1\phi} \exp[n_1 n_2 \phi F(E_2^\circ - E_1^\circ)/RT] \quad (3.229)$$

It can also be shown that the mixed potential is given by:

$$(F/RT)(n_1 + n_2)E_m = (F/RT)(n_1 E_1^\circ + n_2 E_2^\circ) + \ln C_B/C_A + \ln (k'_{dD}/k'_{dC}) + \ln [(1 - i_m/i_{LB})/(1 - i_m/i_{LA})] \quad (3.230)$$

EXAMPLE: The platinum-catalyzed hexacyanoferrate(III) plus iodide reaction

The reaction between $Fe(CN)6^{3-}$ and I^- is strongly catalyzed by platinum metal. The overall reaction is:

$$Fe(CN)6^{3-} + 3/2I^- \to Fe(CN)6^{4-} + 1/2I_3^- \quad (1)$$

The kinetics of this reaction was investigated by Freund and Spiro (J. Chem. Soc., Faraday Trans. 1, 79, 491-504 (1983)); the platinum catalyst was used in the form of a rotating disc.

(a) Experiments conducted to examine the effect of the disc stirring rate on the reaction rate gave the following results:

Rotation speed (rev min^{-1})	100	200	300	500	1000	2000
Reaction rate (10^{-6} mol m^{-2} s^{-1})	2	2.75	3.65	4.43	6.65	9.65

Show that these results are consistent with a completely mass transfer-controlled process.

(b) The potential of the disc was monitored in the course of the reaction and it was found to be independent of the rotation speed. Rationalize this observation, assuming (as found in (a) above) a transport-controlled process.

(c) Presented below are experimental data which give the effects of the reactant concentrations on the reaction rate (r). With the aid of these data, determine the reaction order for $Fe(CN)6^{3-}$ and for I^-.

[Feic] (10^{-3} mol dm^{-3})	0.2	0.5	1.0	2.0	5.0	1.0	1.0	1.0	1.0	1.0
[I$^-$] (10^{-3} mol dm^{-3})	50	50	50	50	50	30	50	80	150	300
r (10^{-6} mol m^{-2} s^{-1})	1.27	2.59	4.43	6.64	12.2	2.59	4.43	6.57	10.4	10.4
Emix (mV)	279	286	295	299	307	307	294	282	265	244

(d) The experimental results presented above in part (c) also include data on the effects of the reactant concentrations on the mixed potential indicated by the platinum metal. Show that these trends are consistent with an electrochemical mechanism of the platinum catalysis.

Solution

(a) Figure shows a plot of reaction rate, r, vs. stirring rate. Recalling Equation 3.229, we can write:

$$W = (k'_{dC})^{n_2\phi} (k'_{dD})^{n_1\phi} f \quad (2)$$

where

$$f = C_A^{n_2\phi} C_B^{n_1\phi} \exp[n_1 n_2 \phi F(E_2^o - E_1^o)/RT] \quad (3)$$

Also, in view of Equation 3.211, we can write:

$$k'_{dC} = k''_{dC}\omega^{1/2} \quad (4)$$

$$k'_{dD} = k''_{dD}\omega^{1/2} \quad (5)$$

From Equations 2, 4, and 5,

$$W = f'\omega^{1/2} \quad (6)$$

where

$$f' = (k''_{dC})^{n_2\phi} (k''_{dD}) n_1{}^{\phi} f \quad (7)$$

Also, recall Equation 3.228:

$$1/i_m = 1/W + \phi n_2/i_{LA} + \phi n_1/i_{LB} \quad (3.228)$$

Using Equations 3.108a, 3.109b, and 6 to substitute for i_{LA}, i_{LB}, and 6 respectively in Equation 3.228 gives the mixed current density as:

$$i_m = \beta_m \omega^{1/2} \quad (8)$$

where

$$i/\beta_m = 1/f' + \phi n_2/\beta_A + \phi n_1/\beta_B \quad (9)$$

It follows from Equation 9 that a plot of i_m vs. $\omega^{1/2}$ should give a straight line.

It can be seen from Equation 8 that for a complete mass transport-controlled process, a plot of the reaction rate vs. the square root of the disc rotation rate should give a straight line passing through zero.

(b) The mixed potential that corresponds to total mass transfer control is given by Equation 3.230. Inspection of this equation reveals that it has no dependence on the speed of rotation. Therefore the experimental observations are consistent with the assumed total mass transfer control. Inserting Equations 3.212a, 3.212b, 3, 4, and 7 into Equation 3.230, we get:

$$(F/RT)(n_1 + n_2)E_m = (F/RT)(n_1E_1^o + n_2E_2^o) + \ln (C_B/C_A) + \ln (k^2_{dD}/k^2_{dC})$$
$$+ \ln [(1 - \beta_m/\beta_B)/(1 - \beta_m/\beta_A)] \quad (10)$$

It follows from Equation 10 that a plot of E_m vs. $w^{1/2}$ should have a zero slope.

(c) Based on the overall reaction (Equation 1), the following half-reactions can be written:

$$3/2I^- = 1/2I_3^- + e^- \quad (11)$$
$$Fe(CN)_6^{3-} + e^- = Fe(CN)_6^{4-} \quad (12)$$

Comparing Equations 1, 11, and 12 Equations 3.179, 3.180, and 3.181, it can be seen that the following correspondence exists: A:I_F^-, B:$Fe(CN)_6^{3-}$ (feic), C:I_3^-, D:$Fe(CN)_6^{4-}$ (feoc).

Closer comparison of Equations 3.179 and 11 reveals, however, that whereas in the former both A and C have the same value of the stoichiometric coefficient (i.e., 1), in the case of Equation 11, I_3^- and I^- have different stoichiometric coefficients, i.e., ½ and 3/2 respectively. In order to use the equations available in Section 9.4.4 properly, we must transform Equation 11 into a form in which both the reactant and product have the same stoichiometric coefficient. We proceed by taking $3I^-$ to be equivalent to a hypothetical species I_3^{3-}. Then we can write:

$$I_3^{3-} = I_3^- + 2e^- \quad (13)$$
$$2Fe(CN)_6^{3-} + 2e^- = 2Fe(CN)_6^{4-} \quad (14)$$
$$I_3^{3-} + 2Fe(CN)_6^{3-} = I_3^- + 2Fe(CN)_6^{4-} \quad (15)$$

It must be noted that Equation 15 is equivalent to:

$$3I^- + 2Fe(CN)_6^{3-} = I_3^- + 2Fe(CN)_6^{4-} \quad (16)$$

where I_3^{3-} in Equation 15 has been replaced with $3I^-$. Adopting Equation 15 as our working Equation, it follows from Equation 3.181 that

$$n_1 = 2, n_2 = 1, \phi = 1/(n_1 + n_2) = 1/3 \quad (17)$$

It must be noted further, that the $3I^-/I_3^{3-}$ substitution involves both a stoichiometric and a thermodynamic equivalence. In the case of the stoichiometric equivalence, we recognize that the concentrations are related as:

$$CI^{3-}_3 = C_{I-}/3 \quad (18)$$

The thermodynamic equivalence can be derived by expressing the redox reaction for the I_3^-/I^- couple in the following two alternative ways:

$$I_3^- + 2e^- = 3I^- \quad (19)$$
$$E_1 = E_1^o + (RT/2F) \ln (C_{I^-_3}/C^3_{I^-}) \quad (20)$$
$$I_3^- + 2e^- = I_3^{3-} \quad (21)$$
$$E_1 = E_1^o + (RT/2F) \ln (C_{I^-_3}/C_{I^{3-}_3}) \quad (22)$$

It follows from Equations 20 and 22 that:

$$C_{I^{3-}_3} = C^3_{I^-} \quad (23)$$

We now turn to Equation 3.228b:

$1/r_{cat} = n_1n_2F/W + \phi n_1n_2^2/i_{LA} + \phi n_1^2n_2/i_{LB}$ (3.228b)

Bearing in mind Equation 17, as well as the correspondence A:I_3^{3-}, B:$Fe(CN)_6^{3-}$ (feic), we can write

$1/r_{cat} = (2)(1)F/W + (1/3)(2)(1)^2F/i_{LA} + (1/3)(1)(2)^2F/i_{LB}$
$= 2F/W + (2/3)F/i_{LA} + (4/3)F/i_{LB}$ (24)

Now, using Equations 3.198 and 3.200 to substitute for i_{LA} and i_{LB}, we get:

$1/r_{cat} = 2F/W + (2/3)F/k'_{dA}C_A + (4/3)F/k'_{dB}C_B$ (25)

Referring to the stoichiometric equivalence (Equation 18),

$C_A = C_{I^{3-}_3} = C_{I^-}/3$ (26)

Using Equation 26 to substitute for C_A in Equation 25 and noting that C_B corresponds to C_{Feic}, we can write:

$1/r_{cat} = 2F/W + 2F/k'_{dA}C_I^- + (4/3)F/k'_{dB}C_{Feic}$ (27)

Recalling Equation 3.229,

$W = (k'_{dC})^{n_2\phi}(k'_{dD})^{n_1\phi}C_A^{n_2\phi}C_B^{n_1\phi}\exp[n_1n_2\phi F(E^o_2 - E^o_1)/RT$ (19.311)

we can write,

$W = (k'_{dC})^{1/3}(k'_{dD})^{2/3}C_A^{1/3}C_{Feic}^{2/3}\exp[2F(E_2^o - E_1^o)/3RT]$ (28)

We note again that C_A refers to CI_3^{3-}. However, now we recognize that the parameter W is related to the thermodynamic treatment of the redox couples (see Equations 3.220a and 3.220b). Thus, in Equation 3.229 we must use the thermodynamic equivalence (Equation 23), i.e.,

$C_A = CI^{3-}_3$ (29)

Accordingly, Equation 3.229 becomes:

$W = (k'_{dC})^{1/3}(k'_{dD})^{2/3}\, C_I^- C_{Feic}^{2/3}\exp[2F(E_2^o - E_1^o)/3RT]$ (30)

or

$W = f^2 C_I^- C_{Feic}^{2/3}$ (31)

Combining Equations 27 and 31,

$1/r_{cat} = 2F/f''C_I^-C_{Feic}^{2/3} + (4/3)F/k'_{dB}C_{Feic} + 2F/k'_{dA}C_I^-$ (32)

If the last term on the right hand side is relatively small, we can write:

$q = [1/r_{cat} - (4/3)F/k'_{dB}C_{Feic}] = 2F/f''C_I^-C_{Feic}^{2/3}$ (33)

Figure shows a plot of log q vs. log C_{Feic} for constant C_I^-. The slope obtained, i.e., 0.66, is consistent with the reaction order of 2/3 for C_{Feic} in Equation 33. The corresponding plot of log q vs. log C_I^- for constant C_{Feic}. The slope of 1.0 is also in consonance with the reaction order of unity for C_I^- in Equation 33.

(d) Referring to Equation 3.207, we can see that for constant C_B,

$dE_m/d\ln C_A = =aRT/(1 + \alpha_1 - \alpha_2)F$ (34)

Similarly, for constant C_A,

$dE_m/d\ln C_B = bRT/(1 + \alpha_1 - \alpha_2)F$ (35)

At the temperature of the experiments (5°C), and assuming $a_1 = a_2 = 0.5$, we expect

$$dE_m/d \ln C_A = -RT/F = -24.0 \text{ mV} \tag{36}$$
$$dE_m/d \ln C_B = RT/3F = 7.99 \text{ mV} \tag{37}$$

A plot of E_m vs. ln I^- with a slope of -23.2 mV, consistent with theory (Equation 36). The corresponding E_m vs. ln Feic plot, it shows a slope of 8.2 mV also in agreement with theory (Equation 37).

Electron Transfer at Semiconductor Electrodes

Energy Levels in Electron and Hole Transfer

The kinetics of electrochemical reactions at the semiconductor/aqueous interface can be considered in terms of the transfer of carriers (holes or electrons) from energy levels in the solid to those in the aqueous phase, and vice-versa. In order to satisfy the principle of conservation of energy, radiationless electron transfer is permissible only if the initial and final locations of the electron are at the same energy level.

Consider that Equation 19.1 now refers to a reaction taking place at the semiconductor/electrolyte interface. Two different reaction paths are available, depending on whether electron transfer is with the conduction band or the valence band. Electron transfer in the valence band can be visualized in terms of the transfer of holes. Thus, we have an electron-transfer mechanism (Equation 3.230a), and a hole-transfer mechanism (Equation 3.230b):

$$A+ + e- = B \tag{3.230a}$$
$$A+ = B + h^+ \tag{3.230b}$$

It can be seen that whether the electron or hole transfer pathway predominates depends on the relative positions of the band edges of the semiconductor with respect to the energy levels of the redox couple in the electrolyte.

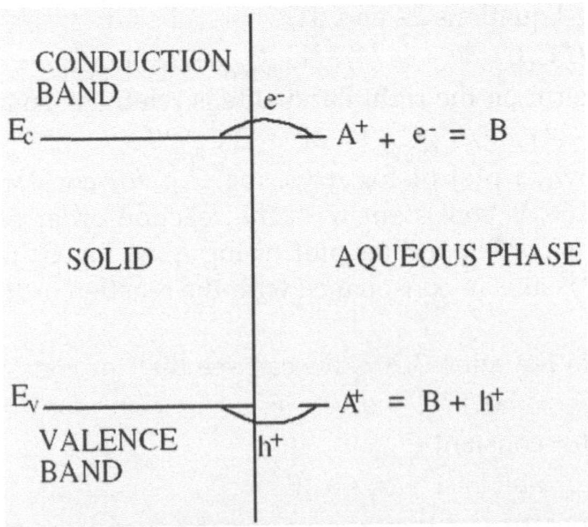

Fig. 3.8: Electron transfer at a semiconductor electrode

In the case of the conduction band electron transfer (Equation 3.230), we can envisage the electrode reaction thus:

$A^{z+}(aq)$ + (Occupied State) e^- (s) ↔ B(aq) + (Vacant State) (s) (3.231)

The rate of electron transfer will be expected to be proportional to the density of empty states on the aqueous species (A+) and the density of occupied energy states at the same energy level in the solid phase. It will be recalled that the energy states in the semiconductor are spread over a wide range of energies. Thus, consideration of all the energy levels will require an integration to be performed. However, in general, only a few states are occupied in the conduction band while most of the energy states in the valence band are occupied. Thus, as far as electron transfer is concerned, only the energy bands in the neighborhood of the band edges Ec and Ev are relevant. Accordingly, for the conduction band process, we can express the rate as:

$$ic = ic_+ + ic_- \quad (3.232a)$$

$$= kc+^o\kappa(Ec)^oCBs^oW_B(E_c)^oNc - kc-^o\kappa(E_c)^oC_{As}{}^oW_A(Ec)^on_s \quad (3.232b)$$

where k_{c+} and k_{c-} are respectively the proportionality constants for the anodic and cathodic conduction band electron reactions, $\kappa(E_c)$ is the probability that the collision of an aqueous species with the surface will result in electron transfer, C_{As} and C_{Bs} are the surface concentrations of the oxidized and reduced aqueous species, $W_A(E_c)$ and $W_B(E_c)$ represent respectively, the probability of finding the oxidized and the reduced species at an energy state that corresponds to E_c, N_c is the density of energy states in the conduction band, and ns is the electron density at the surface.

Similarly, for a valence band process,

$$i_v = i_{v+} + i_{v-} \quad (3.233a)$$

$$= kv+^o\kappa(Ev)^oCB_s{}^oW_B(E_v)^ops - kv-^o\kappa(E_v)^oC_{As^o}W_A(E_v)_oN_v \quad (3.233b)$$

where k_{v+} and k_{v-} are respectively the proportionality constants for the anodic and cathodic valence band hole reactions, Nv is the density of energy states in the valence band, and ps is the hole density at the surface.

Current-Potential Relations

At equilibrium, there is no net conduction band or valence band electron transfer. That is,

$$i_v = i_c = 0 \quad (3.234)$$

If the surface concentrations of electrons and holes at equilibrium are denoted by nseq and pseq respectively, then it follows from Equations 3.232 - 3.234 that:

$$i_c = i_{c,o}\,[C_{Bs}/C_B - (C_{As}/C_A)(n_s/n_{seq})] \quad (3.235)$$

$$i_v = i_{v,o}\,[(CB_s/C_B)(p_s/p_{seq}) - (C_{As}/C_A)] \quad (3.236)$$

where CA and CB are respectively the bulk aqueous phase concentrations of the oxidized and reduced species, while ic,o and iv,o represent respectively the exchange currents for the conduction band and valence band processes and are given by:

$$i_{c,o} = k_c{+}^o\kappa(E_c)^oC_B{}^oW_B(E_c)_oN_c \quad (3.237a)$$
$$= kc{-}^o\kappa(Ec)^oC_A{}^oW_A(E_c)^on_{seq} \quad (3.237b)$$
$$i_{v,o} = k_v{+}^o\kappa(E_v)^oC_B{}^oW_B(E_v)^op_{seq} \quad (3.238)$$
$$= kv{-}^ok(Ev)^oCA^oWA(Ev)^oNv \quad (3.239)$$

Equations 3.235 and 3.236 take into consideration the fact that at equilibrium the bulk and surface concentrations of the aqueous reactants must be equal, i.e., $C_{As} = C_A$ and $C_{Bs} = C_B$.

When there is no concentration gradient,

$$C_{As}/C_A = C_{Bs}/C_B = 1 \quad (3.240)$$

Therefore Equations 3.235 and 3.236 become:

$$i_c = i_{c,o}\ [1 - (n_s/n_{seq})] \quad (3.241)$$
$$i_v = i_{v,o}\ [(p_s/p_{seq}) - 1)] \quad (3.242)$$

Recall Equation

$$n_s = n_b \exp{-e}\ \Delta\phi_s/kT \quad (3.243)$$

where nb is the bulk concentration of electrons in the conduction band of the semiconductor. It follows that

$$n_s/n_{seq} = [n_b \exp(-e\ \Delta\phi_s/kT)]/[n_b \exp(-e\Delta\phi_{seq}/kT)] \quad (3.244)$$
$$= \exp(-\eta_{sc}e/kT) \quad (3.245)$$

where η_{sc} is the overpotential given by

$$\eta_{sc} = \Delta\phi_s - \Delta\phi_{seq} \quad (3.246)$$

and $\Delta\phi_{seq}$ is the equilibrium value of $\Delta\phi$. Combination of Equations 3.241 and 3.245 gives:

$$i = i_{c,o}\ [1 - \exp(-\eta_{sc}e/kT)] \quad (3.247)$$

Also, recall that the bulk and surface hole concentrations are related thus:

$$p_s = p_b \exp e\Delta\phi_s/kT \quad (3.248)$$

It follows from Equations 3.242 and 3.248 that:

$$i_v = i_{v,o}\ [\exp(\eta_{sc}e/kT) - 1)] \quad (3.249)$$

A comparison of the Butler-Volmer equation (Equation 19.21) with Equation 3.247 indicates that for electron exchange with the conduction band, the apparent transfer coefficient is zero. On the other hand, a similar comparison with the expression obtained for hole exchange with the valence band (Equation 3.249) reveals that in this case the apparent transfer coefficient is unity. Further examination of Equation 3.247 reveals that for a conduction band electron transfer, the applied potential affects the cathodic current but not the anodic current. The reverse situation occurs in the case of a valence band electron transfer. Here, as can be seen from Equation 3.249, the anodic current is potential-dependent whereas the cathodic current has no potential dependence.

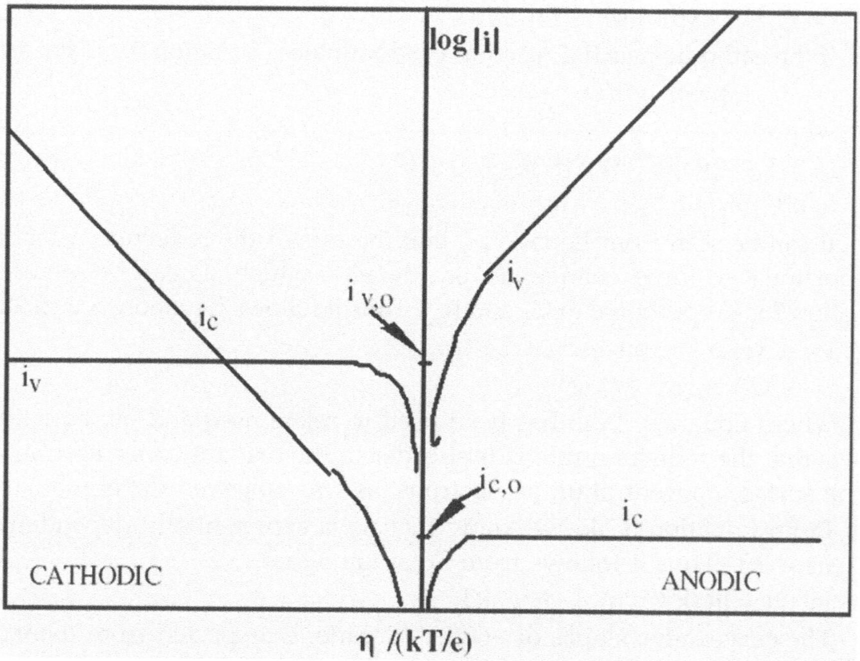

Fig. 3.9: A Current-voltage curves for conduction-band and valence-band electron transfers at the semiconductor/electrolyte interface (after Gerrischer, 1970, p.498)

Figure shows a graphical representation of the current-voltage relations for conduction band and valence band charge transfers, as described by Equations 3.247 and 3.249 respectively.

EXAMPLE: Reduction of oxidizing agents on n-ZnO

(a) Ferricyanide ions were reduced at the n-ZnO electrode by applying a cathodic potential:

$Fe(CN)^{3-}_6 + e^- = Fe(CN)^{4-}_6$

The cathodic current was found to vary in direct proportion to the surface concentration of electrons and to the ferricyanide concentration. Rationalize these observations in the light of the above discussion of conduction band electron transfer. (see Freund and Morrison, Surf. Sci., 9, 119 (1968); Morrison, Surface Sci., 15, 363 (1969))

(b) Figure presents cathodic currents obtained from the reduction of a number of one-equivalent oxidizing agents at a ZnO electrode. Show that the observed results are consistent with a first-order dependence of the cathodic current on the surface electron density.(see van den Berghe *et al.*, Surf. Sci., 39, 368 (1973)).

Solution

(a) Recall the expression derived above for the current-potential relation for a conduction band electron transfer:

$$i = i_{c,o} [1 - \exp(-\eta sc^{e}/kT)] \quad (3.247)$$

If the cathodic paartial reaction predominates, Equation 3.247 becomes:

$$i = -i_{c,o} \exp(-\eta_{sc}e/kT) \quad (1)$$

where

$$i_{c,o} = k_c\text{-}^{o}\kappa(Ec)^{o}C_A{}^{o}WA(E_c)^{o}n_{seq} \quad (3.237b)$$

$$= k^{o}C_A{}^{o}n_{seq} \quad (2)$$

It can be seen from Equation 1 that the rate of the reduction reaction is proportional to the exchange current density, which, as can be seen from Equation 2 is proportional to C_A and n_{seq}. Thus it follows Equations 1 and 2 that

$$i = -k^{o}C_A{}^{o}n_{seq} \exp(-\eta sc^{e}/kT) \quad (3)$$

$$= -k^{o}CA^{o}n_s \quad (4)$$

where Equation 3.245 has been used to relate nseq and ns. Equation 4 shows that the reduction rate is first order in the oxidant concentration and in the surface concentration of electrons, as was observed experimentally.

(b) From Equation 3.245 we know that ns is exponentially dependent on hsce/kT. Thus it follows from Equation 3 that

$$\ln |i| = \ln (k^{o}C_A{}^{o}n_{seq}) - \eta_{sc}e/kT \quad (5)$$

The curves give slopes of ~60mV/decade, as expected from theory.

EXAMPLE: Reduction of Fe^{3+} on CdS

Show that for the CdS/Fe^{3+} system a slope of 60 mV/decade is obtained from the experimental data. (see G, p.506, also V. A. Tyagai, Elecktrokhimiya, 1, 377 (1965))

Transport of Charge Carriers in Semiconductors

Where a surface reaction involves the consumption of a minority carrier, the rate at which this carrier is transported to the semiconductor electrolyte interface can determine the rate of the overall reaction. It is therefore of interest to develop a quantitative description of carrier diffusion in a semiconductor. In order to accomplish this, we must first determine the rate at which holes and electrons are produced in the bulk of the semiconductor. Once the carriers have been produced, they must then be transported to the solid/aqueous interface where the electrochemical reaction takes place.

In the presence of current flow, the semiconductor electrode can be divided into three regions: the bulk region, the diffusion region, and the space charge region, as illustrated in figure for an n-type semiconductor (see Green, p.386). In this case, holes constitute the minority carriers. In the bulk region, the equilibrium hole and electron distributions are preserved. Between the bulk and space charge regions is the diffusion region, characterized by a concentration gradient of holes. As a result of the hole-consuming surface reaction, the hole concentration at the edge of the space charge region (x=x1) will be lower than its equilibrium value. A concentration gradient of holes therefore arises outside the space charge region.

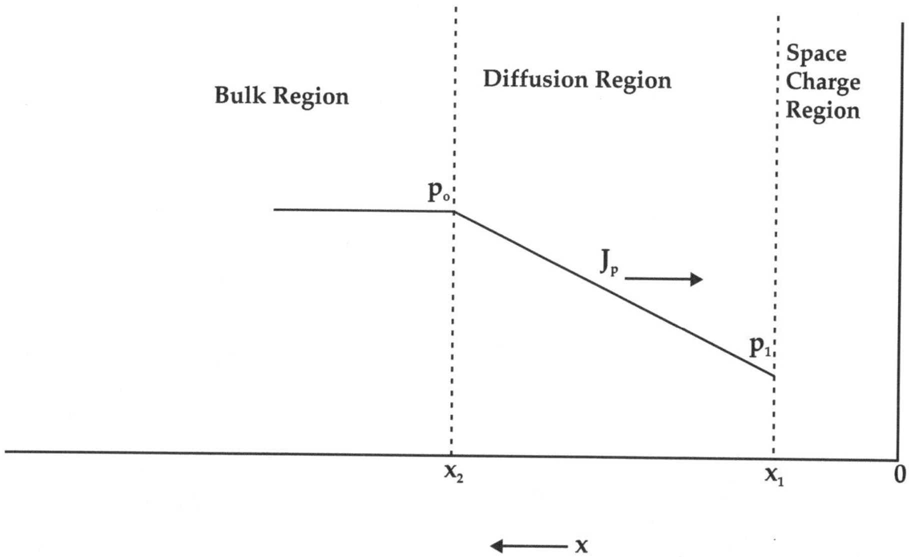

Fig. 3.10: The diffusion of holes in an n-type semiconductor

Recalling Equation 3.12a, it can be stated that, under steady-state conditions, the hole concentration must satisfy the following differential equation:

$$D_p d^2p/dx^2 + r_p = 0 \quad (3.250)$$

where D_p is the diffusion coefficient of a hole, and rp is the net rate of hole production inside the semiconductor. As noted previously, inside a semiconductor, electrons and holes can undergo recombination. This process can be viewed in terms of a homogeneous reaction of the form:

$$e^- + h^+ = 0 \quad (3.251)$$

The forward reaction represents recombination, while the reverse represents the generation of an electron-hole pair. Assuming that Equation 3.251 represents an elementary reaction, the corresponding rate equation can be expressed as:

$$r = dp/dt = dn/dt = r_{gen} + r_{rec} = k_{gen} - k_{rec}np$$
$$= k_{rec}(n_o p_o - np) = k_{rec}(ni^2 - np) \quad (3.252)$$

Let us now consider an n-type semiconductor. Let us suppose that an excess of holes is introduced by some means. Then the rate of recombination will be given by:

$$dp/dt = - k_{rec} n_o p \quad (3.253)$$

In writing Equation 3.253, it has been assumed that since for an n-type semiconductor, electrons are the majority carriers, the approximation n=no can be made. It follows from Equation 3.253 that,

$$\ln(p/p_{initial}) = -k_{rec} n_o t \quad (3.254)$$

We can define the *lifetime* of a minority carrier as the time it takes to decrease the concentration of non-equilibrium holes or electrons to 1/e of its original value. Therefore, substituting $(p/p_{initial}) = 1/e$ at $t = t_p$ in Equation 3.254 gives the lifetime of holes, t_p as:

$$t_p = 1/k_{rec}n_o \quad (3.255)$$

The lifetime of the minority carrier (tp) can also be viewed as the average time excess minority carriers remain in their excited state after generation (Morrison, p.11). It follows from Equations 3.252 and 3.255 that,

$$r_p = dp/dt = (p_o - p)/t_p \quad (3.256)$$

Combining Equations 3.250 and 3.256, we get:

$$D_p d^2p/dx^2 + (p_o - p)/t_p = 0 \quad (3.257)$$

The relevant boundary conditions are:

$$x \rightarrow \infty,\ p = po \quad (3.258)$$

$$x = x_1,\ p = p1 \quad (3.259)$$

Applying these boundary conditions to Equation 3.257 gives:

$$(p - po) = (p1 - po)\exp[(x_1 - x)/L_p] \quad (3.260)$$

where

$$L_p = (D_p t_p)^{1/2} \quad (3.261)$$

The parameter Lp is termed the *diffusion length*. It represents the average distance the minority carrier (a hole in this case) diffuses before recombination occurs. It follows from the definition of the diffusion length that any holes generated in the region between $x=(x_1+ L_p)$ and x_1 will enter the space charge region without recombining.

It follows from Equation 3.261 that

$$dp/dx = [(p1 - p_o)/L_p]\exp[(x_1 - x)/L_p] \quad (3.262)$$

Therefore, for $x=x_1$,

$$dp/dx = (p1 - p_o)/L_p \quad (3.263)$$

The hole current at $x=x_1$ is then given by:

$$i_p = -eD_p dp/dx \quad (3.264a)$$

$$= -eD_p(p1 - p_o)/L_p \quad (3.264b)$$

When p1 = 0, a limiting current (ip,lim) is attained, i.e.,

$$i_p,lim = eD_p po/L_p \quad (3.265)$$

It follows from Equations 3.264b and 3.265 that:

$$i_p = -(p_1 - p_o)i_{p,lim}/p_o \quad (3.266a)$$

or

$$(p_1/p_o) = 1 - (i_p/i_{p,lim}) \quad (3.266b)$$

With the aid of Equation 3.266b, we can obtain a relationship between the surface concentration of holes and the space charge potential in the presence of current flow. The surface reaction results in current flow between the bulk regions of the semiconductor and the surface. This current flow results in a departure of the hole and electron distributions from their respective equilibrium values. That is, the condition np = ni2 is no longer satisfied. If the departure from equilibrium is not too drastic, the resulting situation can be viewed as a "quasi-equilibrium". Under these conditions, the holes and electrons are not in mutual equilibrium. However, it can be assumed that the holes (or electrons) at the surface are in equilibrium with the holes (or electrons) at the edge of the space charge layer:

$$p_s = p_1 \exp(e\Delta\phi_s/kT) \quad (3.267)$$

$$n_s = n_1 \exp(-e\Delta\phi_s/kT) \quad (3.268)$$

Also, since the region outside the space charge consitutes an electroneutral region, n1 and p1 are related to their equilibrium values, no and po as:

$$(n_1 - n_2) = (p_1 - p_o) \quad (3.269)$$

Recalling Equation 3.267, we can write:

$$\Delta\phi_s = (kT/e)\ln(p_s/p_1) = (kT/e)\ln[(p_s/p_o)(p_o/p1)]$$
$$= (kT/e)\ln(p_s/p_o) - (kT/e)\ln(p_1/p_o) \quad (3.270)$$

Combining Equations 3.266b and 3.270 gives:

$$\Delta\phi_s = (kT/e)\ln(p_s/p_o) - (kT/e)\ln[1 - (i_p/i_{p,lim})] \quad (3.271)$$

We can define a *hole-transport overvoltage*, hTp, as

$$H_{Tp} = (kT/e)\ln[1 - (i_p/i_{p,lim})] \quad (3.272)$$

The hole-transport overvoltage can be viewed as the contribution which hole transport makes to the space-charge overvoltage. Using Equation 3.272, we can rewrite Equation 3.271 as:

$$\Delta\phi_s = (kT/e)\ln(p_s/p_o) - \eta_{Tp} \quad (3.273)$$

At equilibrium, there is no net current flow and the corresponding space-charge potential is then given by:

$$\Delta\phi_{s,eq} = (kT/e)\ln(p_{s,eq}/po) \quad (3.274)$$

Therefore, with the aid of Equations 3.273 and 3.274, the space charge overvoltage can be expressed as:

$$\eta_s = \Delta\phi_s - \Delta\phi_{s,eq} = (kT/e)\ln(p_s/p_o) - \eta Tp - (kT/e)\ln(p_{s,eq}/p_o)$$
$$= (kT/e)\ln(p_s/p_{s,eq}) - \eta_{Tp} \quad (3.275)$$

Now, the total overvoltage is given by:

$$\eta = \eta_s + \eta_H \quad (3.276)$$

From 3.275 and 3.276,

$$(p_s/p_{s,eq}) = \exp[e(\eta - \eta_H + \eta_{Tp})/kT] \quad (3.277)$$

Alternatively, using Equation 3.272 to substitute for hTp in Equation 3.277, we get:

$$(p_s/p_{s,eq}) = [1 - (i_p/i_{p,lim})] \exp[e(\eta-\eta_H)/kT] \quad (3.278)$$

4

Electrometry

INTRODUCTION

Electroanalytical methods are a class of techniques in analytical chemistry which study an analyte by measuring the potential (volts) and/ or current (amperes) in an electrochemical cell containing the analyte. These methods can be broken down into several categories depending on which aspects of the cell are controlled and which are measured. The three main categories are potentiometry (the difference in electrode potentials is measured), coulometry (the cell's current is measured over time), andvoltammetry (the cell's current is measured while actively altering the cell's potential).

Potentiometry

Potentiometry passively measures the potential of a solution between two electrodes, affecting the solution very little in the process. The potential is then related to the concentration of one or more analytes. The cell structure used is often referred to as an electrode even though it actually contains *two* electrodes: an *indicator electrode* and a *reference electrode* (distinct from the reference electrode used in the three electrode system). Potentiometry usually uses electrodes made *selectively* sensitive to the ion of interest, such as a fluoride-selective electrode. The most common potentiometric electrode is the glass-membrane electrode used in a pH meter.

A variant of potentiometry is chronopotentiometry which consists in using a constant current and measurement of potential as a function of time. It has been iniatiated by Weber.

Coulometry

Coulometry uses applied current or potential to completely convert an analyte from one oxidation state to another. In these experiments, the total current passed is measured directly or indirectly to determine the number of electrons passed. Knowing the number of electrons passed can indicate the concentration of the analyte or, when the concentration is known, the number of electrons transferred in the redox reaction. Common forms of coulometry include bulk electrolysis, also known as *Potentiostatic coulometry* or*controlled potential coulometry*, as well as a variety of coulometric titrations.

Voltammetry

Voltammetry applies a constant and/or varying potential at an electrode's surface and measures the resulting current with a three electrode system. This method can reveal the reduction potential of an analyte and its electrochemical reactivity. This method in practical terms is nondestructive since only a very small amount of the analyte is consumed at the two-dimensional surface of the working and auxiliary electrodes. In practice the analyte solutions is usually disposed of since it is difficult to separate the analyte from the bulk electrolyte and the experiment requires a small amount of analyte. A normal experiment may involve 1-10 mL solution with an analyte concentration between 1 and 10 mmol/L. Chemically modified electrodes are employed for high sensitive electrochemical determination of organic molecules as well as metal ions.

Polarography

Polarography is a subclass of voltammetry that uses a dropping mercury electrode as the working electrode.

Amperometry

Amperometry is the term indicating the whole of electrochemical techniques in which a current is measured as a function of an independent variable that is, typically, time or electrode potential. Chronoamperometry is the technique in which the current is measured, at a fixed potential, at different times since the start of polarisation. Chronoamperometry is typically carried out in unstirred solution and at fixed electrode, i.e., under experimental conditions avoiding convection as the mass transfer to the electrode. On the other hand, voltammetry is a subclass of amperometry, in which the current is measured at varying the potential applied to the electrode. According to the waveform that describes the way how the potential is varied as a function of time, the different voltammetric techniques are defined. Confusion arose recently about the correct use of many terms proper of electrochemistry/electroanalysis, often owing to the diffusion of electroanalytical techniques in fields where they constitute an instrument to use, not being the 'core business' of the study. Though electrochemists are pleased about this, they invite to use the terms properly, in order to avoid fatal misunderstandings. We shall now discuss the above methods in detail

The potentiometry includes the potentiometric methods that is as follows.

Potentiometric methods are concerned with the measurement of potential as a function of analyte activity or concentration. The basic principles of potentiometry will be discussed later through the text in details but some introductory information may be necessary at this point.

Oxidation - Reduction Reactions

Look at a zinc electrode immersed in a solution of zinc sulfate. Zinc will tend to dissolve forming more Zn_2^+ in solution

$$Zn\ (s) = Zn_2^+ + 2\ e \qquad (1)$$

Electrons will be accommodated within the metallic bond of the zinc metal and the zinc electrode will acquire a negative potential.

In equation 1, the oxidation number of zinc has increased and the process is termed an oxidation process.

The reverse of the behavior described above is observed when a copper electrode is immersed in a solution of copper (II) sulphate. Cu^{2+} ions tend to deposit on the copper electrode as solid copper atoms, by gaining 2e each as in equation 2

$$Cu^{2+} + 2e = Cu\ (s) \qquad (2)$$

This is a reduction reaction since the oxidation number on C_u^{2+} has decreased to zero in Cu (s). The copper electrode will increase in weight and acquire a positive potential.

Electrochemical Cells

There are two types of electrochemical cells in the concept whether the cell generates potential (called a galvanic cell) or consumes potential (called an electrolytic cell). A cell is simply constructed from two electrodes immersed in solution. The electrode at which reduction occurs is called the cathode (-) while that at which oxidation occurs is called the anode (+).

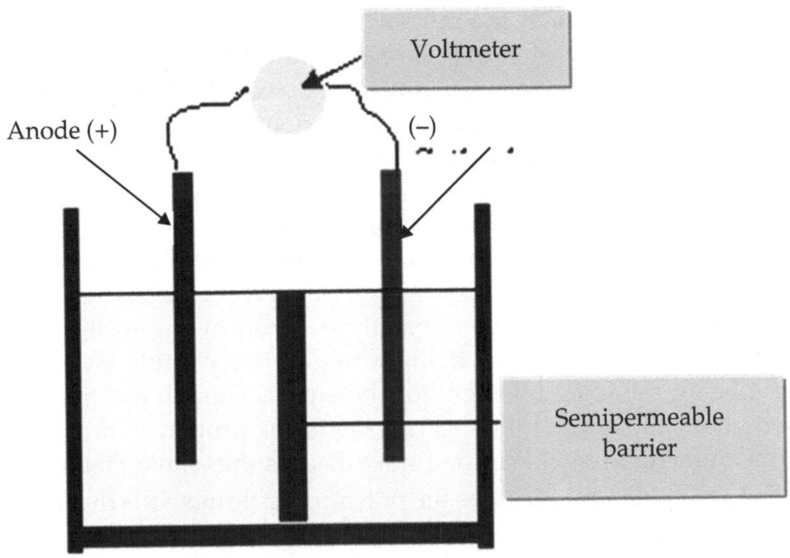

Fig. 4.1: A schematic representation of an electrochemical cell (Zinc is the cathode and copper is the anode)

The cells we will study in this chapter are of the first type where electrons generated by one half reaction will be consumed by the other half reaction forcing the current to flow.

Calculating the Cell Potential

The process of calculating the cell potential is simple and involves calculation of the potential of each electrode separately, then the overall cell potential can be determined from the simple equation:

Ecell = Ecathode - Eanode (3)

Ecell = EZn^{2+}/Zn (s) - EC_u^{2+}/Cu (s) (4)

Sometimes, this relation is written as:

$$E_{cell} = E_{right} - E_{left}$$

This is true since the convention is to place the cathode to the right of the cell while the anode is placed to the left of the cell.

If the E_{cell} is a positive value, the reaction is spontaneous and if the value is negative, the reaction is nonspontaneous in the direction written and will be spontaneous in the reverse direction. Note that electrode potentials are always written as reductions.

Electrode Potentials

It should be clear that the cell mentioned above can be looked at as two separate half cells. The first half cell is the Cu^{2+}/Cu (s) (anode) and the other is the Zn(s)/Zn^{2+}(cathode). For comparative purposes, all reduction potentials are written for the reduction process.Separate electrode potentials can be found by comparison with a reference standard hydrogen electrode (SHE) that is given an arbitrary zero value. The unknown half-cell is made as the anode and is placed to the right of the half-cell which is placed to the left.

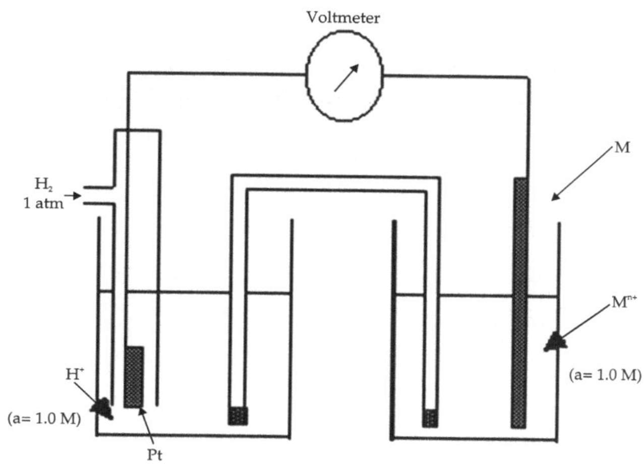

Fig. 4.2: Diagrammatic cell for measurement of standard electrode potential

Since the standard electrode potential for the SHE is zero, the potential displayed by the potentiometer is a direct measure of the standard electrode potential (Es).

Cell Representation and Spontaneity

For the purpose of saving time and effort, a simple method is used to represent potentiometric cells where the representation starts with the cathode and end up with the anode, passing through the different solutions and the salt bridge. The cell can be written as

Zn (s)/Zn^{2+}(a = 1.0 M)//Cu^{2+}(a = 1.0 M)/Cu (s)

Where the single vertical line represents a phase boundary and double parallel lines represents the salt bridge. In some cases, a semipermeable barrier is used rather than a salt bridge; this is represented by a dashed vertical line.

The cell in Figure 4.2 can be represented as

Pt/H_2 (1 atm), H^+(a = 1.0 M)//Mn^+(a = 1.0 M)/M (s)

The reaction will occur spontaneously when Es (cell) is positive while it will proceed in the reverse direction when Es (cell) is negative according to the equation for the standard free energy, ΔGs

$\Delta Gs = - nFEs$

Negative ΔGs Values indicate a spontaneous reaction while positive values indicate reactions in reverse direction.

Liquid Junction Potential

When a semipermeable membrane or barrier separates two solutions of different concentrations, the more concentrated solution tends to diffuse through the barrier according to Le Chatelier principle.

If it is the case where mobilities of the positive ions are different from those of the negative ions; then a potential difference between the two solutions is developed. Figure 4.3 shows an example for this behavior using more concentrated HCl solution to the left of the semipermeable barrier.

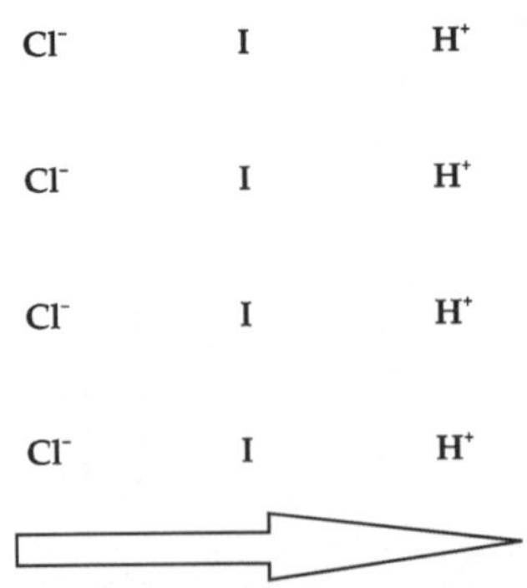

Fig. 4.3: Development of liquid junction potential

Since H+ ions have much higher mobilities than Cl^- ions, more H^+ ions will cross the barrier than Cl^- ions in a certain time which results in the development of the liquid junction potential. This type of potential is most encountered when the system involves H^+ ions. It is for the sake of decreasing liquid junction potential that KCl is used in salt bridges. K+ ion have comparable mobilities to Cl^- ions.

The Nernst Equation

Standard electrode potentials are measured when the activity of the oxidized form equals 1.00 M. If the activity of the oxidized form is different from 1.00, an electrode acquires a different potential. This potential can be determined from the very useful Nernst equation.

$$E = E_s - \frac{2.303RT}{nF}\log\frac{a_{red}}{a_{ox}}$$

Where a_{red} and a_{ox} are activities of the reduced and oxidized forms, respectively.

R is the gas censtant (8.314 J K^{-1} mol^{-1}), T is the temperature expressed in Kelvin, F is the Faraday constant (9.6484 × 104 C mol-1), and n is the charge on the ion of interest.

For example, when Zn(s) is immersed in a Zn^{2+} solution that is 0.01 M, the potential can be calculated as

$$E = E_s[Zn^{2+}/Zn(s)] - \frac{2.303RT}{nF}\log\frac{a[(Zns)]}{a[(Zn^{2+})]}$$

$$E = -0.763 \ \frac{2.303RT}{nF}\log\frac{1}{10^2}$$

$$E = -0.763\,\frac{2\times 2.303RT}{2F}$$

Depending on temperature, the value of the electrode potential can be determined at an activity of 0.01 M Zn^{2+}. Note that the activity of any substance present at its standard state is given the value of 1. Also, note that when the activity of Zn^{2+} is 1.0 M then the value of the electrode potential becomes the same as the value of the standard electrode potential because the log term becomes zero.

The Nernst equation can be used for the calculation of the potential of each half cell. Combination of the two half cell potentials yields the overall cell potential. This is the point of interest in doing potentiometry because simple effort and manipulation of the various conditions will lead to very valuable quantitative data, as will be discussed below.

Consider the conventional cell which was referred to in previous sections:

Zn (s) / Zn^{2+} (a = x) // Cu^{2+}(a = y) / Cu (s)

The Nernst equation for each half cell can be written

$$E = E_s - \frac{2.303RT}{nF}\log\frac{1}{x} \qquad (6)$$

$$E\,(Cu^{2+}/Cu) - \frac{2.303RT}{2F}\log\frac{1}{y} \qquad (7)$$

Equations 6 and 7 can be combined yielding equation 8 since

$E_{cell} = E_{right} - E_{left}$

$$E\,(Cu^{2+}/Cu) - \frac{2.303RT}{2F}\log y - E_{zn^{2+}/Zn} \qquad (8)$$

The idea of potentiometric methods rely on fixing the potential of one half cell (by fixing the activity) and measuring the activity of the ion in question. Therefore, if the activity of Zn^{2+} is kept constant, EZn^{2+}/Zn will be constant. Combination of Es (Cu^{2+}/Cu) and EZn^{2+}/Zninto one constant E′ allows for the determination of the Cu2+ activity (Y) as shown in equation 9.

$$E\,(Cu^{2+}/Cu) - \frac{2.303RT}{2F}\log y \qquad (9)$$

Only Y (Cu^{2+} activity) is the factor that affects the value of Ecell. At least two measurements of Ecell at different Y values are required to determine Y. However, it is a routine work to construct a calibration plot and then determine the unknown activity from the curve rather than direct calculation using two points only.Ion - selective electrodes are based on this principle where a general equation for the calculation of the activity of ions can be written as:

$$E_{cell} = E' + \frac{2.303RT}{nF}\log ai \qquad (10)$$

Where ai is the activity of ion i.

The pre log term can be written as 0.0591/n at 25 °C (298K). If Ecell is plotted versus log ai, a straight line is obtained, the slope of which is 0.0591/n. Therefore, electrodes which yield comparable slopes to this value are said to have Nernstian response while others which give slopes below 0.054/n are said to have either sub-Nernstian response or unaccepted performance.

Activity versus Concentration

Analytical chemists prefer to use concentration terms rather than activity, since most analytical methods are concerned with the calculation and use of concentration. Also, preparation of solutions of specific concentrations is straight forward while it is very difficult to prepare solutions of specific activities. Therefore, it is an important achievement to obtain concentration values from equations such as equation 10. Activity can be thought of as the effective concentration and is related to concentration by the relation.

$$a_i = c_i f_i \qquad (11)$$

Where fi is the activity coefficient of ion i and is given by the Debye - Huckel relationship:

$$\log f_1 = -AZ_1 2\frac{\pi}{2} \qquad (12)$$

Where A is a constant, Zi is the charge on ion i and I the ionic strength of the solution.

It is clear from equation 12 that fi aquire a constant value at constant ionic strength. Therefore, addition of an ionic strength adjustor to all samples and standards will keep fi constant. The ionic strength adjustor is a concentrated solution of inert ions that do not participate in any electrochemical reaction in the system under consideration. Equation 10 can be rewritten in order to include the concentration term

$$E_{cell} = E' + \frac{2.303RT}{nF}\log c_i f_i \qquad (13)$$

Since fi is constant after addition of a suitable ionic strength adjustor, equation 13 can be rewritten as

$$E_{cell} = E' + \frac{2.303RT}{nF}\log c_i \qquad (14)$$

$$E_{cell} = E' + \frac{2.303RT}{nF}\log f_i$$

Equation 14 suggests that when Ecell is plotted versus log ci a straight line is obtained and direct determination of concentration is possible.

Reference Electrodes

In developing equation 14, an important assumption that the left hand half cell potential being constant was made. This is practically achieved by using a reference electrode which can be simply defined as an electrode of constant potential. Three main formulations of reference electrodes are most widely used.

1. Silver/silver Chloride Electrode

This is the simplest reference electrode available which is composed of a silver wire coated with a surface of silver chloride and dipped in a saturated KCl solution. Few AgCl crystals or few drops of $AgNO_3$ are added to the KCl solution. The electrode can be represented by the half cell:

KCl(sat), AgCl (sat)/ Ag

The electrode contents are placed in a glass tube that contains a porous barrier at the lower part to allow for ion exchange and thus potential development. The potential of the Ag/AgCl electrode is 0.204 V at 25 °C.

The half cell reaction taking place is

$AgCl\ (s) + e = Ag(s) + Cl^-$

The potential of the electrode is a function of the activity of the Cl-. Since a saturated solution of KCl is used, Cl- activity is constant and thus the potential of the electrode is constant.

2. The Saturated Calomel Electrode (SCE)

The saturated calomel electrode is an excellent reference electrode that is usually very stable and reliable. The heart of the electrode is the calomel paste which is a paste of mercurous chloride, Hg, and KCl. The half cell can be represented as:

$KCl\ (sat)/Hg_2\ Cl_2\ (sat)/Hg$

Where two liquid junctions are involved since the electrode is composed of a paste of solid KCl, solid Hg_2Cl_2 and Hg placed in a small tube the bottom of which is plugged with porous glass or cotton wool (See experimental section for details of electrode preparation). This tube is dipped into a saturated KCl solution with excess solid KCl in a larger tube that also contains a porous barrier at the lower part to allow for ion mobilities through the barrier. The electrode reaction is

$Hg_2\ Cl_2 + 2\ e = 2\ Hg + 2\ Cl^-$

The electrode potential is dependent on the Cl^- concentration accounting for the saturated KCl solution used. Fixed constant potential (0.242 V) is obtained.

3. Mercury/Mercury (I) Sulphate Electrode

In cases where Cl^- concentration is sought, the Ag/AgCl or the calomel electrode can not be used. An electrode that contains no Cl^- ions should be used.

The Hg/Hg_2SO_4 electrode is composed of a paste of solid K_2SO_4, solid Hg_2SO_4 and Hg in a small tube placed cencentric to a larger tube containing saturated K_2SO_4 solution to which some solid K_2SO_4 crystals were added. Both tubes contain a porous barrier to allow for the mobilities of the ions across the barrier in the same mannar as the calomel electrode. The half cell and electrode reaction can be represented as:

$K_2SO_4\ (sat)/Hg_2SO_4\ (s)/Hg$

$Hg_2SO_4\ (s) + 2\ e = 2\ Hg + SO_4^{2-}$

Again, saturated K_2SO_4 solution is used in order to get fixed SO_4^{2-} activity and thus constant potential.

Examples of Ion-Selective Electrodes

(a) The Glass pH Electrodes

Several types of ion-selective electrodes (ISE) had been developed. Among these is the very famous glass pH electrode which responds to H+ concentration. The glass pH electrode is composed of two reference electrodes one called the internal reference electrode which is usually an Ag/Agcl electrode. This is placed in a glass tube the bottom of which is a thin glass bulb containing 1M HCl. The second reference electrode can also be an Ag/AgCl electrode dipped in a saturated KCl solution and is called the external reference electrode. This type of configuration is the combined pH electrode. However, the external reference can be completely separated from the glass electrode in a different configuration where a calomel reference electrode can be used. Almost all glass pH electrodes in current use are combined pH electrodes.

$$E_{cell} = E^{*} + \frac{2.303RT}{F}\log aH^{+} \qquad (15)$$

$$pH = \frac{E^{*} + E_{cell}}{0.0591} \qquad (16)$$

E* contains all contributing potentials like liquid junction potential, asymmetry potential, reference electrode potential and others.

(b) Solid State Electrodes

Among the very best and reliable solid state electrodes is the fluoride ion-selective electrode. The heart of this electrode is a very insoluble lanthanum fluoride crystal.

The electrode can be represented as

Sample/LaF_3 membrane/Internal reference

The internal reference electrode is an Ag/AgCl electrode and the F-ISE is coupled to a calomel reference electrode.

The Nernst equation for the F- ISE can be written in a similar fashion as equation 15 replacing F- for H+ and changing the sign. The pF can be calculated from the equation:

$$pH = \frac{E^{*} - E_{cell}}{0.0591} \qquad (17)$$

APPLICATIONS OF POTENTIOMETRY

Experiment 1: Construction of Reference Electrodes

Background

The need for a reference electrode in an electrochemical cell is surely required. A reference electrode is simply one which does not change potential as electrochemical reactions take place. The most widely used reference electrodes are the saturated calomel (SCE) and the silver/silver chloride electrodes. The construction of both electrodes is relatively simple but requires good experience when long-term stability of these electrodes is required. However, electrodes that may be stable for several years can be prepared in the laboratory.

Electrode Half Reaction

Hg/Hg_2Cl_2, KCl (saturated)

Chemicals and Reagents

(a) Provided

1. Solid Hg_2Cl_2.
2. Mercury.
3. Solid KCl.
4. Saturated KCl solution.
5. 1 M KCl solution.
6. 0.1 M HCl solution.
7. 2 M Nitric acid solution.

(b) Need Preparation

None

Other materials

1. Platinum wire.
2. Silver wire.
3. Copper wire.
4. Glass wool.
5. Glass tubes (about 2.5 and 7 mm in diameter).
6. Silicon glue or equivalent.

I. Saturated Calomel Reference Electrode

Procedure

1. Soak all glass components to be used in the construction of the SCE in a detergent solution (like Teepol) for at least 10 min. Wash thoroughly with tap and distilled water, respectively.
2. Fix a platinum wire to the end of the smaller diameter glass tube allowing about 4 mm of the wire to emerge inside the tube for contact with mercury in a later step.
3. Prepare the calomel paste by grinding about 1 g of Hg_2Cl_2, 1 g of KCl, few drops of Hg, and dropwise addition of saturated KCl solution with continuous grinding till a moderately thick paste is obtained.
4. Carefully place few drops of Hg into the tube mentioned in step 2 and pack the paste. Packing should be as compact as possible where the Hg and the paste should look like a single unit free of air bubbles or discontinuity.

5. Seal the end of the tube constructed in step 4 with glass wool in order to keep the tube contents in place.
6. Place the smaller loaded tube into the wider one which should contain saturated KCl solution and have a fine porosity sintered glass seal at one of its ends (well packed glass wool is OK). The assembly should look like that in the attached figure, after proper sealing of the two tubes together.
7. The assembly (SCE) should be stored in saturated KCl solution and is left to equilibrate for 24 hours.
8. At all times, never allow the inner KCl solution to drop belowthe level of the inner tube.

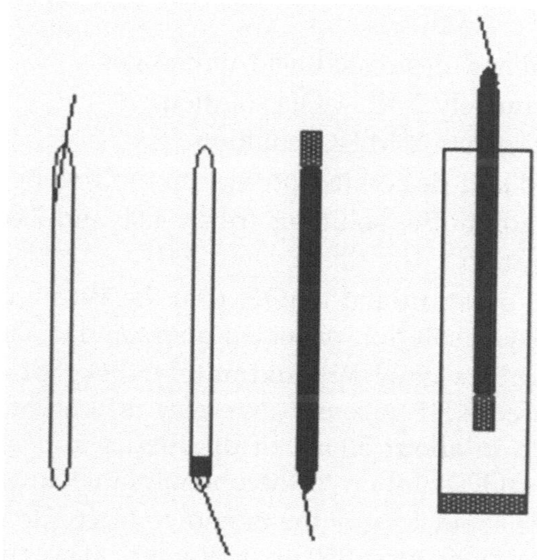

Fig. 4.4: A platinum wire is sealed to the inner tube (a), inner tube with Hg (b), calomel paste filling with glass wool seal (c), and complete assembly of the SCE (d)

II. Silver / Silver Chloride Reference Electrode

Procedure

1. Clean the silver wire by dipping in 2 M nitric acid solution for about 30 sec, rinse with distilled water followed by immediate dipping in 0.1 M HCl for 20 min.
2. If the wire is not coated by a layer of AgCl from step 1, anodize the wire at a small current for about 20 min.
3. Insert the AgCl coated silver wire into a glass tube containing a saturated KCl solution and a fine porosity sintered glass end.
4. Equilibrate the electrode in saturated KCl solution for 24 hours after which it should be ready for use.

5. The Ag/AgCl wire should not be allowed to dry and must always be kept in enough inner electrode filling solution.

Experiment 2: Potentiometric Derivation of Acid-Base Titration Curve

Background

Titration of weak acids with strong bases, and vice versa, is routinely conducted using potentiometry. The pH is measured through the course of the titration by a pH meter. The number of acidic protons in the acid can be determined from the amount of acid and volume of base consumed in the titration process. The molecular weight and ionization constant(s) may also be determined from results of such an experiment.

Chemicals and Reagents

(a) Provided
   1. Predried and desiccated acid unknown.
   2. Approximately 5 M NaOH solution.
   3. Approximately 2 M HCl solution.
   4. Predried and desiccated potassium hydrogenphthalate (KHP).
   5. Calibration buffer solutions (pH = 4.00 and 7.00).

(b) Need Preparation
   1. 250 mL of standard NaOH that is about 0.1 M. Dilute the stock NaOH solution provided and standardize against KHP.
      Method: Transfer approximately 0.6 g of the predried and desiccated KHP (accurate weight) into a 250 mL conical flask, dissolve in about 50 mL of distilled water and titrate against dilute NaOH solution to the phenolphthalein end point.
   2. Dissolve about 1.5 g of the unknown (accurate weight) in distilled water, transfer into a 250 mL volumetric flask and adjust to volume using distilled water.

Apparatus and Materials

1. pH Meter.
2. Combined pH electrode.
3. Magnetic stirrer.
4. Stirring magnet.

Caution: Glasss electrodes are fragile, therefore do not jam the electrode into the bottom of the beaker and allow no possibility for the stirring bar to hit it.

Procedure

1. Follow instructions from your supervisor on the procedure for the correct operation and calibration of the pH meter available in the laboratory.
2. Transfer, exactly, 50 mL of the unknown weak acid sample into a 250 mL beaker, dilute to about 100 mL, drop a stirring bar and place the beaker on the magnetic stirrer.

3. Immerse the combined glass electrode into the solution and start the magnetic stirrer at a suitable rate. Record the initial pH.
4. Start addition of the NaOH standardized solution from the buret and record the pH after each addition of 1 mL increments of the base.
5. When the pH starts to increase significantly with NaOH addition, allow dropwise addition of NaOH and record the pH after each addition.
6. After the rate of change in pH with NaOH addition becomes small again, record the pH values as in step 4.
7. Continue addition of NaOH till the pH meter reads a value of about 12.
8. Report your results and plot the titration curve between pH and volume of NaOH added. Calculate the ionization constant(s) of the acid at 25%, 50%, and 75% of the end point as well as the molecular weight of the acid.

Experiment 3: Construction of a Chloride Ion-Selective Electrode and Determination of Chloride

Background

Solid state ion-selective electrodes (ISE) are of significant value for fast and inexpensive determinations of analytes. Chloride, bromide, iodide, sulfide, and cyanide are just few examples of analytes for which solid state ISE were constructed. The basis of the solid state chloride electrode is a pressed disc of a mixture of silver sulfide and silver chloride. Such a disc has enough electrical conductivity to be used without an internal filling solution. The disc is prepared in the same manner like a KBr disc prepared for IR spectroscopic studies, using a conventional hydraulic die system.

The disc is glued to the end of a glass tube and a platinum wire is allowed to come in contact with the disc through few drops of mercury. The resulting working electrode, in conjunction with a reference electrode, is properly connected to a pH meter. The signal is measured in millivolts (mV) and is related to chloride ion concentration.

Chemicals and Reagents

(a) Provided

1. Predried and desiccated silver sulphide.
2. Predried and desiccated silver chloride.
3. Mercury.
4. Total ionic strength adjustment buffer (TISAB) solution.
5. Predried and desiccated sodium chloride.
6. Chloride sample of unknown concentration.

(b) Need Preparation

1. 250 mL of 0.1 M NaCl standard solution.

2. By dilution of solution 1, prepare 5X10-2, 1X10-2, 5X10-3, 1X10-3, 5X10-4, and 1X10-4 M NaCl solution (100 mL each).

Apparatus and Materials

1. pH Meter.
2. Platinum wire.
3. Reference electrode.
4. Open ends glass tube.
5. Silicon glue.
6. Magnetic stirrer.
7. Stirring bar.
8. Hydraulic die assembly.

Procedure

1. Soak all glass tubings to be used in this experiment in a detergent solution for 10 min then wash with plenty of distilled water. Allow for the tube to dry in a drying oven followed by desiccation.
2. Prepare the Ag2S/AgCl disc by mixing about 0.05 g of each. Finely grind the mixture and follow instructions on the correct use of the available hydraulic die assembly. In general, a pressure of about 10 tons should be applied for about 1 min.
3. Release the pressure slowly and remove the disc from the die assembly.
4. Carefully handle the disc from its wedges and glue to the bottom of the glass tube using silicon glue or equivalent and allow to air dry.
5. Place few drops of Hg in the tube and immerse a clean platinum wire into the Hg pool. Seal the other end of the tube by proper gluing.
6. Allow the resulting electrode to equilibrate in distilled water till a constant signal, versus the reference electrode, is obtained. The electrode is ready for use.
7. Transfer 25 mL (exactly) of the least concentrated NaCl solution into a 100 mL beaker placed on a magnetic stirrer. Add 10 mL of the TISAB solution and dilute to 50 mL with distilled water. Drop a stirring bar into the solution and immerse the reference and chloride electrodes in this solution. Start the magnetic stirrer and record the potential in mV when a stable signal is reached.
8. Repeat step 7 for the other standard chloride solution and repeat for the unknown chloride sample.
9. Plot the potential in mV versus log [Cl-] and construct the calibration curve. Find the slope of the resulting line, in the linear region, and determine the concentration of the unknown chloride sample.
10. Report your results as ppm NaCl in the original sample.

CHRONOPOTENTIOMETRY

In chronopotentiometry, a current pulse is applied to the working electrode and itsresulting potential is measured against a reference electrode as a function of time.At the moment when the current is first applied, the measured potential is abruptlychanged due to the iR loss, and after that it gradually changes, because a concentrationoverpotential is developed as the concentration of the reactant is exhausted at the electrode surface. If the current is larger than the limiting current, the required flux for the current cannot be provided by the diffusion process and, therefore, the electrode potential rapidly rises until it reaches the electrode potential of the next available reaction, and so on.The different types of chronopotentiometric techniques are depicted in figure 4.5 In constant current chronopotentiometry, the constant anodic/cathodic current appliedto the electrode causes the electroactive species to be oxidized/reduced at a constant rate. The electrode potential accordingly varies with time as the concentration ratio of reactant to product changes at the electrode surface. This process is sometimes used for titrating the reactant around the electrode, resulting in a potentiometric titration reactant might be insufficiently supplied to the surface to accept all of the electrons being forced by the application of a constant current. The electrode potential will then sharply change to more anodic/cathodic values. The shape of the curve is governed by the reversibility of the electrode reaction. The applied current can be varied with time, rather than being kept constant. For example, the current can be linearly increased or decreased (chronopotentiometry with linearly rising current in the figure) and can be reversed after some time (current reversal chronopotentiometry in the figure). If the current is suddenly changed from an anodic to cathodic one, the product formed by the anodic reaction (i.e., anodic product) starts to be reduced. Then, the potential moves in the cathodic direction as the concentration of the cathodic product increases. On the other hand, the current is repeatedly reversed in cyclic chronopotentiometry.

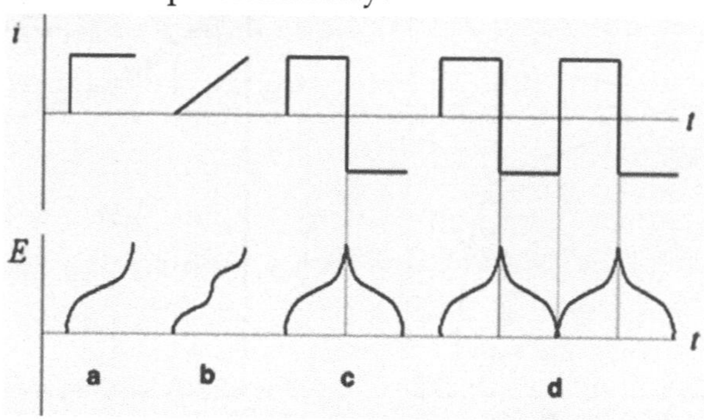

Fig. 4.5: Different types of chronopotentiometric experiments.
(a) Constant current chronopotentiometry. (b) Chronopotentiometry with linearly rising current. (c) Current reversal chronopotentiometry. (d) Cyclic chronopotentiometry

The typical chronopotentiometric techniques can be readily extended to characterize the electrochemical properties of insertion materials. In particular, current reversal and cyclic chronopotentiometries are frequently used to estimate the specific capacity and to evaluate the cycling stability of the battery, respectively.

Shown in figure 4.6a is a typical galvanostatic charge/discharge profile of LiMn powders at a rate of 0.2 C (In battery field, nC rate means the discharging/charging rate at which the battery is virtually fully discharged/ charged for 1/n h.). The total quantity of electricity per mass available from a fully charged cell (or storable in a fully discharged cell) can be calculated at a specific C rate from the charge transferred during the discharging (or charging) process in terms of $C{\cdot}g^{-1}$ or $mAh{\cdot}g^{-1}$. Alternatively, the quantity of electricity can be converted to the number of moles of inserted atoms as long as the electrode potential is obtained in a (quasi-) equilibrium state (Fig. 4.6b; for more details, please see the explanation below on the galvanostatic intermittent titration technique). The specific capacity is frequently measured at different discharging rates to evaluate the rate capability of the cell (Fig. 4.7).

The voltage profile, obtained by current reversal or cyclic chronopotentiometry, can be effectively used to characterize the multi-step redox reactions during the insertion process. An example is given in figure 4.8 for Cu_6Sn which is one of the anodic materials that can be used in rechargeable lithium batteries. The differential capacity curve dC/dE which is reproduced from the voltage versus specific capacity curve, clearly shows two reduction peaks and the corresponding oxidation peaks. The reduction peaks, R1 and R2, are caused by the phase transformation of Cu_6Sn_5–Li_2CuSn and the subsequent formation of LiSn, while the oxidation peaks, O1 and O2, are ascribed to the corresponding reverse reactions for the formation of $Li_{4{\cdot}4}Sn$ Cu_6Sn_5 and Cu_6Sn_5 respectively.

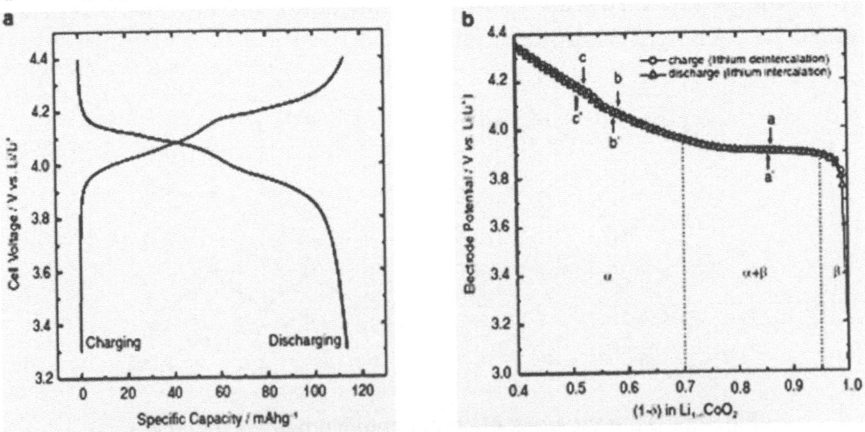

Fig. 4.6: (a) Galvanostatic charge/discharge curve of $LiMn_2O_4$and (b) open-circuitpotential versus lithium stoichiometry plot of $LiCoO_2$

The galvanostatic intermittent titration technique (GITT) is considered to be one of the most useful techniques in chronopotentiometry. In the GITT, a constant current is applied for a given time to obtain a specific charge increment and then it is interrupted to achieve open circuit condition until the potential change is virtually zero. This process is repeated until the electrode potential reaches the cut-off voltage. Eventually, the equilibrium electrode potential is obtained as a function of lithium content. Another important usage of the GITT is the estimation of the chemical diffusion coefficient of the species in the insertion materials. When the diffusion process in the material is assumed to obey Fick's diffusion equations for a planar electrode, the chemical diffusion coefficient can be expressed as follows:

$$D = \frac{4}{\pi}\left(\frac{I_0 V_m}{z_i F S}\right)^2 \left[\left(\frac{dE}{d\delta}\right) / \left(\frac{dE}{d\sqrt{t}}\right)\right]^2 \text{ for } t << \frac{l^2}{D} \quad (18)$$

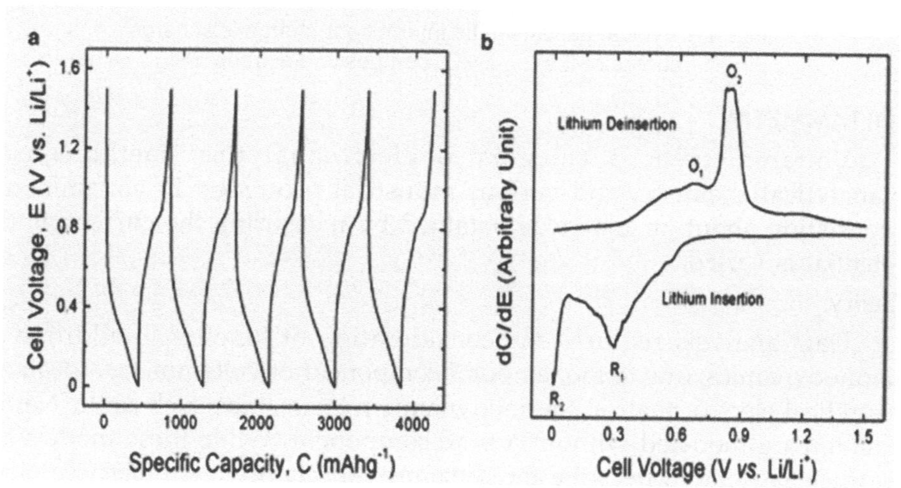

Fig. 4.7: (a) Voltage profiles of the electrodeposited Ni-Sn foam with nanostructured walls at different discharging (lithium dealloying) rates, and (b) dependence of specific capacity on discharging rate, obtained from the samples created at different deposition times

where Vmis the molar volume of the active material; z, the valence number of diffusing species; F, the Faraday constant; S, the surface area of the material; Ii, the applied constant current,

$dE/d\delta$

the dependence of electrode potential on the stoichiometry of the inserted atoms;

$dE/d\sqrt{t}$

The dependence of the electrode potential on the square root of time; and l, the thickness of the electrode (or solidstate-diffusion length).

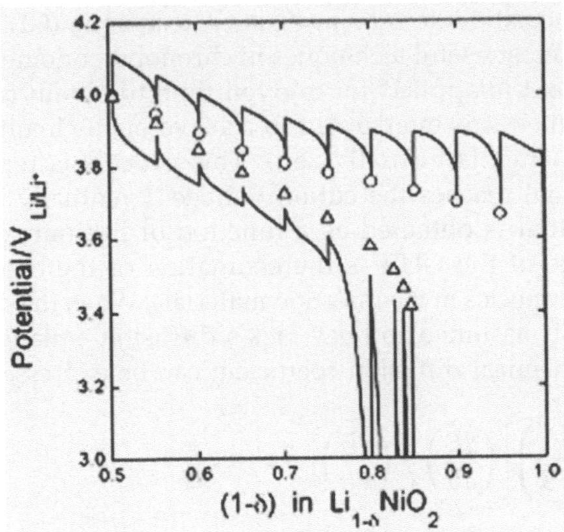

Fig. 4.8: Typical galvanostatic intermittent charge–discharge curves of the $Li_{1-\delta}NiO_2$ composite electrode

VOLTAMMETRY

Voltammetry is a category of electroanalytical methods used in analytical chemistry and various industrial processes. In voltammetry, information about an analyte is obtained by measuring the current as the potential is varied.

Theory

Data analysis requires the consideration of kinetics in addition to thermodynamics, due to the temporal component of voltammetry. Idealized theoretical electrochemical thermodynamic relationships such as the Nernst equation are modeled without a time component. While these models are insufficient alone to describe the dynamic aspects of voltammetry, models like the Tafel equation and Butler-Volmer equation lay the groundwork for the modified voltammetry relationships that relate theory to observed results.

The Three Electrode System

Voltammetry experiments investigate the half cell reactivity of an analyte. Voltammetry is the study of current as a function of applied potential. These curves I = f(E) are called voltammograms. The potential is varied arbitrarily either step by step or continuously, and the actual current value is measured as the dependent variable. The opposite, i.e., amperometry, is also possible but not common. The shape of the curves depends on the speed of potential variation (nature of driving force) and on whether the solution is stirred or quiescent (mass transfer). Most experiments control the potential (volts) of an electrode in contact with the analyte while measuring the resulting current (amperes). To conduct such an experiment

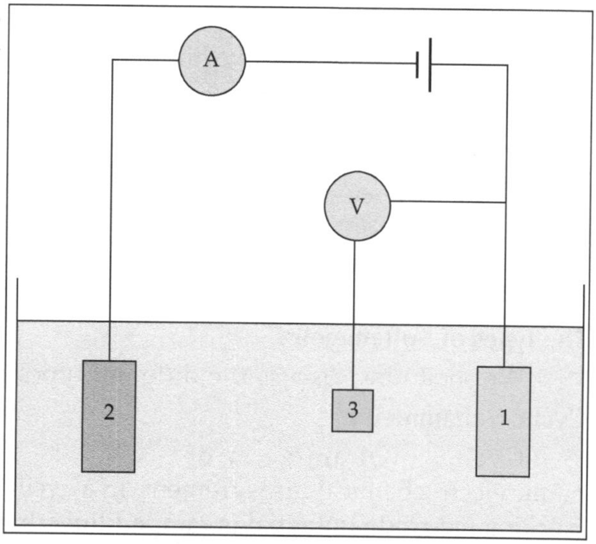

Fig. 4.9: Three-electrode setup: (1) working electrode; (2) auxiliary electrode; (3) reference electrode

requires at least two electrodes. The working electrode, which makes contact with the analyte, must apply the desired potential in a controlled way and facilitate the transfer of charge to and from the analyte. A second electrode acts as the other half of the cell. This second electrode must have a known potential with which to gauge the potential of the working electrode, furthermore it must balance the charge added or removed by the working electrode. While this is a viable setup, it has a number of shortcomings. Most significantly, it is extremely difficult for an electrode to maintain a constant potential while passing current to counter redox events at the working electrode. To solve this problem, the roles of supplying electrons and providing a reference potential are divided between two separate electrodes. The reference electrode is a half cell with a known reduction potential. Its only role is to act as reference in measuring and controlling the working electrodes potential and at no point does it pass any current. The auxiliary electrode passes all the current needed to balance the current observed at the working electrode. To achieve this current, the auxiliary will often swing to extreme potentials at the edges of the solvent window, where it oxidizes or reduces the solvent or supporting electrolyte. These electrodes, the working,reference, and auxiliary make up the modern three electrode system. There are many systems which have more electrodes, but their design principles are generally the same as the three electrode system. For example, the rotating ring-disk electrode has two distinct and separate working electrodes, a disk and a ring, which can be used to scan or hold potentials independently of each other. Both of these electrodes are balanced by a single reference and auxiliary combination for an overall four electrode design. More complicated experiments may add working electrodes as required and at times reference or auxiliary electrodes. In practice it can be very important to have a working electrode with known dimensions and surface characteristics. As a result, it is common to clean and polish working electrodes regularly. The auxiliary electrode can be almost anything as long as it doesn't react with the bulk of the analyte solution and conducts well.

The reference is the most complex of the three electrodes; there are a variety of standards used and it is worth investigating elsewhere. For non-aqueous work, IUPAC recommends the use of the ferrocene/ferrocenium couple as an internal standard. In most voltammetry experiments, a bulk electrolyte (also known as a supporting electrolyte) is used to minimize solution resistance. It is possible to run an experiment without a bulk electrolyte, but the added resistance greatly reduces the accuracy of the results. With room temperature ionic liquids, the solvent can act as the electrolyte.

The types of Voltammetry

We shall now discuss the different types of Voltammetry

Cyclic Voltammetry

Cyclic voltammetry or CV is a type of potentiodynamic electrochemical measurement. In a cyclic voltammetry experiment the working electrode potential is ramped linearly versus time like linear sweep voltammetry. Cyclic voltammetry takes the experiment a step further than linear sweep voltammetry which ends when it reaches a set potential. When cyclic voltammetry reaches a set potential, the working electrode's potential ramp is inverted. This inversion can happen multiple times during a single experiment. The current at the working electrode is plotted versus the applied voltage to give the cyclic voltammogram trace. Cyclic voltammetry is generally used to study the electrochemical properties of an analyte in solution.

Experimental Method

In cyclic voltammetry, the electrode potential ramps linearly versus time as shown. This ramping is known as the experiment's scan rate (V/s). The potential is applied between the reference electrode and the working electrode and the current is measured between the working electrode and the counter electrode. These data are then plotted as current (i) vs. potential (E). As the waveform shows, the forward scan produces a current peak for any analytes that can be reduced (or oxidized depending on the initial scan direction) through the range of the potential scanned. The current will increase as the potential reaches the reduction potential of the analyte, but then falls off as the concentration of the analyte is depleted close to the electrode surface. If the redox couple is reversible then when the applied potential is reversed, it will reach the potential that will reoxidize the product formed in the first reduction reaction, and produce a current of reverse polarity from the forward scan. This oxidation peak will usually have a similar shape to the reduction peak. As a result, information about the redox potential and electrochemical reaction rates of the compounds are obtained.

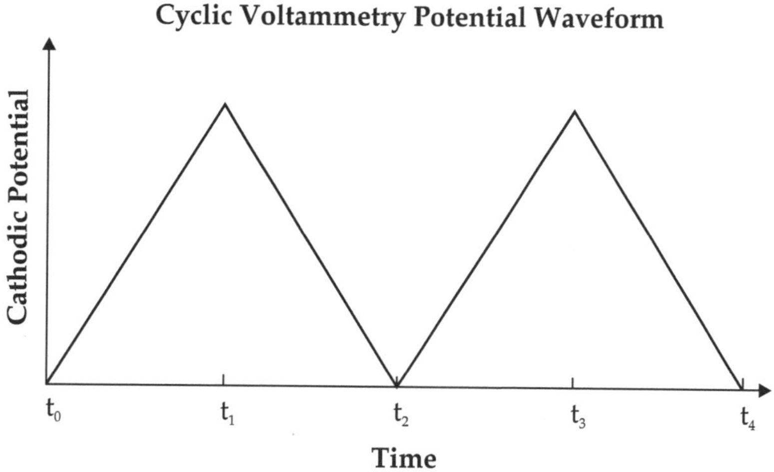

Fig. 4.10: A typical Cyclic Voltammetry Waveform

For instance if the electronic transfer at the surface is fast and the current is limited by the diffusion of species to the electrode surface, then the current peak will be proportional to the square root of the scan rate. This relationship is described by the Cottrell equation. The CV experiment then samples only a small portion of the solution, the material within the diffusion layer.

Characterization

The utility of cyclic voltammetry is highly dependent on the analyte being studied. The analyte has to be redox active within the experimental potential window. It is also highly desirable for the analyte to display a reversible wave. A reversible wave is when an analyte is reduced or oxidized on a forward scan and is then reoxidized or rereduced in a predictable way on the return scan as shown in the first figure.

Even reversible couples contain polarization overpotential and thus display a hysteresis between absolute potential between the reduction (E_{pc}) and oxidation peak (E_{pa}). This overpotential emerges from a combination of analyte diffusion rates and the intrinsic activation barrier of transferring electrons from an electrode to analyte. A theoretical description of polarization overpotential is in part described by the Butler-Volmer equation and Cottrell equation. Conveniently in an ideal system the relationships reduces to $\left|E_{pc} - E_{pa}\right| = \frac{57\,\text{mV}}{n}$, for an n electron process.

Reversible couples will display ratio of the peak currents passed at reduction (i_{pc}) and oxidation (i_{pa}) that is near unity ($1 = i_{pa}/i_{pc}$). This ratio can be perturbed for reversible couples in the presence of a following chemical reaction, stripping wave, or nucleation event. When such reversible peaks are observed thermodynamic information in the form of half cell potential $E^0_{1/2}$ can be determined. When waves are semi-reversible such as when i_{pa}/i_{pc} is less than or greater than 1, it can be possible to determine even more information especially kinetic processes like following chemical reaction. When waves are non-reversible it is impossible to determine what their thermodynamic $E^0_{1/2}$ is with cyclic voltammetry. This $E^0_{1/2}$ can be determined, however it often requires equal quantities of the analyte in both oxidation states. When a wave is non-reversible cyclic voltammetry can not determine if the wave is at its thermodynamic potential or shifted to a more extreme potential by some form of overpotential. The couple could be irreversible because of a following chemical process, a common example for transition metals is a shift in the geometry of the coordination sphere. If this is the case, then higher scan rates may show a reversible wave. It is also possible that the wave is irreversible due to a physical process most commonly some form of precipitation as discussed below. Some speculation can be made in regards to irreversible waves however they are generally outside the scope of cyclic voltammetry.

Differential Pulse Voltammetry

Differential Pulse Voltammetry, DPV, (or Differential Pulse Polarography, DPP) is often used to make electrochemical measurements. It can be considered as a derivative of linear sweep voltammetry or staircase voltammetry, with a series of regular voltage pulses superimposed on the potential linear sweep or stairsteps. The current is measured immediately before each potential change, and the current difference is plotted as a function of potential. By sampling the current just before the potential is changed, the effect of the charging current can be decreased.

By contrast, in normal pulse voltammetry the current resulting from a series of ever larger potential pulses is compared with the current at a constant 'baseline' voltage. Another type of pulse voltammetry is squarewave voltammetry, which can be considered a special type of differential pulse voltammetry in which equal time is spent at the potential of the ramped baseline and potential of the superimposed pulse.

Electrochemical Cell Set-Up

The system of this measurement is usually the same as that of standard voltammetry. The potential between the working electrode and the reference electrode is changed as a pulse from an initial potential to an interlevel potential and remains at the interlevel potential for about 5 to 100 milliseconds; then it changes to the final potential, which is different from the initial potential. The pulse is repeated, changing the final potential, and a constant difference is kept between the initial and the interlevel potential. The value of the current between the working electrode and auxiliary electrode before and after the pulse are sampled and their differences are plotted versus potential.

Characteristics

Differential pulse voltammetry has these characteristics:

1. Reversible reactions show symmetrical peaks, and irreversible reactions show asymmetrical peaks.
2. The peak potential is equal to $E_{1/2}^{r}$-ΔE in reversible reactions, and the peak current is proportional to the concentration.
3. The detection limit is about 10^{-8} M.

Uses

These measurements can be used to study the redox properties of extremely small amounts of chemicals because of the following two features:

1. In these measurements, the effect of the charging current can be minimized, so high sensitivity is achieved.
2. Faradaic current is extracted, so electrode reactions can be analyzed more precisely.

Linear Sweep Voltammetry

Linear sweep voltammetry is a voltammetric method where the current at a working electrode is measured while the potential between the working electrode and a reference electrode is swept linearly in time. Oxidation or reduction of species is registered as a peak or trough in the current signal at the potential at which the species begins to be oxidized or reduced.

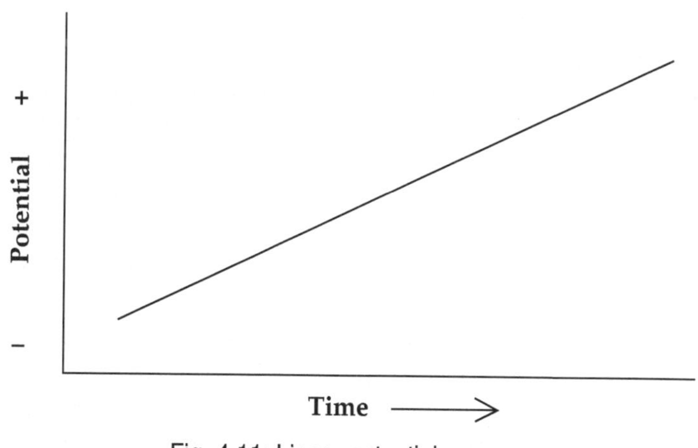

Fig. 4.11: Linear potential sweep

Experimental method

The experimental setup for linear sweep voltammetry utilizes a potentiostat and a three-electrode setup to deliver a potential to a solution and monitor its change in current. The three-electrode setup consists of a working electrode, an auxiliary electrode, and a reference electrode. The potentiostat delivers the potentials through the three-electrode setup. A potential, E, is delivered through the working electrode. The slope of the potential vs. time graph is called the scan rate and can range from mV/s to 1,000,000 V/s. At higher scan rates the current is found to increase which improves the signal to noise ratio. Therefore higher scan rates lead to better signal to noise ratios.

The working electrode is where the oxidation/reduction reactions occur. The equation below gives an example of an oxidation occurring at the surface of the working electrode. ES is the standard reduction potential of A. As E approaches ES the current on the surface increases and when E=ES then the concentration of [A] = [A-] at the surface. As the molecules on the surface of the working electrode or oxidized/reduced they move away from the surface and new molecules come into contact with the surface of the working electrode. This flow of molecules to and from the working electrode causes the current.

$A + e^- = A^-$ E_s=0.00V

Oxidation of molecule A at the surface of the working electrode

The auxiliary and reference electrode work in unison to balance out the charge added or removed by the working electrode. The auxiliary electrode balances the working electrode, but in order to know how much potential it has to add or remove it relies on the reference electrode. The reference electrode has a known reduction potential. The auxiliary electrode tries to keep the reference electrode at a certain reduction potential and to do this it has to balance the working electrode.

Characterization

Linear sweep voltammetry can identify unknown species and determine the concentration of solutions. E1/2 can be used to identify the unknown species while the height of the limiting current can determine the concentration. The sensitivity of current changes vs. voltage can be increased by increasing the scan rate. Higher potentials per second result in more oxidation/reduction of a species at the surface of the working electrode.

Variations

For reversible reactions cyclic voltammetry can be used to find information about the forward reaction and the reverse reaction. Like linear sweep voltammetry, cyclic voltammetry applies a linear potential over time and at a certain potential the potentiostat will reverse the potential applied and sweep back to the beginning point. Cyclic voltammetry provides information about the oxidation and reduction reactions.

Applications

While cyclic voltammetry is applicable to most cases where linear sweep voltammetry is used, there are some instances where linear sweep voltammetry is more useful. In cases where the reaction is irreversible cyclic voltammetry will not give any additional data that linear sweep voltammetry would give us. In one example, linear voltammetry was used to examine direct methane production via a biocathode. Since the production of methane from CO_2 is an irreversible reaction, cyclic voltammetry did not present any distinct advantage over linear sweep voltammetry. This group found that the biocathode produced higher current densities than a plain carbon cathode and that methane can be produced from a direct electrical current without the need of hydrogen gas.

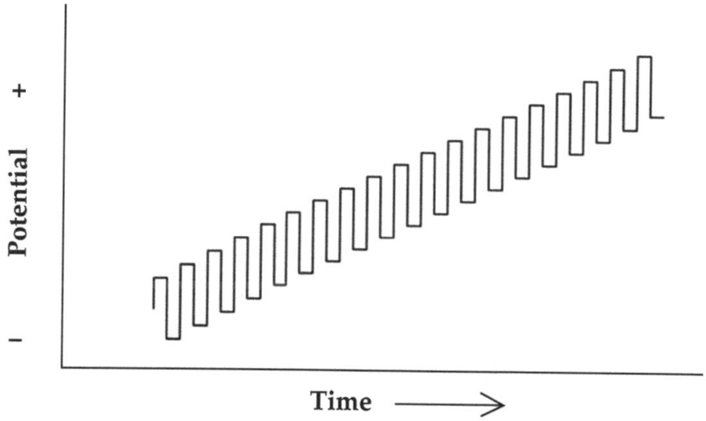

Fig. 4.12: Showing the wave form of the square wave voltammetry

Square wave Voltammetry

Square wave voltammetry (SWV) is a further improvement of staircase voltammetry which is itself a derivative of linear sweep voltammetry. In linear sweep voltammetry the current at a working electrode is measured while the potential between the working electrode and a reference electrode is swept linearly in time. In squarewave voltammetry, asquarewave is superimposed on the potential staircase sweep. Oxidation or reduction of species is registered as a peak or trough in the current signal at the potential at which the species begins to be oxidized or reduced. In staircase voltammetry the potential sweep is a series of stair steps. The current is measured at the end of each potential change, right before the next, so that the contribution to the current signal from the capacitive charging current is minimized. The differential current is then plotted as a function of potential, and the reduction or oxidation of species is measured as a peak or trough. Due to the lesser contribution of capacitative charging current the detection limits for SWV are on the order of nanomolar concentrations.

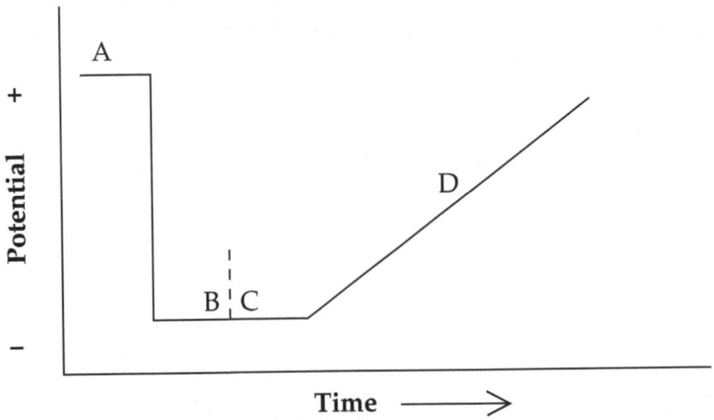

Fig. 4.13: The steps of Anodic Stripping Voltammetry (a) Cleaning step, (b) Electroplating step, (c) Equilibration step, (d) Stripping step

Anodic Stripping Voltammetry

Anodic stripping voltammetry is a voltammetric method for quantitative determination of specific ionic species. The analyte of interest is electroplated on the working electrode during a deposition step, and oxidized from the electrode during the stripping step. The current is measured during the stripping step. The oxidation of species is registered as a peak in the current signal at the potential at which the species begins to be oxidized. The stripping step can be either linear, staircase, squarewave, or pulse.

Electrochemical Cell Set-Up

Anodic stripping voltammetry usually incorporates three electrodes, a working electrode, auxiliary electrode (sometimes called the counter electrode), and reference electrode. The solution being analyzed usually has an electrolyte added to it. For most standard tests, the working electrode is a bismuth or mercury film electrode (in a disk or planar strip configuration). The mercury film forms an amalgam with the analyte of interest, which upon oxidation results in a sharp peak, improving resolution between analytes. The mercury film is formed over a glassy carbon electrode. A mercury drop electrode has also been used for much the same reasons. In cases where the analyte of interest has an oxidizing potential above that of mercury, or where a mercury electrode would be otherwise unsuitable, a solid, inert metal such as silver, gold, or platinum may also be used.

Steps

Anodic stripping voltammetry usually incorporates 4 steps if the working electrode is a mercury film or mercury drop electrode and the solution incorporates stirring. The solution is stirred during the first two steps at a repeatable rate. The first step is a cleaning step; in the cleaning step, the potential is held at a more oxidizing potential than the analyte of interest for a period of time in order to fully remove it from the electrode. In the second step, the potential is held at a lower potential, low enough to reduce the analyte and deposit it on the electrode. After the second step, the stirring is stopped, and the electrode is kept at the lower potential. The purpose of this third step is to allow the deposited material to distribute more evenly in the mercury. If a solid inert electrode is used, this step is unnecessary. The last step involves raising the working electrode to a higher potential (anodic), and stripping (oxidizing) the analyte. As the analyte is oxidized, it gives off electrons which are measured as a current. Stripping analysis is an analytical technique that involves (i) preconcentration of a metal phase onto a solid electrode surface or into Hg (liquid) at negative potentials and (ii) selective oxidation of each metal phase species during an anodic potential sweep.

Stripping analysis has the following properties:

- Very sensitive and reproducible (RSD<5%) method for trace metal ion analysis in aqueous media.
- Concentration limits of detection for many metals are in the low ppb to high pptrange (S/N=3) and this compares favorably with AAS or ICP analysis.
- Field deployable instrumentation that is inexpensive.
- Approximately 12-15 metal ions can be analyzed for by this method.
- The stripping peak currents and peak widths are a function of the size, coverage and distribution of the metal phase on the electrode surface (Hg or alternate)

Sensitivity

Anodic stripping voltammetry can detect µg/L concentrations of analyte. This method has an excellent detection limit (typically 10^{-9} - 10^{-10} M)

Applications

Stripping voltammetry (Anodic, Cathodic and Adsorptive) have been employed for analysis of organic molecules as well as metal ions. Carbon paste, glassy carbon paste, glassy carbon etc electrodes when modified are termed as chemically modified electrodes. Chemically modified electrodes have been employed for the analysis of organic molecules (viz., Paracetamol, aspirin, caffeine, phenol, catechol, resorcinol, hydroquinone, dopamine, L-dopa, epinephrine, nor epinephrine, methyl parathion, ethyl parathion, venlafaxine, desvenlafaxine, imipramine, trimipramine, desipramine etc) as well as metal ions (bismuth, antimony etc.)

Cathodic Stripping Voltamemetry

Cathodic stripping voltammetry is a voltammetric method for quantitative determination of specific ionic species. It is similar to the trace analysis method anodic stripping voltammetry, except that for the plating step, the potential is held at an oxidizing potential, and the oxidized species are stripped from the electrode by sweeping the potential positively. This technique is used for ionic species that form insoluble salts and will deposit on or near the anodic, working electrode during deposition. The stripping step can be either linear, staircase, square wave, or pulse.

AMPEROMETRY

Amperometry in chemistry and biochemistry is detection of ions in a solution based on electric current or changes in electric current.

Amperometry is used in electrophysiology to study vesicle release events using a carbon fiber electrode. Unlike patch clamp techniques, the electrode used for amperometry is not inserted into or attached to the cell, but brought in close proximity of the cell. The measurements from the electrode originate from an oxidizing reaction of a vesicle cargo released into the medium. Another technique used to measure vesicle release is capacitive measurements.

History

Electrochemical or amperometric detection as it was first used in ion chromatography was single-potential or DC amperometry, useful for certain electrochemically active ions such as cyanide, sulphite, and iodide. The development of pulsed amperometric detection (PAD) for analytes that fouled electrode surfaces when detected eventually helped create a new category of ion chromatography for the determination of carbohydrates. Another advancement, known as integrated amperometry, has increased the sensitivity for other electrochemically active species, such as amines and many compounds that contain reduced sulphur groups that are sometimes weakly detected by PAD. It was established that neurotransmitters could be electrochemically detected by placing a carbon electrode into tissue and recording the current from oxidizing neurotransmitters. One of the first measurements was made using an implanted carbon fiber electrode in the neostriatum of rats. Further work was done in chromaffin cells to investigate catecholamine release from large dense core vesicles.

Principle

In order to record vesicle fusion, a carbon fiber electrode is brought close to the cell. The electrode is held at a positive potential, and when the cargo from a fused vesicle is near the electrode, oxidation of the cargo transfers electrons to the electrode. This causes a spike, the size of which can be used to estimate the number of vesicles, and the frequency gives information about the release probability.

Detection Methods

Single-Potential Amperometry

Any analyte that can be oxidized or reduced is a candidate for amperometric detection. The simplest form of amperometric detection is single-potential, or direct current (DC), amperometry. A voltage (potential) is applied between two electrodespositioned in the column effluent. The measured current changes as an electroactive analyte is oxidized at the anode or reduced at the cathode. Single-potential amperometry has been used to detect weak acid anions, such as cyanide and sulphide, which are problematic by conductometric methods. Another, possibly more important advantage of amperometry over other detection methods for these and other ions, such as iodide, sulfite, and hydrazine, is specificity. The applied potential can be adjusted to maximize the response for the analyte of interest while minimizing the response for interfering analytes.

Pulsed Amperometry (pulsed amperometric detection, PAD)

An extension of single-potential amperometry is pulsed amperometry, most commonly used for analytes that tend to foul electrodes. Analytes that foul electrodes reduce the signal with each analysis and necessitate cleaning of the electrode. In pulsed amperometric detection (PAD), a working potential is applied for a short time (usually a few hundred milliseconds), followed by higher or lower potentials that are used for cleaning the electrode. The current is measured only while the working potential is applied, then sequential current measurements are processed by the detector to produce a smooth output. PAD is most often used for detection of carbohydrates after an anion exchange separation, but further development of related techniques show promise for amines, reduced sulfur species, and other electroactive compounds.

Chronoamperometry

Chronoamperometry is an electrochemical technique in which the potential of the working electrode is stepped and the resulting current from faradaic processes occurring at the electrode (caused by the potential step) is monitored as a function of time. Limited information about the identity of the electrolyzed species can be obtained from the ratio of the peak oxidation current versus the peak reduction current. However, as with all pulsed techniques, chronoamperometry generates high charging currents, which decay exponentially with time as any RC circuit. The Faradaic current—which is due to electron transfer events and is most often the current component of interest—decays as described in the Cottrell equation. In most electrochemical cells this decay is much slower than the charging decay—cells with no supporting electrolyte are notable exceptions. Most commonly investigated with a three electrode system. Since the current is integrated over relatively longer time intervals, chronoamperometry gives a better signal to noise ratio in comparison to other amperometric technique.

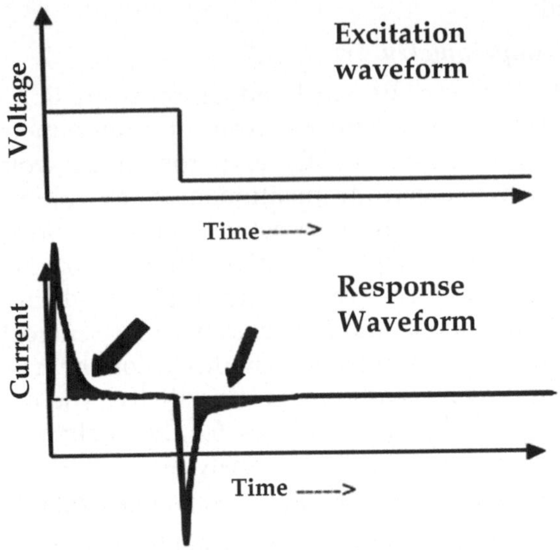

Fig. 4.14: Double-pulsed chronoamperometry waveform showing integrated region for charge determination

Example

Anthracene in deoxygenated dimethylformamide (DMF) will be reduced (An + e^- -> An^-) at the electrode surface that is at a certain negative potential. The reduction will be diffusion-limited, thereby causing the current to drop in time (proportional to the diffusion gradient that is formed by diffusion). You can do this experiment several times increasing electrode potentials from low to high. (In between the experiments, the solution should be stirred.) When you measure the current i(t) at a certain fixed time point τ after applying the voltage, you will see that at a certain moment the current i(τ) does not rise anymore; you have reached the mass-transfer-limited region. This means that anthracene arrives as fast as diffusion can bring it to the electrode.

5

Electrowetting and Surface Chemistry

INTRODUCTION

Miniaturization has been a technological trend for several decades. What started out initially in the microelectronics industry long ago reached the area of mechanical engineering, including fluid mechanics. Reducing size has been shown to allow for integration and automation of many processes on a single device giving rise to a tremendous performance increase, e.g. in terms of precision, throughput, and functionality. One prominent example from the area of fluid mechanics the 'lab-on-a-chip' systems for applications such as DNA and protein analysis, and biomedical diagnostics. Most of the devices developed so far are based on continuous flow through closed channels that are either etched into hard solids such as silicon and glass, or replicated from a hard master into a soft polymeric matrix. Recently, devices based on the manipulation of individual droplets with volumes in the range of nanolitres or less have attracted increasing attention.

From a fundamental perspective the most important consequence of miniaturization is atremendous increase in the surface-to-volume ratio, which makes the control of surfaces and surface energies one of the most important challenges both in microtechnology in general a well as in microfluidics. For liquid droplets of submillimetre dimensions, capillary forces dominate. The control of interfacial energies has therefore become an important strategy for manipulating droplets at surfaces. Both liquid–vapour and solid–liquid interfaces have been influenced in order to control droplets, as recently reviewed by Darhuber and Troian. Temperature gradients as well as gradients in the concentration of surfactants across droplets give rise to gradients in interfacial energies, mainly at the liquid–vapour interface, and thus produce forces that can propel droplets making use of the thermocapillary and Marangoni effects.

Chemical and topographical structuring of surfaces has received even more attention. Compared to local heating, both of these two approaches offer much finer control of the equilibrium morphology. The local wettability and the substrate topography together provide boundary conditions within which the droplets adjust their morphology to reach the most energetically favourable configuration. For complex surface patterns, however, this is not always possible as several metastable morphologies may exist. This can lead to rather abrupt changes in the droplet shape, so-called morphological transitions, when the liquid is forced to switch from one family of morphologies to another by varying a control parameter, such as the wettability or the liquid volume.

The main disadvantage of chemical and topographical patterns is their static nature, which prevents active control of the liquids. Considerable work has been devoted to the development of surfaces with controllable wettability—typically coated with self-assembled monolayers. Notwithstanding some progress, the degree of switchability, the switching speed, the long term reliability, and the compatibility with variable environments that have been achieved so far are not suitable for most practical applications. In contrast, electrowetting (EW) has proven very successful in all these respects: contact angle variations of several tens of degrees are routinely achieved. Switching speeds are limited (typically to several milliseconds) by the hydrodynamic response of the droplet rather than the actual switching of the equilibrium value of the contact angle. Hundreds of thousands of switching cycles were performed in long term stability tests without noticeable degradation. Nowadays, droplets can be moved along freely programmable paths on surfaces; they can be split, merged, and mixed with a high degree of flexibility. Most of these results were achieved within the past five years by a steadily growing community of researchers in the field.

Electrocapillarity, the basis of modern electrowetting, was first described in detail in 1875 by Gabriel Lippmann. This ingenious physicist, who won the Nobel prize in 1908 for the discovery of the first colour photography method, found that the capillary depression of mercury in contact with electrolyte solutions could be varied by applying a voltage between the mercury and electrolyte. He not only formulated a theory of the electrocapillary effect but also developed several applications, including a very sensitive electrometer and a motor based on his observations. In order to make his fascinating work, which has only been available in French up to now, available to a broader readership, we included a translation of his work in the appendix of this review. The work of Lippmann and of those who followed him in the following more than a hundred years was devoted to aqueous electrolytes in direct contact with mercury surfaces or mercury droplets in contact with insulators. A major obstacle to broader applications was electrolytic decomposition of water upon applying voltages beyond a few hundred millivolts. The recent developments were initiated by Berge in the early 1990s, who introduced the idea of using a thin insulating layer to separate the conductive liquid from the metallic electrode in order to eliminate the problem of electrolysis. This is the concept that has also become known as electrowetting on dielectric (EWOD).

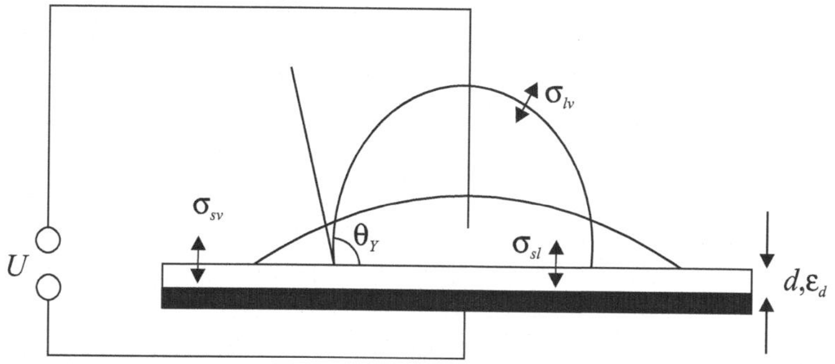

Fig. 5.1: Generic electrowetting set-up. Partially wetting liquid droplet at zero voltage (dashed)and at high voltage (solid). See the text for details

In the present review, we are going to give an overview of the recent developments in electrowetting, touching only briefly on some of the early activities that were already described in a short review by Quilliet and Berge. The article is organized as follows. We discuss the theoretical background of electrowetting, comparing different fundamental approaches, and present some extensions of the classical models. It is devoted to materials issues. We discuss the phenomenon of contact angle saturation, which has probably been the most fundamental challenge in electrowetting for some time. It is devoted to the fundamental principles of electrowetting on complex surfaces, which is the basis for most applications. It deals with some aspects of dynamic electrowetting, and finally, before concluding, a variety of current applications ranging from lab-on-a-chip to lens systems and display technology.

Theoretical Background

Electrowetting has been studied by researchers from various fields, such as applied physics, physical chemistry, electrochemistry, and electrical engineering. Given the various backgrounds, different approaches were used to describe the electrowetting phenomenon, i.e. to determine the dependence of the contact angle on the applied voltage. In this section, we will— after a few introductory remarks about wetting the main approaches of electrowetting theory: the classical thermodynamic approach (2.2.1), the energy minimization approach (2.2.2), and the electromechanical approach (2.2.3). We will describe some extensions of the basic theories that give more insight into the microscopic surface profile near the three-phase contact line (2.3.1), the distribution of charge carriers near the interface (2.3.2), and the behaviour at finite frequencies (2.3.3).

Basic aspects of wetting

In electrowetting, one is generically dealing with droplets of partially wetting liquids on planar solid substrates. In most applications of interest, the droplets are aqueous salt solutions with a typical size of the order of 1 mm or less. The ambient medium can be either air or another immiscible liquid, frequently an oil. Under these conditions, the Bond number Bo = g ρ R2/σlv, which measures the strength of gravity with respect to surface tension, is smaller than unity. Therefore we neglect gravity throughout the rest of this paper. In the absence of external electric fields, the behaviour of the droplets is then determined by surface tension alone. The free energy F of a droplet is a functional of the droplet shape. Its value is given by the sum of the areas Ai of the interfaces between three phases, the solid substrate (s), the liquid droplet (l), and the ambient phase, which we will denote as vapour (v) for simplicity, weighted by the respective interfacial energies σi, i.e. σsv (solid–vapour), σsl (solid–liquid), and σlv (liquid–vapour):

$$F = F_{if} = \sum_i A_i \sigma_i - \lambda V \qquad (1)$$

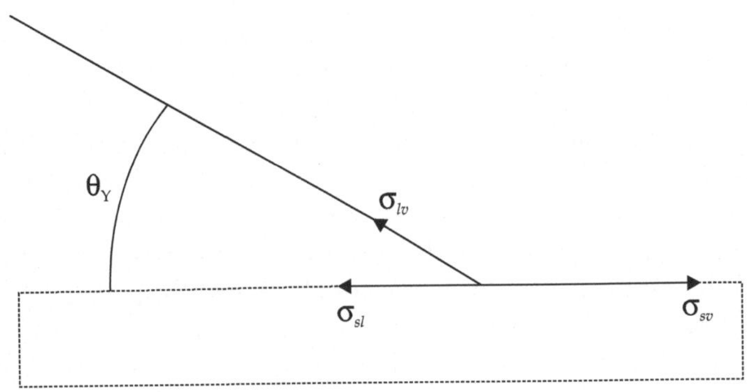

Fig. 5.2: Force balance at the contact line (for θY approximately 30°)

Here, λ is a Lagrangian variable present to enforce the constant volume constraint. λ is equal to the pressure drop p across the liquid–vapour interface. Variational minimization of equation (1) leads to the two well-known necessary conditions that any equilibrium liquid morphology has to fulfil: the first one is the Laplace equation, stating that p is a constant, independent of the position on the interface:

$$\Delta_p = \sigma_{lv}\left(\frac{1}{r_1}+\frac{1}{r_2}\right) = \sigma_{lv} \cdot \kappa. \qquad (2)$$

Here, r1 and r2 are the two—in general position dependent—principal radii of curvature of the surface, and κ is the constant mean curvature. For homogeneous substrates, this means that droplets adopt a spherical cap shape in mechanical equilibrium. The second condition is given by Young's equation

$$\cos\theta_Y = \frac{\sigma_{sv} - \sigma_{sl}}{\sigma_{lv}} \tag{3}$$

which relates Young's equilibrium contact angle θY to the interfacial energies. Alternatively to this energetic derivation, the interfacial energies σi can also be interpreted as interfacial tensions, i.e. as forces pulling on the three-phase contact line. Within this picture, equation (3) is obtained by balancing the horizontal component of the forces acting on the three-phase contact line (TCL); see figure 5.2.

Note that both derivations are approximations intended for mesoscopic scales. On the molecular scale, equilibrium surface profiles deviate from the wedge shape in the vicinity of the TCL. Within the range of molecular forces, i.e. typically a few nanometres from the surface, the equilibrium surface profiles are determined by the local force balance (at the surface) between the Laplace pressure and the disjoining pressure, in which the molecular forces are subsumed. Despite the complexity of the profiles that arise, these details are not relevant if one is only interested in the apparent contact angle at the mesoscopic scale. On that latter scale, the contact line can be considered as a one-dimensional object on which the interfacial tensions are pulling. As we will see below, a comparable situation arises in electrowetting.

Note that the ambient phase can be another liquid, immiscible with the droplet, instead of vapour.

Note that these conditions are only necessary and not sufficient. In addition, the second variation of F must be positive. In the presence of complex surfaces, some morphologies may indeed be unstable although both necessary conditions are fulfilled.

The vertical force component is balanced by normal stresses in the stiff solid substrate.

Electrowetting Theory for Homogeneous Substrates

The thermodynamic and electrochemical approach. Lippmann's classical derivation of the electrowetting or electrocapillarity equation is based on general Gibbsian interfacial thermodynamics. Unlike in the recent applications of electrowetting where the liquid is separated from the electrode by an insulating layer, Lippmann's original experiments dealt with direct metal (in particular mercury)–electrolyte interfaces. For mercury, several tenths of a volt can be applied between the metal and the electrolyte without any current flowing. Upon applying a voltage dU, an electric double layer builds up spontaneously at the solid–liquid interface consisting of charges on the metal surface on the one hand and of a cloud of oppositely charged counter-ions on the liquid side of the interface. Since the accumulation is a spontaneous process, for instance the adsorption of surfactant molecules at an air–water interface, it leads to a reduction of the (effective) interfacial tension σ_{sl}^{eff}

$$d\sigma_{sl}^{eff} = -\rho_{sl}\, dU \tag{4}$$

surface charge density of the counter-ions.) (Our reasons for denoting the voltage dependent tension as 'effective' will become clear below.) The voltage dependence of sl is calculated by integrating equation (4). In general, this integral requires additional knowledge about the voltage dependent distribution of counter-ions near the interface. The equation below describes such a calculation on the basis of the Poisson–Boltzmann distribution. For now, we make the simplifying assumption that the counter-ions are all located at a fixed distance dH (of the order of a few nanometres) from the surface (Helmholtz model). In this case, the double layer has a fixed capacitance per unit area, cH = ε0 εl / dH, where εl is the dielectric constant of the liquid. We obtain

$$\sigma_{sl}^{eff}(U) = \sigma_{sl} - \int_{pzc}^{U} \rho_{sl}\, d\tilde{U} = \sigma_{sl} - \int_{pzc}^{U} c_H \tilde{U}\, d\tilde{U} = \sigma_{sl} - \frac{\varepsilon_0 \varepsilon_1}{2d_H}(U - U_{pzc})^2. \tag{5}$$

Here, Upzc is the potential (difference) of zero charge. (Note that mercury surfaces—like those of most other materials—acquire a spontaneous charge when immersed into electrolyte solutions at zero voltage. The voltage required to compensate for this spontaneous charging is UPZC. The chemical contribution σsl to the interfacial energy, which appeared previously in Young's equation, is assumed to be independent of the applied voltage. To obtain the response of the contact angle, equation (5) is inserted into Young's equation (3). For an electrolyte droplet placed directly on an electrode surface we find

$$\cos\theta = \cos\theta_Y + \frac{\varepsilon_0 \varepsilon_1}{2d_H \sigma_{lv}}(U - U_{pzc})^2 \tag{6}$$

For typical values of dH (2 nm), εl (81), and σlv (0.072 mJ m–2) we find that the ratio on the rhs of equation is on the order of 1 V–2 . The contact angle thus decreases rapidly upon the application of a voltage. It should be noted, however, that equation is only applicable within a voltage range below the onset of electrolytic processes, i.e. typically up to a few hundred millivolts. As mentioned already in the introduction, modern applications of electrowetting usually circumvent this problem by introducing a thin dielectric film, which insulates the droplet from the electrode. In this EWOD configuration, the electric double layer builds up at the insulator–droplet interface. Since the insulator thickness d is usually much larger than dH, the total capacitance of the system is reduced tremendously. The system may be described as two capacitors in series, namely the double at the solid–insulator interface (capacitance cH) and the dielectric layer with cd = ε0 εd / d (εd is the dielectric constant of the insulator). Since cd cH, the total capacitance per unit area c ≈ cd. With this approximation, we neglect the finite penetration of the electric field into the liquid, i.e. we treat the latter as a perfect conductor. As a result, we find that the voltage drop occurs within the dielectric layer, and equation (5) is replaced by

$$\sigma_{sl}^{eff}(U) = \sigma_{sl} - \frac{\varepsilon_0\varepsilon_d}{2d}U^2 \tag{7}$$

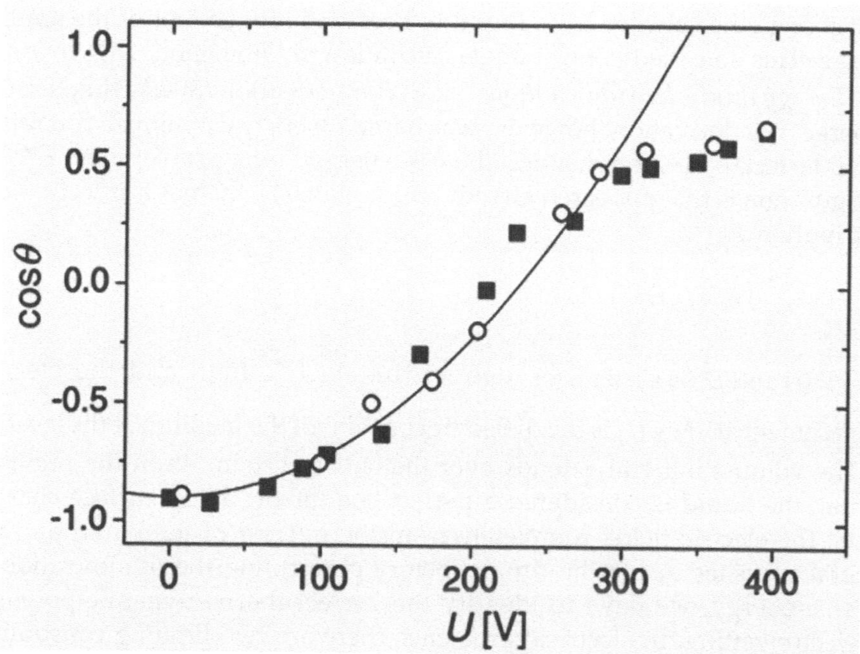

Fig. 5.3: Contact angle versus applied (RMS) voltage for a glycerol–salt (NaCl) water droplet (conductivity: 3 mS cm–1 ; AC frequency: 10 kHz) with silicone oil as the ambient medium. Insulator: Teflon AF 1601 (d ≈ 5 μm). Note that θY is almost 180° for this system. Filled(open) symbols: increasing (decreasing) voltage. Solid line: parabolic fit according to equation (8)

(Here and in the following, we assume that the surface of the insulating layer does not give rise to spontaneous adsorption of charge in the absence of an applied voltage, i.e. we set ($U_{pzc} = 0$.) In this equation the entire dielectric layer is considered part of one effective solid–liquid interface with a thickness of the order of d, i.e. in practice typically O(1 μm). In that sense, the interfacial energy in equation (7) is clearly an 'effective' quantity. Combining equation (7) with equation (3), we obtain the basic equation for EWOD:

$$\cos\theta = \cos\theta_Y + \frac{\varepsilon_0\varepsilon_d}{2_d\sigma_{lv}}U^2 = \cos\theta_Y + \eta. \tag{8}$$

Here, we have introduced the dimensionless electrowetting number $\eta = \varepsilon_0\varepsilon_r U^2/(2d\sigma_{lv})$ which measures the strength of the electrostatic energy compared to surface tension. The ratio in the middle part of equation (8) is typically four to six orders of magnitude smaller than that in equation (6), depending on the properties of the insulating layer. Consequently, the voltage required to achieve a substantial contact angle decrease in EWOD is much higher. Figure 5.3 shows a typical experimental example. As in many other experiments, equation (8) is found to hold as long as the voltage is not too high. Beyond a certain system dependent threshold voltage, however, the contact angle has always been found to become independent of the applied voltage. This so-called contact angle saturation phenomenon.

Energy minimization method. For EWOD, equation (8) was first derived by Berge. His derivation, however, was based on energy minimization rather than interfacial thermodynamics: the free energy F of a droplet in an EWOD configuration is that appeared already in equation (1), there is an electrostatic contribution F_{el}:

$$F_{el} = \frac{1}{2} \int \vec{E}(\vec{r}) \cdot \vec{D}(\vec{r})\, dV. \qquad (9)$$

$\vec{E}(\vec{r})$ and $\vec{D}(\vec{r})\ \varepsilon_0\varepsilon(\vec{r})\ \vec{E}(\vec{r})$ denote the electric field and the electric displacement at $\vec{r}$. $\varepsilon(\vec{r})$ is the dielectric constant of the medium at the location $\vec{r}$. The volume integral extends over the entire system. As in the previous section, the liquid is considered a perfect conductor; hence surface charges screen the electric fields completely from the interior of the liquid and the integral vanishes inside the droplet.Before performing the minimization of the free energy, we have to identify the correct thermodynamic potential for electrowetting. In electrical problems, there are two limiting constraints: constant charge and constant voltage. The corresponding thermodynamic potentials are related by a Legendre transformation. In electrowetting, the voltage is controlled. The thermodynamic potential corresponding to this situation is given by

$$F = F_{if} - F_{el} = \sum_i A_i\sigma_i - \Delta pV - \frac{1}{2} \int \vec{E}(\vec{r}) \cdot \vec{D}(\vec{r})\, dV. \qquad (10)$$

Before computing the contact angle decrease, one usually introduces another simplification: the electrostatic energy may be split into two parts. The first part arises from the parallel plate capacitor formed by the droplet and the electrode, with C = cd Asl . Thesecond part is due to the stray capacitance along the edge of the droplet. The fringe fields are mainly localized within a small range around the contact line. Therefore, their contribution to the total energy is negligible for sufficiently large droplets. (we will consider the effect of fringe fields in more detail.) Hence, we find

$$F_{el} \approx CU^2/2 = \varepsilon_0\varepsilon_d U^2 A_{sl}/(2d). \qquad (11)$$

Apart from this formal explanation, the negative sign in equation (10) can also beunderstood intuitively by considering the entire system consisting of both the droplet and the power supply (the 'battery') required to apply the voltage. Upon connecting the initially uncharged droplet to the battery, the charge δ Q flows from the battery ($\delta Q_b = -\delta Q$) to the droplet (and to the electrode). The work done on the droplet–electrode capacitor is given by $\delta W = U(Q)\,\delta Q = Q/C\delta Q$ with U (Q) being the charge dependent voltage on the capacitor. The electrostatic energy stored in the droplet in the final state is

$$E_{\text{drop}} = \int \delta W = Q^2/(2C) = CU_b^{\,2}/2. \tag{12}$$

The work done on the battery is $\delta W_b = U_b \delta Q_b = -U_b \delta Q$. In contrast to U (Q), the battery voltage Ub is constant, such that we obtain a release of electrostatic energy of

$$\Delta E_{\text{batt}} = \int \delta W_b = \int U_b \delta Q_b = -\int U_b \delta Q = -CU_b^{\,2} \tag{13}$$

Hence the electrostatic contribution to the free energy is $-CU^b{}_2/2$. Electrowetting is thus driven by the energy gain upon redistributing charge from the battery to the droplet. The contact angle decreases because this increases C and thus allows for the redistribution of even more charge.

For homogeneous electrodes, the free energy thus reads

$$F = A_{\text{lv}}\sigma_{\text{lv}} + A_{\text{sv}}\sigma_{\text{sv}} + A_{\text{sl}}\left(\sigma_{\text{sl}} - \frac{\varepsilon_0\varepsilon_{\text{d}}U^2}{2d}\right) - \Delta pV$$

Equation (11) has the same structure as the free energy in the absence of electric fields (equation (1)). On comparing the coefficients, the electrowetting equation (8) is rediscovered. As in the previous section, this derivation is based on the assumptions that (i) the σi are voltage independent, (ii) the liquid is perfectly conductive, and (iii) contributions from the region around the contact line (due to fringe fields) can be neglected. An important additional insight from this derivation is the fact that the energy gain in electrowetting is actually taking place in the battery, i.e. quite remotely from the droplet itself. This illustrates again the effective character of the definition in (equation (7)).

Electromechanical approach. Both methods discussed so far predict the same contact angle reduction. However, they do not provide a physical picture of how the contact angle reduction is achieved in mechanical terms. Such a picture can be obtained by considering the forces exerted on the liquid by the electric field. These forces contain contributions due to the response of the free electric charge density of and the polarization density ρf in the presence of electric field gradients. This approach was introduced to the field of electrowetting by Jones and recently reviewed by Zeng and Korsmeyer. In the case of simple liquids, one of the most frequently used formulations is the Korteweg–Helmholtz body force density

$$\vec{f}_k = \rho_f \vec{E} - \frac{\varepsilon_0}{2}E^2\,\nabla\varepsilon + \nabla\left[\frac{\varepsilon_0}{2}E^2\frac{\partial\varepsilon}{\partial\rho}\rho\right]$$

where ρ and ε are the mass density and the dielectric constant of the liquid, respectively. The last term in equation (12) describes electrostriction and can be neglected in the present context. The net force acting on a volume element dV of the fluid is obtained by a volume integration over equation (12). As a fundamental consequence of momentum conservation, the same force can also be obtained by an integration along the surface of dV over the momentum flux density of the electric fields, i.e. the Maxwell stress tensor. It seems particularly appropriate because in the perfect conductor limit of electrowetting the entire 'body' force actually acts at the surface: ρf is zero within the bulk, and free surface charges screen the electric field from the interior. The second term on the rhs of equation (12), the so-called ponderomotive force density, $\propto \nabla\varepsilon$, vanishes everywhere except at the surface. Neglecting electrostriction, the Maxwell stress tensor consistent with equation (12) is

$$T_{ik} = \varepsilon_0\varepsilon(E_iE_k - \frac{1}{2}\delta_{ik}E^2)$$

Here, δik is the Kronecker delta function, and i, k = x, y, z. Let us now consider a volume element dV at the liquid–air interface of a perfectly conductive liquid droplet.

The tangential component of the electric field at the surface vanishes and the normal component is related to the local surface charge density by $\rho_s = \varepsilon_0\vec{E} \cdot \vec{n}$, , where n is the (outward) unit normal vector. Furthermore, E vanishes within the liquid. To obtain the net force acting on the liquid volume element, we calculate

$$F_i = \oint_{\Sigma} T_{ik}\, n_k\, \mathrm{d}A \tag{14}$$

using the Einstein summation convention. We find that the only non-vanishing contribution is a force per unit surface area d A directed along the outward surface normal n :

$$\vec{F}/\mathrm{d}A = P_{el}\vec{n} = \frac{\varepsilon_0}{2}E^2\vec{n} = \frac{\rho_0}{2}\vec{E} \tag{15}$$

where we have introduced the electrostatic pressure $P_{el} = \varepsilon_0 E^2/2$ acting on the liquid surface.P_{el} is thus a negative contribution to the total pressure within the liquid. How does this local pressure at the surface affect the contact angle of a sessile droplet? The solution of the problem requires a calculation of the field (and charge) distribution along the surface of the droplet. Far away from the contact line, the charge density at the solid–liquid interface is $\rho_{sl} = \varepsilon_0\varepsilon_d U/d$ and the liquid–vapour surface charge density vanishes. As the three-phase contact line is approached, both charge densities increase due to sharp edge effects, as first pointed out in. The force arising from the charges at the solid–liquid interface leads to a normal stress on the insulator surface, which is balanced by the elastic stress. The forces at the liquid–vapour interface, however, contain both a vertical and a horizontal component pulling on the liquid. Kang assumed that the droplet remains wedge shaped and calculated the net horizontal force acting on the liquid by integrating the horizontal component of equation (15).

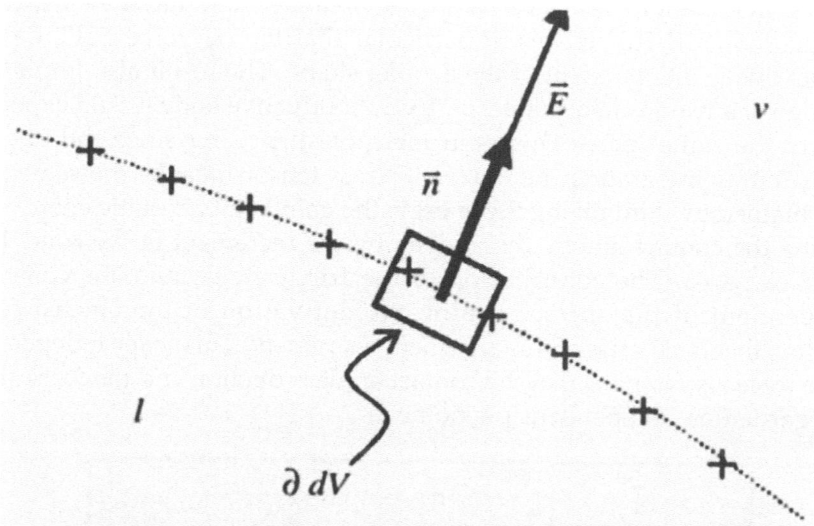

Fig. 5.4: Force acting on a volume element dV at the liquid–vapour interface with surface charges('+'). Solid box: area for surface integral

along the liquid–vapour interface. The field and charge distribution are found by solving the Laplace equation for an electrostatic potential φ with appropriate boundary conditions. For the wedge geometry, an analytic solution can be obtained using conformal mapping as first described by Vallet et al in the context of electrowetting. Both the field and charge distribution are found to diverge algebraically upon approaching the contact line. The resulting Maxwell stress is thus maximal at the contact line and decays to a practically negligible value at a distance of a few d from the TCL. Integrating the horizontal component of the Maxwell stress, we obtain the net force acting on the droplet. For the horizontal component, the result reads.

$$Fx = \frac{\varepsilon_0 \varepsilon_d}{2d} U^2 = \sigma_{lv} \eta. \quad (16)$$

Given the rapid decay of the Maxwell stress, this force can be considered as localized at the contact line, in a coarse grained sense—on a length scale much larger than d. Expression (16) can thus be used in the force balance at the contact line in the spirit of Young. As a result, we rediscover equation (8) for the third time. All three methods are thus equivalent.

It is worth pointing out that the result in equation (16) can be obtained much more easily if we presuppose that the force is localized close to the contact line, as we did implicitly in the previous section when we neglected the contribution of fringe fields. Adapting the ideas of Jones et al, we can calculate the net force by choosing a sufficiently large box around the contact line that the electric field vanishes along most sections of the closed area α. For such a box, only the section along A–B (in figure 5.5) contributes to the integral in equation (14). As a result, we obtain exactly the same expression as equation (16). This means in particular that the net force pulling on the contact line is independent of the droplet shape. The result also implies that the edge of any non-deformable, perfectly conductive body would experience exactly the same force. This is in fact not surprising since the net force calculated by integrating the Maxwell stress tensor must be the same as the one obtained by minimizing the energy: the gain in electrostatic energy upon moving the contact line by dx is given by the increment in the solid–liquid interfacial area. The contribution of the fringe fields remains constant—independent of the surface profile. (A derivation of the electrowetting equation that makes use of this argument was given.) This shape independence of the force also implies that the contact angle reduction and the force should be regarded as independent phenomena.

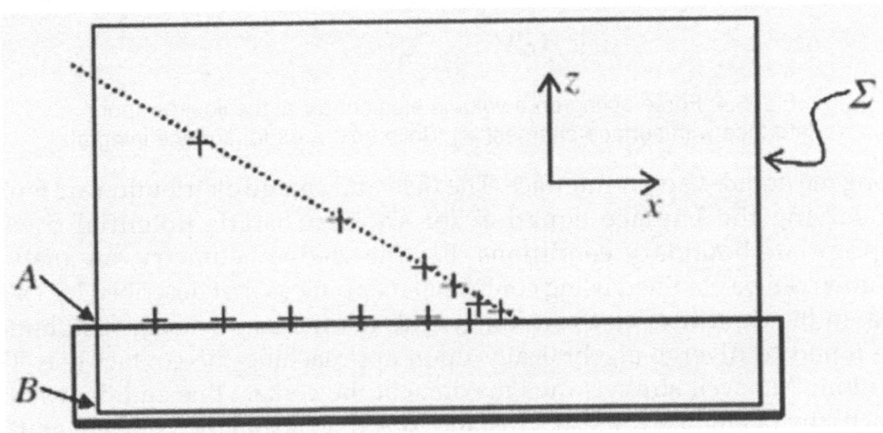

Fig. 5.5: Integration box for the calculation of the net force acting on the contact line

Extensions of the Classical Electrowetting Theory

Fine structure of the triple line. In the previous section, we discussed the response of the liquid on a mesoscopic scale. The impact of the fringe fields on the liquid surface in the vicinity of the TCL was ignored. If we look at the surface profile within that range, the liquid surface is expected to be deformed, as first noted by Vallet et al. In order to calculate the equilibrium surface profile, Buehrle et al proceeded in analogy with conventional wetting theory in the presence of molecular forces: in mechanical equilibrium, the pressure p across the liquid–vapour interface must be independent of the position on the surface. Therefore any electrostatic pressure Pel (r) = ε0 E (r)2/2 close to the TCL must be balanced by an additional curvature of the surface such that

$$\sigma_{lv}\kappa(\vec{r}) - P_{el}(\vec{r}) = \Delta p = \text{const.} \tag{17}$$

Compared to conventional wetting theory, there is one major difference: while the disjoining pressure at a given position r depends only on the film thickness at that position, the electric field and thus Pel (r) depends on the global shape of the droplet. Thus the droplet shape and the field distribution have to be determined self-consistently. Buehrle et al addressed this question for the case of droplets of infinite radius. They chose an iterative numerical procedure, which involved a finite element calculation of the field distribution for a trial surface profile followed by a numerical integration of equation (17) to obtain a refined surface profile. The calculation was a two-dimensional one, i.e. possible modulations of the profile along the contact line were not included. The procedure was found to converge to an equilibrium profile after a few iteration steps. The following main results were found. (i) The surface profiles are indeed curved, as sketched. The curvature of the surface profiles and thus the electric field diverges algebraically at the TCL, as in (with a different exponent, however). (ii) The asymptotic slope of the profile at the substrate remains finite and corresponds to δY, independently of the applied voltage. This is only possible because the divergence of the curvature is very weak. In fact, Buehrle et al confirmed analytically that Pel ∝ r ν with an exponent "1 < ν < 0. (iii) The apparent contact angle δ is in agreement with the electrowetting equation (equation (8)) up to the highest values of η investigated (corresponding to θ = 5°). In view of the discussion in the previous section, this result is not unexpected. It also implies that contact angle saturation does not occur within a two-dimensional electromechanical model—in contrast to some arguments in the literature. Recently, Papathanasiou and Boudouvis repeated the same calculation for droplets of finite size using a slightly different numerical scheme. Except for small deviations from the electrowetting equation, which may be due to the finite size of their system, they reproduced most of the results presented in. Despite the striking difference between the apparent contact angle and the local one at the contact line, the calculations showed that the surface distortions are significant only within a rather small region of O(d) around the TCL. From an applied point of view, this allows for the comforting conclusion that the simple models are sufficient as long as the phenomena of interest occur on a length scale larger than d.

Electrolyte properties. Typical liquids used in electrowetting are aqueous salt solutions. They are conventionally described as perfect conductors with surface charges perfectly screening any external electric field. Microscopically, however, external fields are screened by an inhomogeneous distribution of ions close to the electrolyte surface. For typical ion concentrations, the penetration depth of the electric field is of the order of a few nanometres, given by the Debye length κ^{-1}, with $\kappa = \sqrt{(\Sigma\, n_i^b\, q_i^2)/\varepsilon_0\varepsilon_1/k_BT}$. (The sum runs over all the i, with n_i^b and q_i being the bulk concentration and the charge of the i th species. kB is the Boltzmann constant and T is the temperature.) The local ion concentration and the electrostatic potential φ are coupled via the Poisson–Boltzmann equation.

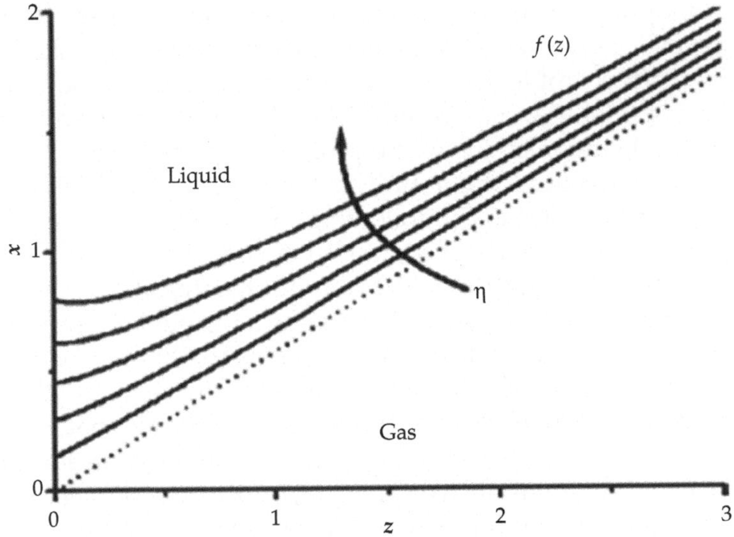

Fig. 5.6: Equilibrium surface profiles (θ = 60η) = 0.2, 0.4, ... 1.0; ε_d = 1)

$$\nabla^2 \phi = -\sum_i \frac{q_i n_i^b}{\varepsilon_0 \varepsilon_1} \exp(-q_i\phi/k_BT). \tag{18}$$

Within this framework, the osmotic pressure

$$\Delta\Pi = \sum n_i^b\, k_BT\,(\exp(-q_i\phi/k_BT) - 1 \tag{19}$$

of the ions has to be taken into account as an extra contribution to the free energy, such that the last term in equation (10) is replaced by

$$F_{el} = \int \left(\frac{1}{2}\vec{E}\,\vec{D} + \Delta\Pi\right) dV = \int \left(\frac{\varepsilon_0\varepsilon_1}{2}\,(\nabla\phi)^2 + \Delta\Pi\right) \mathrm{d}V \tag{20}$$

In order to calculate Fel, a solution of the Poisson–Boltzmann equation is required. For two specific situations the relation between δ and φ can be simplified considerably: when $q\phi/k_BT << 1\,1$, the Poisson–Boltzmann equation (as well as the expression for δ) can be linearized. In this case, one obtains $\Delta\Pi = \varepsilon_0\varepsilon_1\kappa^2\phi^2/2$. One should note that $k_BT/e \approx 25$ mV (elementary charge) at room temperature. Hence the applicability of the linearized Poisson–Boltzmann equation is limited to situations where the potential drop within the liquid is rather small. (While this is usually fulfilled in the centre of the droplet, deviations should be expected close to the TCL, where the electric field strength diverges (see the preceding section).) Thesecond simple situation corresponds to having monovalent salt solutions with $q_1 = -q_2 = z\,e$ (z: valency) and $n^b{}_1 = n^b{}_2$. In this case, hyperbolic sine and cosine terms appear in equation (18) and in the expression for ΔΠ, respectively.

If we consider only the contributions of these terms to the energy per unit area of the solid– liquid interface (i.e. neglecting fringe field contributions), the problem is a one-dimensional one. Using appropriate boundary conditions (fixed potentials on the electrode and in the bulk liquid), analytic expressions for both φ and Fel/Asl can be obtained. The latter is a correction to the electrostatic contribution in equation (11), which ultimately leads to a correction to the electrowetting number η in the electrowetting equation (8). More specifically, one obtains for the linearized Poisson–Boltzmann equation.

$$F_{el} = \int \left(\frac{1}{2} \vec{E}\,\vec{D} + \Delta\Pi \right) dV = \int \left(\frac{\varepsilon_0 \varepsilon_1}{2} (\nabla\phi)^2 + \Delta\Pi \right) dV \tag{20}$$

where ν = eU/kB T. φ0 is the potential (in units of U) at the solid–liquid interface. It is given by the solution of the equation 1 – φ0 – (2εl κ d)/(εr ν)· sinh(νφ0/2) = 0 (constant potential boundary conditions). With λ d in typical experiments, it is obvious that the correction in equation (21) is small. Numerical solutions for φ0 show that the same is true for the correction in equation (22). Corrections due to the double layer thus have a rather weak effect on the apparent contact angle.

Kang et al as well as Chou went one step beyond the above calculation and analysed specifically the contribution arising from the vicinity of the TCL. They calculated the electrostatic contribution to the line tension τe, i.e. to the excess free energy per unit length on the contact line. This excess energy arises from the overlap of the double layers originating from the solid–liquid and from the liquid–vapour interfaces. In, analytical results for τe were obtained for wedge-shaped surface profiles within the linear approximation of the Poisson–Boltzmann equation. τe was found to be of the same order of magnitude as the molecular line tension, i.e. 10-12 – 10-10 J m–1 . Numerical solutions for the full non-linear Poisson–Boltzmann equation produced similar results. Like the line tension of molecular origin, the impact of this electrostatic line tension will hence be negligible for droplets with a diameter of, for example, a hundred nanometres or more. This conclusion is supported by numerical calculations of equilibrium surface profiles based on the full Poisson–Boltzmann equation in analogy to the discussion.

$$\eta_{lin} = \eta . \frac{1}{1 + \varepsilon_d \lambda / \varepsilon_1 d} \tag{21}$$

where $\lambda = k^{-1}$. In the case of monovalent salts, the result is

$$\eta_{mv} = \eta . \left[(1 - \phi_0)^2 + \frac{16\kappa d}{\nu^2} \frac{\varepsilon_1}{\varepsilon_d} \sinh^2(\nu\phi_0/4) \right] \tag{22}$$

AC Electric Fields

The theoretical treatment of electrowetting as discussed so far was based on static considerations. In the case of slow variations of the applied voltage, the contact angle and droplet shape can follow adiabatically the momentary equilibrium values. If the AC frequency exceeds the hydrodynamic response time of the droplet (for typical millimetre-sized droplets at frequencies exceeding a few hundred hertz), the liquid response depends only on the time average of the applied voltage, i.e. the RMS value has to be used in equation (8). This statement is correct as long as the basic assumptions in the derivation of the Lippmann equation are not violated: one of them, the assumption that the liquid can be treated as a perfect conductor, however, breaks down upon increasing the frequency. While the dissolved ions can follow the applied field at moderate frequencies and thus screen the electric field from the interior of the liquid, they are not able to do so beyond a certain critical frequency ωc . Far below ωc, the liquid behaves as a perfect conductor; far above it behaves as a dielectric. (Electric field-induced actuation of liquids beyond ωc is still possible. However, the forces in that range are dielectric body forces. For a review on dielectrophoresis. For homogeneous bulk liquids, the critical frequency for which ohmic and displacement currents are equal is given by

$$\omega_c = \frac{\sigma_1}{\varepsilon_1 \varepsilon_0} \tag{23}$$

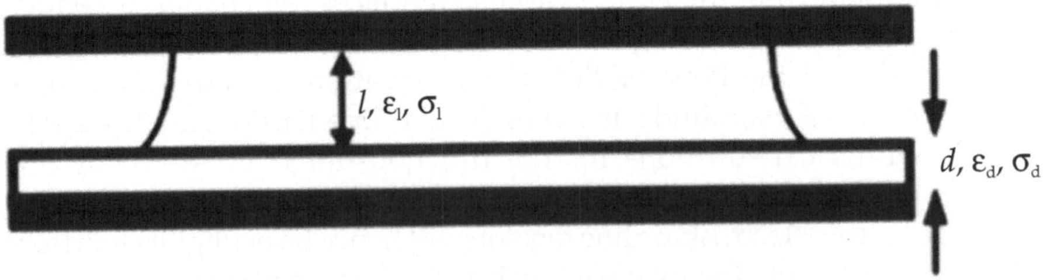

Fig. 5.7: Capillary bridge between bare and insulator-covered electrode (see the text for details)

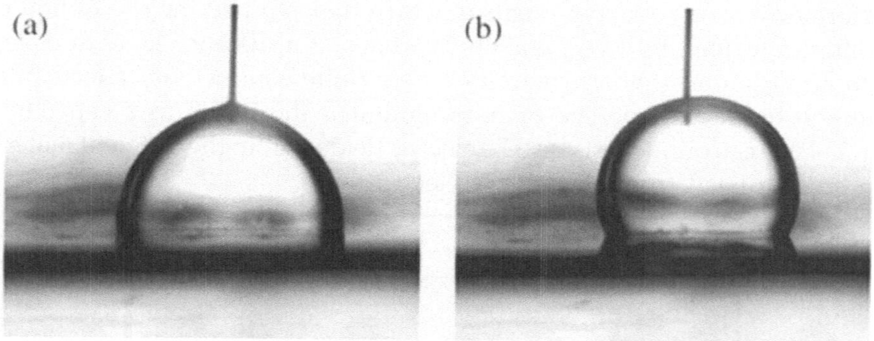

Fig. 5.8: Frequency dependence of contact angle (insulator: 1 μm thermally grown Si oxide, hydrophobized with a monolayer of octadecyltetrachlorosiloxane). Droplet: salt (NaCl) water; conductivity: 0.2 mS cm–1 ; diameter: approximately 2 mm; ambient medium: silicone oil; URMS = 50 V. (a) f = 1 kHz. (b) f = 20 kHz

where σl and εl are the conductivity and the dielectric constant of the liquid, respectively. For an aqueous salt (NaCl) solution with a conductivity of 0.1 S m^{-1} (H≈10^{-4} mol l^{-1}), we have ωc = O(108 s^{-1}). For demineralized water ($\sigma = 4 \times 10^{-6}{}_{S}$ m^{-1}) ωc is as low as 4 × 103 s^{-1}. The relevant critical frequency in electrowetting, however, depends not only on the intrinsic properties of the liquid but also on the geometric and electric properties of the insulating layer. For instance, the characteristic time constant τc for charge relaxation in the configuration sketched in figure 5.7 is given

$$\omega_c = \frac{\sigma_1}{\varepsilon_1 \varepsilon_0}$$

Using, for instance, d = 1 μm, l = 1 mm, εd = 2, εl = 81, σd = 0, and σl = 0.1S m–1(as above), we obtain

$$2\pi/\tau_c^{-1} \approx 4 \times 10^7\ s^{-1}$$

whereas for de mineralized water we have

$$2\pi/\tau_c^{-1} \approx 1.6 \times 10^3\ s^{-1}$$

Figure 5.8 illustrates this breakdown of electrowetting at high frequency for a millimeter-sized droplet of demineralized water. At high frequency, a substantial fraction of the voltage that is applied to the wire drops within the droplet. Therefore, both the voltage at the contact line and thus the energy gain upon moving the latter are reduced. The continuous nature of the transition from conductive to dielectric behaviour as a function of frequency for various salt concentrations. The details of the contact angle response to the electric field are rather complex and geometry dependent when the field penetrates substantially into the liquid.

The transition from low frequency electrowetting behaviour to high frequency dielectrophoretic behaviour is much better illustrated in experiments that measure the forces exerted by the electric fields. Jones et al performed a series of experiments in which they studied the rise of liquid in capillaries formed by two parallel electrodes at a distance D, each covered with an insulator. (Other examples where finite conductivity effects play a role will be discussed. The authors modelled the liquid as a capacitor in parallel with an ohmic resistor. The electric fields within the different materials can be calculated from elementary electrostatics.

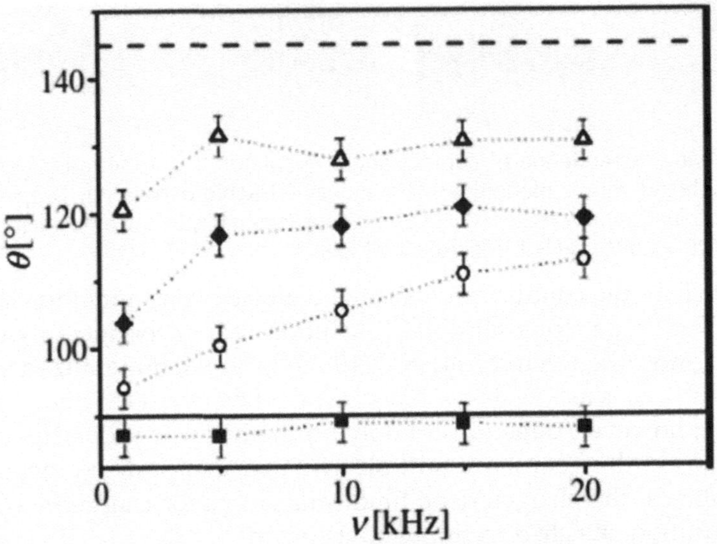

Fig. 5.9: Contact angle θ versus frequency, Conductivity: 1850 μS c m^{-1} (squares), 197 μs cm^{-1} (circles), 91 μS cm^{-1} (diamonds), and 42 μS cm^{-1} (triangles) θY and θ are shown as dashed and solid lines, respectively

Using either the Maxwell stress tensor or the derivative of the total electrostatic energy with respect to the height of the liquid, a frequency dependent expression for the electric force pulling the liquid upwards is obtained. Balancing this force with gravity, Jones et al obtained an expression h = K (ω)U 2 with an analytical function K (ω). The low and high frequency limits are given by

$$h = \begin{cases} \dfrac{\varepsilon_d \varepsilon_0}{4\rho 1 g d D} U^2; & \omega << \omega_c \\ \dfrac{(\varepsilon_1 - 1)\varepsilon_0}{2\rho 1 g D^2} U^2; & \omega >> \omega_c \end{cases}$$

where ρl is the density of the liquid and g is the gravitational acceleration. The critical frequency ωc = 2σ/(D · (2cl + cd)) involves the capacitances per unit area cl and cd of the liquid and of the insulating layer, respectively. K (ω) determined from a series of experimental height of rise versus voltage curves. Good agreement was achieved with model calculations based on independently measured liquid properties.

In addition to this frequency dependent reduction of the rise height, Jones et al also observed a deviation from the predicted parabolic voltage dependence at high voltage. This observation is in qualitative agreement with earlier experiments, in which electrowetting- induced capillary rise was investigated using DC voltage. According to those authors, the deviation from parabolic behaviour in h(U) coincided with the onset of contact angle saturation on a planar substrate made of the same material.

Materials Properties

In classical electrowetting theory, the liquid is treated as a perfect conductor. For aqueous salt solutions this corresponds to the limit of either high salt concentration or low frequency, as discussed in the preceding section. The requirements regarding the concentration and nature of charge carriers are not very stringent. At low frequency ($f < 1$ kHz), even demineralized water displays substantial electrowetting. Frequently, experiments are performed with salt concentrations of the order of 0.01–1 mol l–1. Most authors report no significant influence due to the type or concentration of the salt. However, Quinn et al found systematic pH dependent deviations from equation (8), which they attributed to specific adsorption of hydroxyl ions to the insulator surfaces. Electrowetting was also observed for mixtures of salt solutions with other species (e.g. glycerol, ethanol) without deterioration of electrowetting performance. In particular, electrowetting also occurs in the presence of biomolecules such as DNA or proteins and has even been demonstrated for physiological fluids. One complication with biological fluids is, however, that the performance can be affected by unspecific adsorption of biomolecules to the surfaces. Adsorbed biomolecules generally reduce θY and increase contact angle hysteresis. Room temperature ionic liquids were also shown to display electrowetting. Electrowetting is thus a rather robust phenomenon that depends only weakly on the liquid properties.

In contrast, the properties of the insulating layers are much more critical. Substantial activities have been aimed at optimizing the properties of these layers in order to minimize the voltage required for contact angle reduction. At the same time, the materials used should be chemically inert and stable in order to ensure reproducibility and a long lifetime. Two main criteria can be derived immediately from equation (8): first, the contact angle at zero voltage should be as large as possible, in order to achieve a large tuning range and, second, the dielectric layer should be as thin as possible. The first choice can be met by either using an intrinsically hydrophobic insulator, such as many polymer materials, or by covering hydrophilic insulators with a thin hydrophobic top coating. One possible top coating is self-assembled monolayers (e.g. silanes on glass or SiOx). More frequently, however, thin layers of amorphous fluoropolymer (Teflon AF or Cytop) are used. These materials can be deposited by spin coating or by dip coating. Depending on the solution concentration and on the deposition parameters, layers with a thickness ranging from a few tens of nanometres to several micrometres can be produced. Apart from being hydrophobic, Teflon-like layers can be prepared as very smooth with very small contact angle hysteresis (<10° for water in air). The material is chemically inert and resists both acids and bases. Seyrat and Hayes developed a preparation protocol that leads to very homogeneous Teflon AF layers with high dielectric strength (≈200 V μm–1).

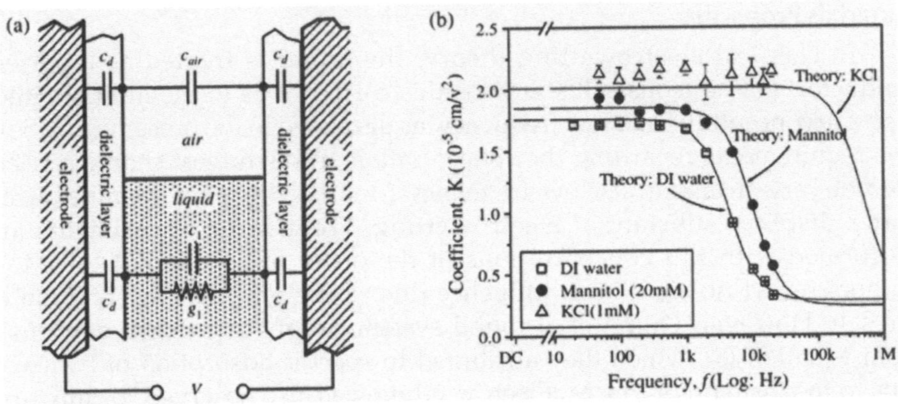

Fig. 5.10: Pellat experiment: electrowetting-induced capillary rise. (a) Schematic set-up and electric equivalent circuit. (b) Frequency dependence of K (w) for DI water, mannitol, and KCl. Reprinted with permission from

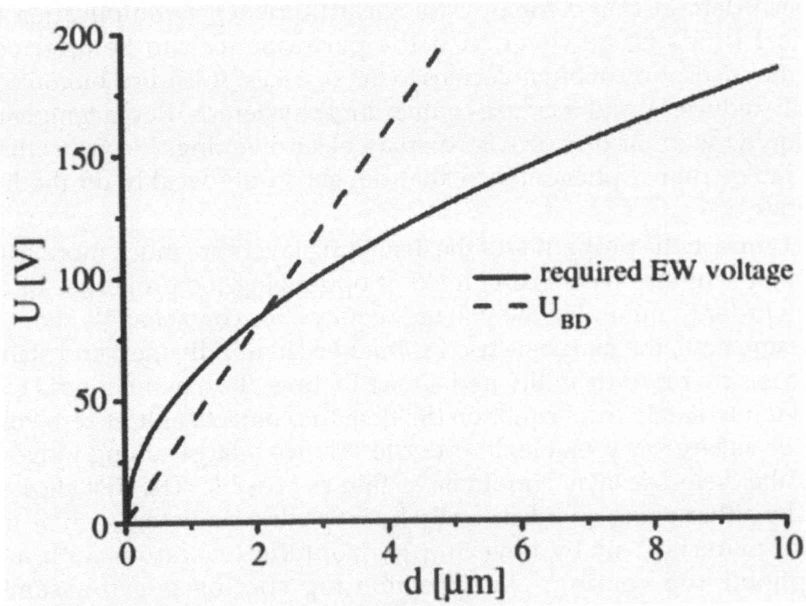

Fig. 5.11: Electrowetting and dielectric breakdown voltage versus insulator thickness. Solid line: voltage required for a contact angle decrease from 120° (0 V) to 70° (for εd = 2; σlv = 0.072 J m–2). Dashed line: critical voltage for dielectric breakdown (for EBD = 40 V μm–1)

Furthermore, amorphous fluoropolymer has become very popular, not only as a top coating but also as an insulating layer.

The critical materials parameter for the insulator is its dielectric strength, or the breakdown field strength EBD. This number limits the minimum thickness of the insulating layer: the voltage required to achieve a desired variation of the contact angle cos θ is given by breakdown occurs at UBD = Ecd. The competition between the two effects is illustrated in figure 5.12. The intersection between the square root function and the straight line determines the minimum insulator thickness required to obtain a certain cos θ for a given dielectric strength—implying a corresponding minimum voltage. The latter can only be reduced by improving the dielectric strength or by using a different material. There are two limitations to this procedure: (i) in view of the diverging electric fields close to the contact line, the breakdown voltage may be exceeded locally, although U/d is still smaller than EBD; and (ii) the dielectric strength of thin layers may differ from the corresponding bulk values.

$$U\,(\Delta \cos \theta) = (d\sigma_{lv}\ \Delta \cos \theta/\varepsilon_0\varepsilon_r)^{1/2} \tag{26}$$

Popular inorganic insulator materials include SiO_2 and SiN. Thin layers with a high dielectric strength can be produced using standard vacuum deposition or growth techniques. In combination with a hydrophobic top coating, they perform well as electrowetting substrates. Compared to Teflon AF (as an insulator), they also offer the advantage of a higher dielectric constant, which contributes to reducing the operating voltage further (see equation (26)). The dependence on the dielectric constant prompted Moon et al to study thin layers of a ferroelectric insulator (barium strontium titanate (BST)) with a specifically high dielectric constant of εd = 180. For a 70 nm BST layer covered by 20 nm Teflon AF, they achieved a contact angle reduction of 40° with an applied voltage of 15 V.

Polymer materials that were used in previous electrowetting studies include parylene-N and parylene-C, conventional Teflon films, polydimethylsiloxane (PDMS), as well as various other commercial polymer foils of variable surface quality. Parylene films are deposited from a vapour phase of monomers, which polymerize upon adsorption onto the substrate. The surfaces are known to be chemically inert and robust and display a high dielectric strength (200 V µm–1).

In electrowetting, Parylene is almost exclusively used in combination with hydrophobic top coatings. One important advantage of the Parylene coatings is that the vapour deposition process allows for uniform conformal coatings on topographically patterned substrates, including the interior of capillaries. Recently, Chiou et al presented an interesting new approach making use of a photoconductive material, which allowed them to switch the electrowetting behaviour optically—a process the authors termed 'optoelectrowetting'. The advantage of this approach is that individual addressing of electrodes in a digital microfluidic chip does not require individual electrical connections to all electrodes. Electrode activation is achieved by directing a laser beam onto the desired electrode.

Contact Angle Saturation

The parabolic relation between the observed contact angle and the applied voltage (equation (8)) was shown experimentally to hold at low voltage. At high voltage, however, the contact angle has always been found to saturate. In particular, no voltage-induced transition from partial to complete wetting has ever been observed. (On the basis of equation (8), such a transition would be expected to occur at $U_{spread} = (2\sigma lv\ d\ (1-\cos\theta Y)/(\varepsilon 0\ \varepsilon d))$. Instead, θ adopts a saturation value θ_{sat} varying between 30° and 80°, depending on the system see also figure 5.3.) It has now become clear that the linear electrowetting models described in cannot explain the phenomenon of contact angle saturation. However, the latter studies showed that the electric field strength diverges close to the TCL. Although the divergence is cut off at small length scales (κ −1, i.e. a few nanometres), the field strength is expected to reach very high values—several tens or hundreds of volts per micrometre. So far, no consistent picture of contact angle saturation has emerged. Nevertheless, a number of mechanisms have been proposed to explain various observations:

(i) Verheijen and Prins found indications that the insulator surfaces were charged after driving a droplet to contact angle saturation. They suggested that charge carriers are injected into the insulators, as sketched. These immobilized charge carriers then partially screen the applied electric field. In order to quantify the effect, they assumed that the immobile charges are located at a fixed depth within the insulating layer and that their density σT is homogeneous within a certain range (≈d) on both sides of the contact line. With these assumptions, they derived a modified version of equation (8):

$$\cos\theta = \cos\theta_Y + \frac{\varepsilon_0\varepsilon_d}{2d\sigma_{lv}}(U - U_T)^2 \tag{27}$$

where UT is the potential of the trapped charge layer outside the droplet, i.e. σT = ε0 εd UT /d. σT and, thus, also UT are unknown functions of the applied voltage that depend on the (non-linear) response of the insulator material. The authors determined these functions by fitting equation (27) to their experimental data. The result was self-consistent, but it was not possible to establish a correlation between this threshold behaviour and other known material parameters or a microscopic process that could be responsible for the charge trapping. Papathanasiou and Boudouvis tried to establish such a correlation by comparing numerically computed values for the electric field strength at the contact line [1](averaged over a certain area) with the dielectric strength of a variety of dielectric materials used in electrowetting experiments. The authors reported good agreement with published experimental saturation contact angles. However, it should be noted that the agreement is sensitive to the size of the box used to average the electric field. The specific choice of 100 nm in is not obviously related to any physical length scale of the system (such as κ −1).

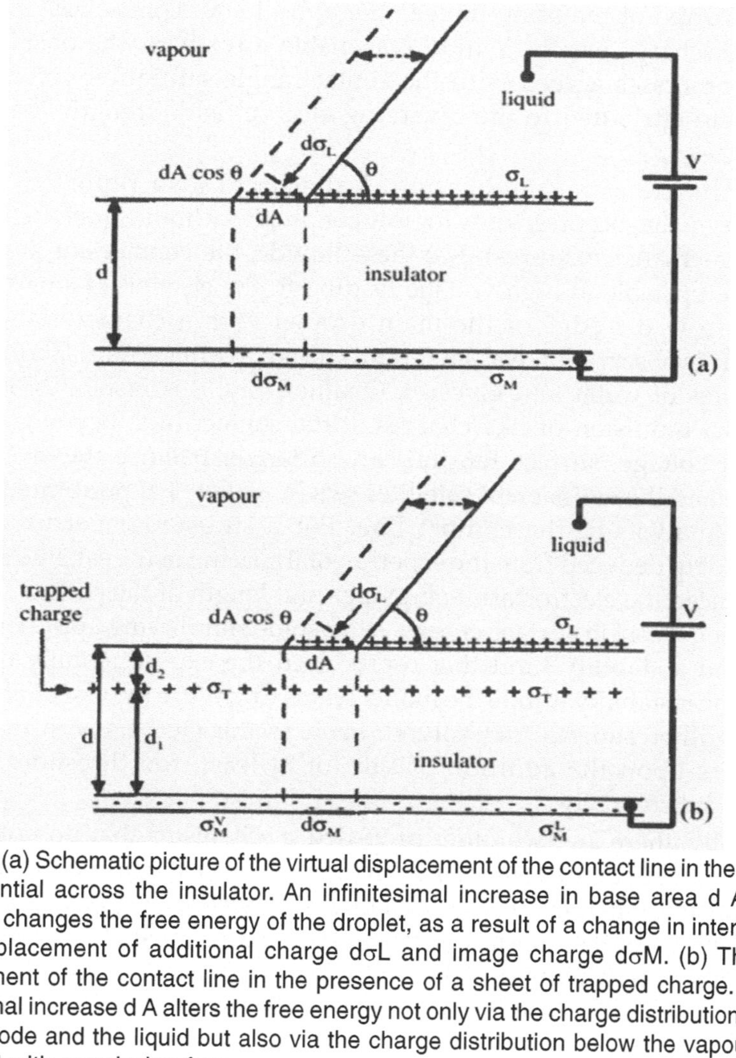

Fig. 5.12: (a) Schematic picture of the virtual displacement of the contact line in the presence of a potential across the insulator. An infinitesimal increase in base area d A at fixed voltage V changes the free energy of the droplet, as a result of a change in interface area and the placement of additional charge dσL and image charge dσM. (b) The virtual displacement of the contact line in the presence of a sheet of trapped charge. Now, the infinitesimal increase d A alters the free energy not only via the charge distribution between the electrode and the liquid but also via the charge distribution below the vapour phase. Reprinted with permission from.

[1] These assumptions seem somewhat artificial for homogeneous dielectric layers. However, it should be recalled that many electrowetting experiments—including that of Verheijen and Prins —are performed on composite substrates made of a thicker main insulating layer and a thin hydrophobic top coating.

(ii) Vallet et al observed two other phenomena that can coincide with contact angle saturation. They found that the contact line of salt solution droplets luminesces at high voltage. Light was found to be emitted in a series of short pulses with durations of less than 100 ns. The wavelength of the emitted light was verified to correspond to known emission characteristics of several ambient gas atmospheres. Simultaneously with the optical observation, the authors measured the current in the system: a series of spikes occurred at the same time as the optical emission pulses, indicating discrete discharge events. Within reasonable error bars, the onset voltage for both processes agreed with the contact angle saturation voltage. Both effects were attributed to the diverging electric field strength close to the contact line.

(iii) In the same publication, Vallet et al also reported another phenomenon that occurred only for low conductivity liquids (deionized water and water–ethanol mixtures). For these liquids, the contact line was found to become unstable at high voltage leading to the ejection of small satellite droplets from the edge of the main droplet with a characteristic lateral spacing. This observation was later reproduced by Mugele and Herminghaus for mixtures of water and glycerol. Qualitatively, this instability is due to the mutual repulsion of like charges at the contact line. Beyond a certain threshold voltage, surface tension can no longer balance the electrostatic repulsion and the emission of satellites sets in. Vallet et al performed a linear stability analysis of the contact line. For a sinusoidal perturbation of wavevector q (deduced from the experimental spacing of the satellite droplets) they balanced the electrostatic energy per unit length of the contact line with the additional cost in surface energy. With some simplifying approximations, they found a stability limit that reproduced the experimentally observed onset of the instability. While the model seems to capture the essential physics, it leaves other aspects unresolved, such as the fact that the instability disappears upon the addition of salt (or at least, the threshold voltage increases substantially.

Finally, there are two other proposed mechanisms that do not refer to the field strength at the contact line: (iv) Peykov et al suggested that equation (8) should fail when $\sigma\ \text{eff}_{sl}$ (see equation (7)) approaches zero. The idea is that the energy of the interface between two phases must always be positive for an interface to remain stable. However, this model has not received broad acceptance because it is not clear whether this criterion is applicable for the effective solid–liquid interfacial energy in electrowetting[2].

[2] Recall that the electrostatic energy gain, which is responsible for the negative term in equation (11), takes place in the battery.

Fig. 5.13: Contact line instability and emitted satellite droplets at high voltage. (Deionized water on silanized glass; droplet diameter: ≈3 mm.) Note the liquid necks between the satellites and the large droplet (inset)

(v) Contact angle saturation can also occur when either the assumption of a perfectly conductive liquid or a perfectly insulating dielectric or both are violated. We saw already that finite conductivity effects reduce the impact of an applied AC voltage on the contact angle: when the voltage partially drops within the bulk of the droplet, the net force acting on the TCL is reduced. The same effect can occur for DC voltage if the dielectric layer is not perfectly insulating. Shapiro et al analysed the field distribution within and around a spherical cap-shaped droplet assuming a finite resistivity ratio $A = \rho d\ d/(\rho l\ R)$ (ρd, ρl : resistivity of the dielectric and the liquid; R: droplet radius). Their calculations showed that the potential drop within the droplet increases with decreasing contact angle, which causes saturation. Overall, the results seem to compare favourably to some published experimental data. However, the general relevance of the approach—in particular for large resistivity ratios—has yet to be demonstrated.

The diversity of explanations indicates that contact angle saturation is still not well understood. Most probably, there may be no unique explanation. It seems clear that diverging electric fields at the contact line can induce several distinct non-linear effects, each of which may independently cause saturation. Which effect dominates depends on the specific conditions of each experiment and identifying these conditions requires more work in the future.

Complex Surfaces and Droplet Morphologies

Morphological Transitions on Structured Surfaces

Classical electrowetting theory was developed for planar substrates with homogeneous electrodes. Applications in microfluidics, however, demand the use of structured substrates. In most cases, the substrates are planar and homogeneous but the electrodes are patterned. Sometimes, the surfaces are chemically patterned in addition and in some cases topographical structuring is also used. In most applications one is interested in the behaviour of the liquid on a scale that is large compared to the insulator thickness. Hence, effects related to the field distribution close to the contact line can be ignored. The effect of electrowetting is then reduced to a variation of the surface wettability on top of the activated electrode(s). The handiness of equation (7) now becomes apparent: with this equation, electrowetting on patterned substrates is mapped onto conventional wetting of chemically (and/ or topographically) patterned substrates.

$$F[A] = \sigma_{lv}\left(A_{lv} - \int \cos\theta(\vec{r})\, dA_{sl}\right) \tag{28}$$

Here, cos θ (r) = cos θY +η(r) with θ(r) depending on the voltage applied to the electrode at the position r. (As in equation (28) has to be supplemented with a constraint of constant volume.) The equilibrium morphology of droplets in electrowetting can thus be calculated by the same methods as the morphology of droplets wetting structured surfaces in the absence of electric fields. The latter subject has attracted considerable attention in recent years both from an experimental and from a theoretical point of view. The presence of either chemical or topographical patterns on surfaces gives rise to complex liquid morphologies. Under favorable conditions, several morphologies may be (meta)stable simultaneously. Abrupt morphological transitions between such competing morphologies can be induced by varying the surface wettability (or some other external control parameter. From an applied perspective, the richness of phenomena gives rise to new opportunities for controlling and manipulating the behaviour of liquids on surfaces. Fundamentally, these phenomena arise from the fact that the prescription of the surface pattern and the liquid volume alone leave substantial freedom for the system to adapt its shape. In particular, the contact angle can assume any value between θA and θB, when the contact line is pinned along the edge between two domains A and B with the respective contact angles.

Except for a few simple geometries, the morphologies of liquid droplets on patterned surfaces have to be computed numerically by minimizing the functional in equation (under the constraint of constant volume). A popular numerical tool is the public domain software package Surface Evolver. Application of the Surface Evolver to electrowetting problems has been demonstrated by several groups.

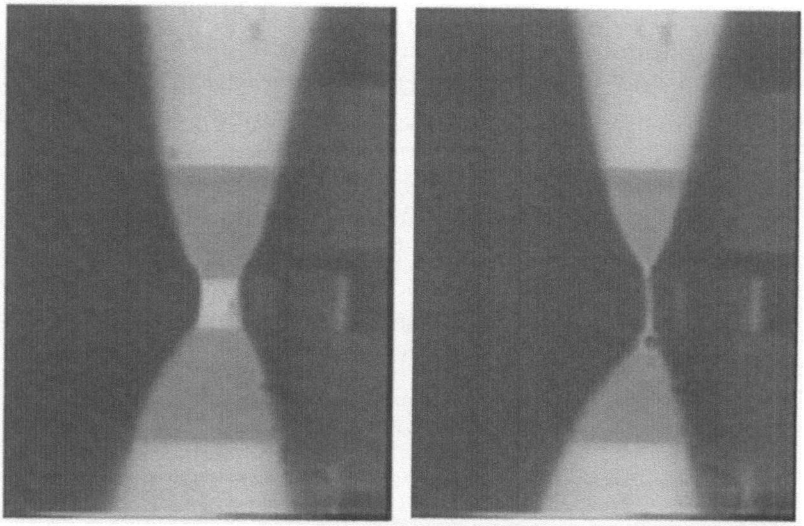

Fig. 5.14: Electrostatic repulsion between adjacent droplets. A voltage applied to the central stripe electrode (width 20 µm) produces a protrusion at moderate voltage (91 V; left image). At high voltage (210 V; right image) the protrusions approach each other and flatten. Droplet coalescence is suppressed by electrostatic repulsion. Reproduced from

There is one notable exception to the analogy between conventional wetting and electrowetting with patterned substrates: changes of the topology of the liquid are affected by long range electrostatic attraction or repulsion at the contact line. For instance, the coalescence of neighboring droplets can be suppressed by electrostatic repulsion. Figure 5.14 illustrates this effect for two adjacent droplets with a specific electrode geometry. For opposing voltages, electrostatic attraction facilitates coalescence (and can even lead to spark generation.

Patterned Electrodes

The simplest patterned substrate on which droplets display a morphological transition is a hydrophobic surface (e.g. $\theta = 180^\circ$) with a stripe of variable wettability (θs). For moderate wettability contrasts, there is only one stable morphology, which is a droplet slightly stretched along the stripe. For stronger wettability contrasts (i.e. $\theta s < \theta c$, with θc being a volume dependent critical angle), a second morphology appears, namely a section of a cylinder with the contact line pinned along the edges of the stripe. Brinkmann and Lipowsky determined a complete morphological diagram describing the stability of both morphologies as a function of the reduced liquid volume (in units of the cube of the stripe width) and θs (see figure 5.15). Klingner and Mugele verified this prediction experimentally using an electrowetting set-up with a stripe electrode. In order to reduce contact angle hysteresis and to achieve a high contact angle at zero voltage as in, they used a system of two immiscible liquids (droplets of salt water in silicone oil). The experiments confirmed the theoretical prediction rather well. Similar experiments using multilayer substrates with various patterned electrodes separated by dielectric layers were performed by Bienia. For the geometrical conditions of those experiments no morphological transitions occurred. However, the authors proposed an approximate method for incorporating corrections due to field enhancement close to the edges of the electrodes into equation. Continuous morphological changes were also observed for droplets confined between two parallel electrodes at a distance D, each covered with a stripe electrode. (This slit pore geometry is most widely used in microfluidic applications) For arbitrary misalignment of the stripes in the azimuthal direction, more complex liquid morphologies can be achieved. Again, morphological variations were found to be continuous and could be described on the basis of equation (28) using the Surface Evolver.

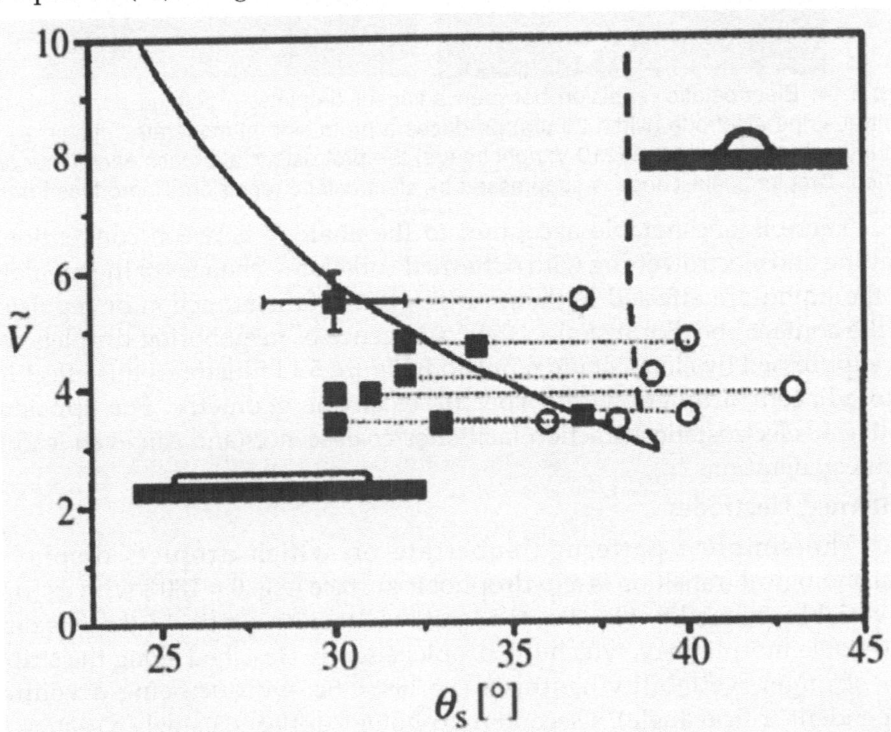

Fig. 5.15: Morphological phase diagram (θs –V plane). The solid and the dashed lines, which were taken from, represent numerically obtained instability lines for the bulge and channel morphologies, respectively. For small angles only the channel cylindrical morphology is stable; for high angles only the stretched droplet morphology is stable (see the sketched side view images of both morphologies). In the region between the solid and dashed lines both morphologies are (meta)stable. Solid squares and open circles represent the experimentally determined values for the stretched droplet instability and cylinder instability, respectively. Thin dotted lines connect data points that were recorded in a single experimental run. Reprinted from.

For slit pores with uniform walls slightly inclined with respect to each other such that the gap width D decreased with increasing height, Wang and Jones reported an instability of a rising meniscus beyond a certain threshold voltage UT. For sufficiently strong inclination, the meniscus height was found to jump abruptly from a certain intermediate height all the way to the top of the electrodes. This bifurcation phenomenon comes about because the energy required to raise the meniscus by h decreases with increasing height h, while the electrostatic energy gain remains constant.

Topographically Patterned Surfaces

The effect of topographical surface patterns on wetting is even more dramatic than that of lateral chemical patterns. Superhydrophobicity and hydrophilicity are amongst the most spectacular consequences of surface roughness. The influence of roughness on wetting is twofold, as illustrated in figure 5.17. On the one hand (figure 5.17(a)), roughness increases the actual solid–liquid interfacial area Asl with respect to the apparent, projected one Asl,p . As a result, the contact angle on a rough surface will be increased or decreased as compared to the contact angle on a smooth surface of the same material, depending on whether θY > 90° or θY < 90°, respectively. This effect is classically described by Wenzel's law, cos θ = r · cos θY, with r = Asl/Asl,p.

Quantitatively, the validity of this picture turns out to limited to a range of θC < θY < 90°, with θC depending on the surface roughness. On the other hand, for θY > 90°, a completely different liquid morphology becomes possible (figure 5.17(b)). In this morphology Asl is dramatically reduced and much of the apparent solid–liquid interface is in fact a liquid–vapour interface. This reduction in Asl gives rise to a very high mobility with extremely small contact angle hysteresis. In this state the contact angle is given by the Cassie–Baxter equation, cos θ = –1+ f · (1+ cos θY), where f is the fractional surface area of the pillar tops. The range of stability for both morphologies depends on the aspect ratio, on the spacing between the pillars, and of course on the contact angle. Krupenkin demonstrated the use of electrowetting to switch a liquid droplet from the Cassie–Baxter to the Wenzel morphology.

They fabricated nanopillars with a diameter of 350 nm and a height of 7 μm by dry etching a Si wafer. Each pillar had a conductive core of Si covered by a thermally grown insulating SiO layer and a hydrophobic top coating. The transition between the two morphologies was induced at a well-defined threshold voltage. Samples with a variety of different pillar spacings showed that cos θ indeed increases linearly with increasing f in the rolling ball state, whereas the opposite tendency was observed in the Wenzel state (as qualitatively expected due to the increase of r with increasing f). In addition, the authors observed another transition from the Wenzel state to a morphology where the droplets spread over the entire surface.

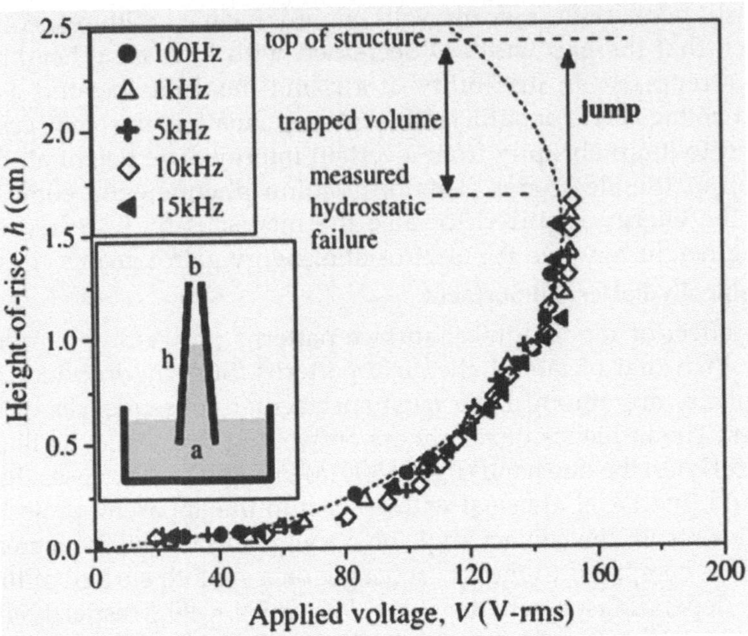

Fig. 5.16: Height of rise versus voltage. Symbols: experimental data for various frequencies for a 1 mM KCl solution (conductivity: 1.4 × 10–2 S m^{-1}) with a = 0.12 mm, b = 0.49 mm, H = 24 mm. Dashed line: model. Inset: geometry

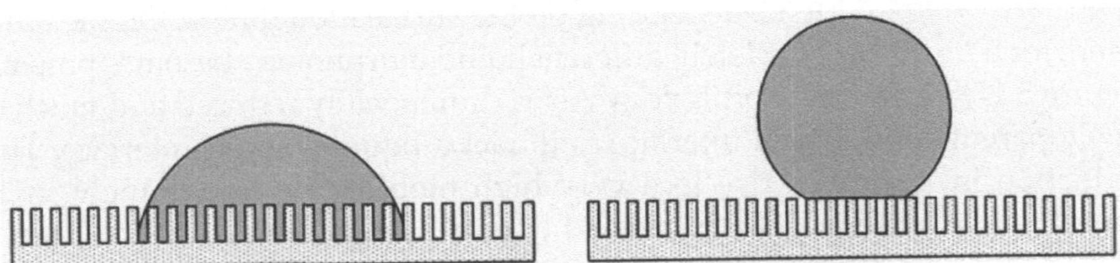

Fig. 5.17: Droplets wetting rough surfaces. (a) Wenzel state with enhanced solid–liquid interfacial area. (b) Cassie–Baxter state with entrapped air underneath the drople

Such a state is indeed expected. In contrast to the morphological transition discussed in the previous section, the transition between the Cassie–Baxter and the Wenzel state in was not reversible. More recently McHale et al investigated electrowetting on similar surfaces, with an emphasis on dynamic phenomena. Baret et al investigated the wetting behaviour of liquids in rectangular trenches with depth and width of 10–20 and 15–50 μm, respectively. The trenches were etched into a Si wafer and subsequently thermally oxidized and hydrophobized using alkyl silane monolayers. Figure 5.19(a) shows a top view of a droplet overlapping with several channels. At zero voltage, there is minimal leakage of the liquid from the droplet into the channels. Beyond a certain threshold voltage, filling of the channels suddenly starts and becomes more and more pronounced as the voltage gets higher (figure 5.19(b)). In fact, the trenches are expected to be empty above a certain critical contact angle and completely filled below it if brought into contact with a reservoir such as the droplet in this experiment.

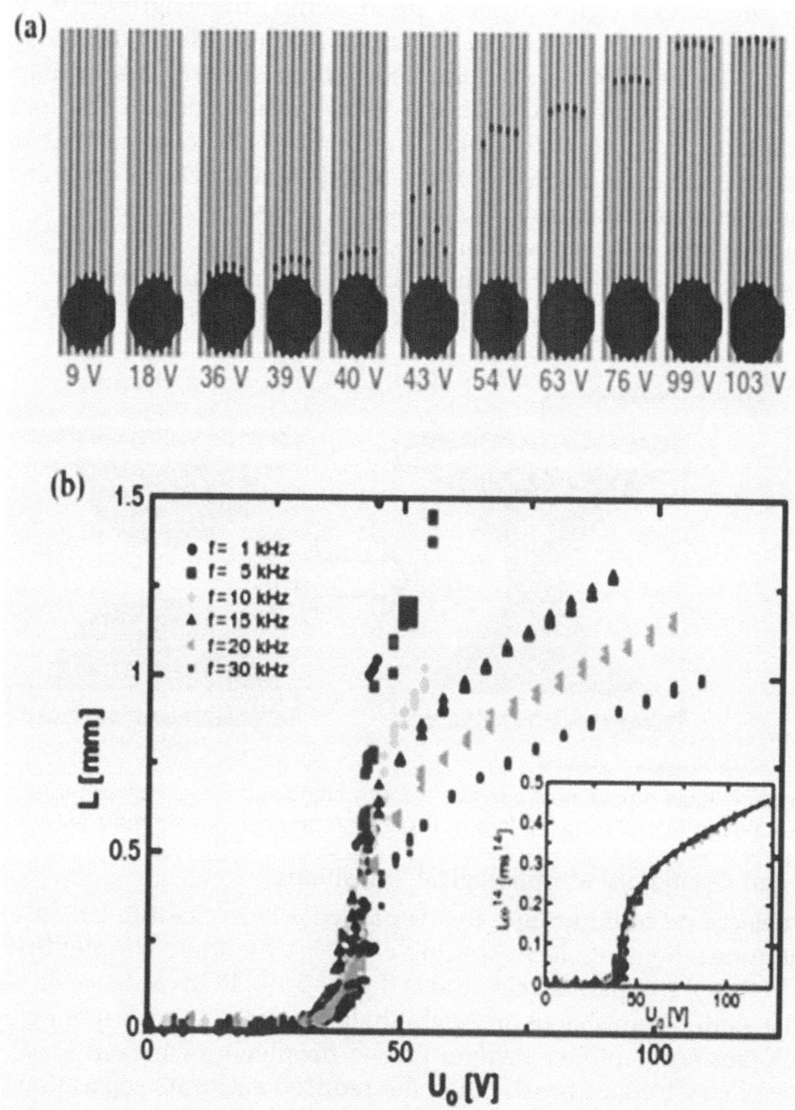

Fig. 5.18: (a) Top view of the channels for different voltages. The frequency of the voltage is 20 kHz and the drop wets five channels. On the right of the drop one, see the contacting electrode. (b) Measurements of the length as a function of the applied voltage for different frequencies. The threshold voltage is obtained at 43 V. Inset: rescaled data (courtesy of Seemann and Baret)

The critical angle is determined by the requirement of equal pressures in the channel and in the reservoir. As the contact angle decrease, the curvature of the surface at the end of the liquid fingers (and thus the pressure) decreases. When it becomes equal to the pressure in the droplet, filling suddenly sets in (see figure 5.19(b)). Interestingly, the length of the liquid fingers remains finite even beyond the critical voltage. Moreover, the length depends on the frequency of the applied voltage. This is due to the finite conductivity effects before: due to the small cross section of the trenches and the finite conductivity of the liquid, the ohmic resistance along the channel is substantial. Since the liquid is also coupled capacitively to the substrate, the liquid-filled channel behaves as an electric transmission line. As a result, the voltage at the tip is smaller than the applied voltage and depends on the length of the channel. By taking these effects into account, Baret et al were able to rescale their frequency dependent data onto a single master curve (see the inset of figure 5.19(b))

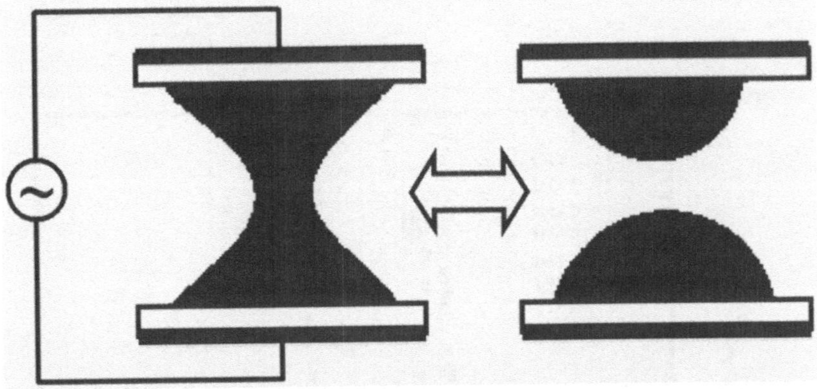

Fig. 5.19: A liquid droplet between two electrowetting substrates can either form a capillary bridge (morphology A; left) or two separate droplets (morphology B; right)

Self-excited Oscillatory Morphological Transitions

An electrode configuration that is particularly relevant to lab-on-a-chip kinds of applications of electrowetting consists of a liquid droplet bridging the gap between two parallel electrodes (figure 5.19). In the absence of electric fields, the equilibrium shapes and stability limits of the two competing liquid morphologies (A: capillary bridge; B: two droplets) have been studied in detail. Capillary bridges break when the reduced substrate separation D (in units of V 1/3) exceeds a certain critical value Dc,A which depends on the contact angle. Two separated droplets become unstable upon geometric overlap, i.e. below another—again contact angle dependent—critical reduced separation Dc,B. Under electrowetting conditions, these two stability limits are affected differently because the topologies of the two morphologies are different. The capillary bridge is simply connected, which means that the liquid is at a fixed potential corresponding to half of the applied voltage and therefore the contact angle decreases with increasing voltage. As a result, Dc,A is a monotonically decreasing function of the applied voltage. In contrast, each of the separate droplets assumes a different potential, namely that of the electrode that the droplet is attached to. As a result, the contact angle remains equal to θY, independent of U. However, the droplets attract each other electrostatically and as a result Dc,B is an increasing function of the applied voltage. Given the opposing slopes, Dc,A and Dc,B cross at a certain critical voltage. Beyond this voltage both morphologies are unstable for plate separations between the two instability limits. Under these conditions, the liquid was found to oscillate periodically between the two morphologies. The oscillation rate (1 s–1) was found to be independent of the applied AC frequency (>1 kHz). It is determined by the relaxation of charge deposited on the separate droplets immediately after break-up: the contact angle slowly relaxes back to θY as the charge disappears via leakage currents. This oscillatory behaviour is reminiscent of the so-called 'beating mercury heart' in which a mercury droplet under an acid solution periodically attaches to and detaches from an Fe nail when the latter is immersed into the acid and brought sufficiently close to the mercury surface. The dynamics of the beating mercury heart, however, are far more complex. They are in fact related to the kinetics of electrochemical reactions at the surfaces of the mercury and the nail, respectively.

More recently, Baret et al found that much faster oscillations can be achieved if the conductivity and the frequency of the applied voltage are matched, such that the charge on the droplet disappears during the pinch-off process when the capillary bridge breaks. The frequency of these oscillations (several tens of hertz) is determined by the hydrodynamic response time of the droplet to (sudden) changes of the contact angle. These fast oscillations were also found to be useful in promoting mixing in droplets. Figure shows a series of snapshots recorded during the oscillation of a droplet that was stained with fluorescent dye in its top half in the initial state. The entire droplet (of millimetre size) was mixed within a few seconds, more than 100 times faster than purely diffusive mixing.

Electrostatic Stabilization of Complex Morphologies

The contact line instability discussed in the context of contact angle saturation can give rise to rather complex liquid morphologies. In particular, the satellite droplets generated by the instability do not necessarily detach from the main droplet. Instead mother and satellite droplet sometimes remain connected by a thin liquid bridge. It is obvious that the curvature of the liquid surface (and thus the Laplace pressure) in the satellite droplet is substantially higher than in the mother droplet. Nevertheless, these complex liquid morphologies were found to be stable for poorly conductive liquids and AC voltages of sufficiently high frequency. The reason is related to the finite conductivity of the liquid. If the ohmic resistance of the liquid channel is larger than the capacitive impedance between the satellite droplet and the substrate electrode, there is a strong electric field around the satellite which causes an additional electrostatic pressure that pulls along the outward direction of the satellite droplet's surface. It turns out that this electrostatic contribution to the total pressure scales with U^2/r^2_{sat}, where r^{sat}_{sat} is the radius of the satellite droplet.

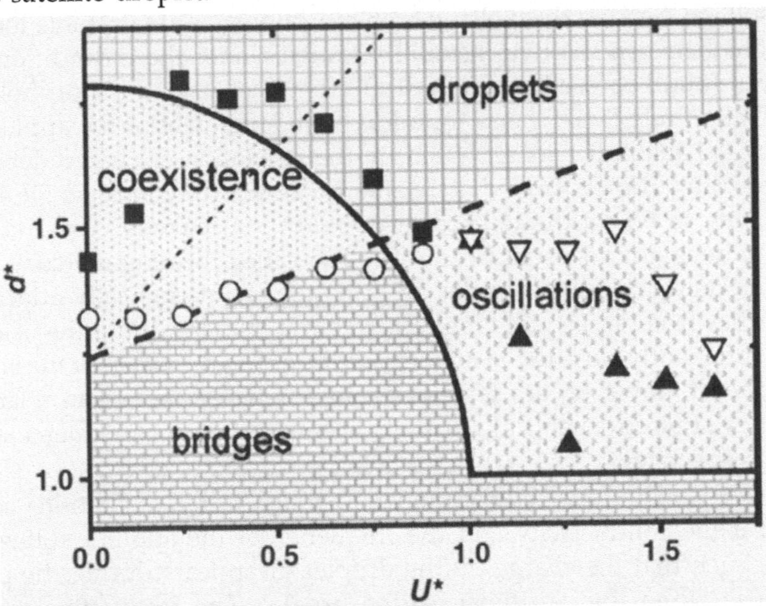

Fig. 5.20: Phase diagram. Normalized plate separation versus normalized voltage. Symbols: experimental results. Lines: model results. Bridge stability limit (solid); droplet phase stability limit for V = 30 nl (dashed) and for V = 30 pl (dotted)

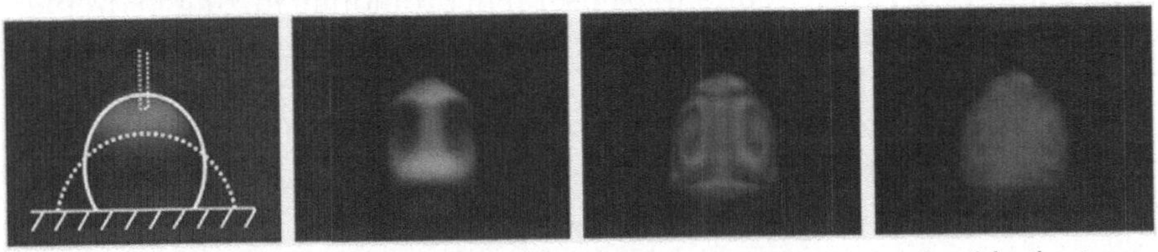

Fig. 5.21: Oscillation-induced mixing. Water droplet, initially dye stained in the top part, oscillating at 81 Hz between the two morphologies indicated in the left picture. Droplet diameter:1 mm. Time between consecutive images: 1 s

Since the Laplace pressure scales only with $1/r_{sat}$, small droplets can be stabilized with respect to larger ones by this mechanism. This experiment illustrates that the class of liquid microstructures eligible for showing mechanical stability is no longer restricted to morphologies with constant mean curvature. In the presence of suitable electric fields, more complex morphologies may also be stabilized.

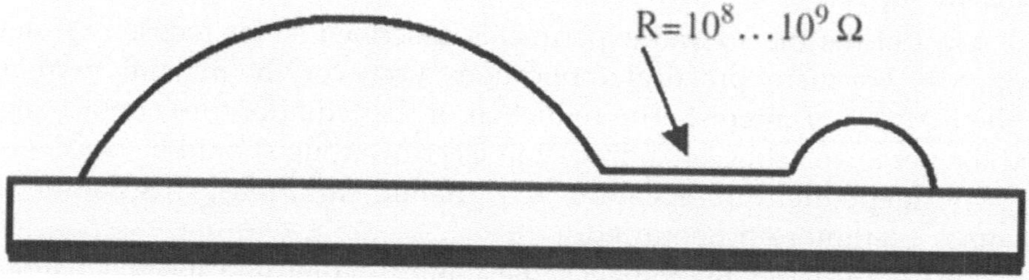

Fig. 5.22: Schematic diagram of a small satellite droplet connected to the reservoir drop via a thin channel. The ohmic resistance of the channel can exceed the capacitive impedance between the satellite and the bottom electrode (thick black line)

Competitive Wetting of Two Immiscible Liquids

Another degree of complexity arises when electrowetting experiments are performed in an ambient oil environment rather than in a gas atmosphere. Both liquids, the oil and the aqueous phase, compete in wetting the solid surface. Depending on the microscopic interactions (e.g. short range chemical forces, long range van der Waals forces), various scenarios are possible. At finite voltage, electrostatic interactions alter the balance of molecular forces. Since electrowetting substrates are typically hydrophobic, complete wetting of the oil phase at zero voltage is frequently observed. In this case, θY is essentially 180° and the aqueous phase is separated from the substrate by a thick oil layer[3]. As the voltage is increased, electrostatic interactions press the aqueous phase towards the substrate and decrease the thickness doil of the oil film. For sufficiently thin oil layers, the free energy (per unit area) of the oil film in a van der Waals system is given by

$$F\,(d_{\text{oil}}) \approx \gamma_{\text{so}} + \gamma_{\text{ow}} + \frac{A}{12\pi d_{\text{oil}}^2} - \frac{c_d U^2}{2}\left(1 - \frac{\varepsilon_d d_{\text{oil}}}{\varepsilon_{\text{oil}} d}\right)$$

where γ_{so} and γ_{ow} are the solid–oil and oil–water interfacial energies, A is the Hamaker constant (>0 for long range wetting) and ε_{oil} is the dielectric constant of the oil. This function has a minimum corresponding to the equilibrium thickness of the oil film at $d_{\text{oil}}^* = (\varepsilon_0 \varepsilon_{\text{oil}} A/(3\pi c_d^2 U^2))^{1/3}$, which can be tuned continuously by varying U . In spite of the obvious practical importance of this oil film—both for reducing contact angle hysteresis as well as for preventing unspecific adsorption of biomolecules onto the substrates [5]—little is known experimentally. Preliminary experiments by Bienia et al indicate that a characterization is possible using ellipsometry.

---

[3] Under these conditions, the droplets are obviously extremely mobile because any surface heterogeneity that might cause pinning and contact angle hysteresis is smeared out by the oil film.

Dynamic Aspects of Electrowetting

Most of the theory and experiments described so far focused on static properties. For many practical applications, however, the dynamic response of the liquid is of interest. The reduction of the (equilibrium) contact angle and the net force acting on a droplet in electrowetting should be considered as two independent observables. In dynamic situations, this distinction becomes even more pronounced.

On the one hand, the contact angle assumes a time and speed dependent value which is determined by local dissipative processes and flow fields in the vicinity of the TCL. On the other hand, the entire droplet also responds on a global scale, e.g. by a translation of its centre of mass, as for instance in lab-on-a-chip kinds of applications to be discussed later. This global response is obviously affected not only by local effects close to the contact line but also by viscous dissipation in the bulk[4]. A consistent hydrodynamic description (ignoring specific effects related to contact line dynamics) was presented.

Let us first consider centre of mass translations. One immediate observation is that Reynolds numbers of electrowetting-induced flows are rather low. With typical velocities of the order of v ≈ 10–2 –10–1 m s–1 and droplet sizes of R ≈ 10–3 m or less, one obtains Re = ρv R/μ ≈ 100 for water and even smaller values for more viscous liquids. Hence, the flow is usually laminar. The forces generated by the electric field have already been discussed. Within the range of validity of the electrowetting equation (equation (8)) EW-induced motion is analogous to the motion of droplets on chemically heterogeneous substrates, which was described e.g. by Brochard and references therein). The driving force (per unit length d y of the contact line) is determined by the energy gain upon displacing the contact line by x: E/d y = (σ eff –σsl) × = –(ε0 εr U 2/d)· x = –σlv η x . Hence the force f (per unit length) is given by f = – E/x = σlv ·η (see equation (16)). This force acts locally perpendicular to the contact line. In order to extract the net force on a droplet, the (vectorial) local force has to be integrated along the contact line using the appropriate local value of η = η(r). As mentioned above, there are several contributions to the net force which oppose the motion. Dissipation contains contributions both from the contact line and from the bulk of the droplet. Two extreme cases can be considered: if the dissipation is dominated by contact line friction, the pressure within the droplet equilibrates quickly and the droplet retains its spherical cap shape but with a time dependent dynamic contact angle θd. If, on the other hand, bulk viscous effects dominate, the contact angle assumes its local equilibrium angle everywhere along the contact line. As a result, the drop shape is non-spherical and a hydrodynamic pressure gradient arises and drives fluid flow within the droplet. In most

[4] For large droplets of low viscosity liquids, inertial effects may also play a role.

practical situations, an intermediate behaviour is expected to be observed with both contributions present simultaneously. Quantitative investigations of the centre of mass motion are presented. Two important findings should be noted: first, liquid motion could only be achieved above some threshold voltage. This observation is attributed to contact angle hysteresis: droplet motion can only set in when the contact angle on the leading (trailing) edge of the droplet exceeds (is smaller than) the local advancing (receding) contact angle. The threshold voltage for initiating droplet motion is found to decrease upon immersing the liquid droplet into an oil environment, as expected on the basis of the discussion. Second, it is found that contact line friction contributes substantially to the dissipation of the sub-millimeter liquid structures investigated.

Contact line friction creates a link between the center of mass motion of the droplet and the dynamic behaviour of the contact angle: it is well known that classical hydrodynamics cannot describe the motion of the TCL. The flow fields required to move the wedge-shaped edge of the droplet give rise to a diverging stress, which in turn requires an infinite force to move the TCL. Several strategies, including employing the phenomenological concept of slip at the solid–liquid interface, were introduced to resolve the problem. In the context of electrowetting, contact line friction was analyzed within the framework of the molecular kinetic model. This model pictures contact line motion as a series of discrete random jumps on a molecular scale involving energy barriers and microscopic adsorption sites. These molecular scale processes give rise to a friction force (per unit length) that is given by the product of a friction coefficient î and the velocity v of the contact line. Blake et al studied the dynamic contact angle of a liquid curtain (glycerol water mixture) wetting a Teflon substrate that was moved at a constant velocity v. The dynamic contact angle increased with increasing substrate speed both in the absence and in the presence of an applied voltage. For any given velocity, the contact angle decreased upon applying a voltage U. For a given U, the variation of cos θ (with respect to zero voltage) turned out to be independent of v, in agreement with the prediction of the molecular kinetic model.

Decamps and DeConinck analysed the response of the contact angle of a glycerol–water droplet on a Teflon surface upon applying a voltage step. The contact angle decreased from θY ≈ 110° to its voltage dependent final value within less than 0.2 s. The time dependence was fitted with a formula based on the molecular kinetic model. For a relatively rough Teflon surface (contact angle hysteresis: ≈ 50°), the authors deduced a contact line friction coefficient $\xi \approx 4$ Pa s. A similar value was recently found for ethylene glycol in capillary rise experiments by Wang and Jones.

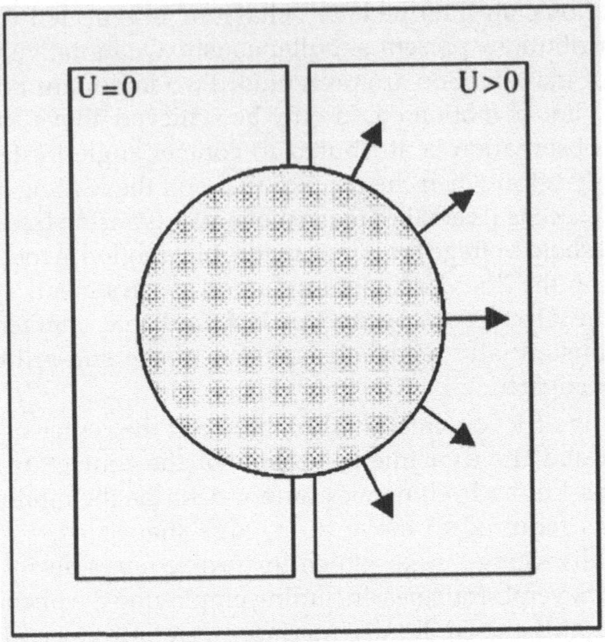

Fig. 5.23: Top view of a droplet partially overlapping with an activated (right) and a deactivated (left) electrode. Arrows indicate the force acting on the contact line

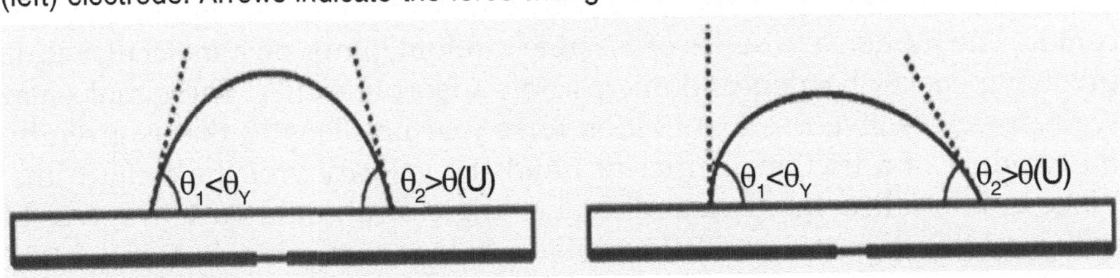

Fig. 5.24: Side view of imbalanced droplets partially overlapping with a deactivated (left) and with an activated (right) electrode. (a) Droplet dominated by contact line friction; (b) droplet dominated by bulk viscous dissipation

While the experimental results discussed above were interpreted within the framework of the molecular kinetic model, this does not rule out the possibility that other approaches to the problem of contact line motion may be equally well suited to explaining the experimental observations.

Applications

Lab-on-a-chip

Lab-on-a-chip applications of electrowetting were mainly promoted by two laboratories, that of Richard Fair at Duke University (for a recent review focused on the activities of this laboratory and that of Kim at UCLA with several other groups joining in more recently.

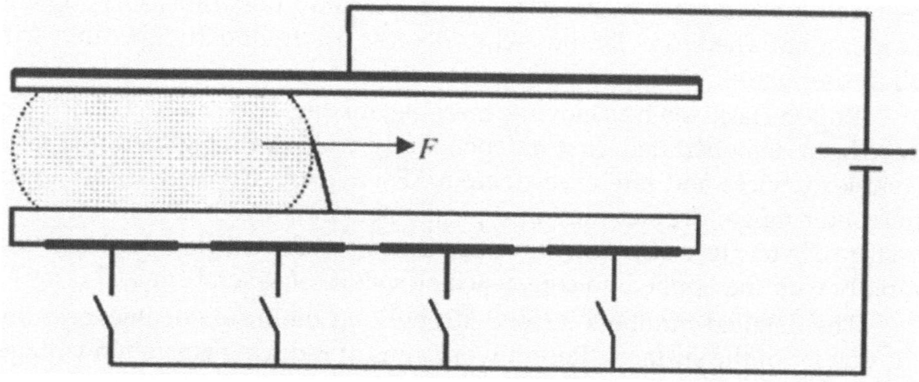

Fig. 5.25: Schematic diagram of a typical lab-on-a-chip system. The thin white layer on the top surface is usually a hydrophobic top coating that is does not insulate the droplet electrically. By activating the second electrode, the bottom right contact angle is reduced and the droplet is distorted accordingly

The principal idea is to provide a substrate with a series—preferentially an array—of individually addressable electrodes that allow for moving droplets around along arbitrary paths, depending on the freely programmable activation sequence of the electrodes. Small droplets can be extracted from larger reservoir droplets transported to specifically designed locations. The small droplets can be merged and mixed to induce chemical reactions. For the practical realization of such a device, several aspects have to taken into account. (i) Electrowetting requires electrical contact to the liquid. The usual procedure of immersing wires into the droplets is not practicable for lab-on-a-chip applications. Therefore, a sandwich design consisting of two parallel substrates with the liquid confined in between has become standard. One of the substrates contains the patterned electrodes required for liquid actuation. The other substrate (the top surface) consists of a homogeneous electrode that provides electrical contact to the droplet(s) independently of its (their) position. The electrode, which is frequently made of a transparent ITO layer on a glass substrate, is usually covered with a thin hydrophobic layer that gives rise to a large contact angle and weak contact angle hysteresis but does not prevent electrical contact. (ii) In order to allow for reliable droplet actuation, droplet edges must overlap with at least two adjacent electrodes. As a consequence, the smallest liquid volume that can be transported is determined by the size of the electrodes. With substrate separations of 100–500 μm and electrode sizes of the order of 1 mm, this means typical droplet volumes of 0.1–1 μl. The reliability of droplet actuation is frequently improved by a zigzag design of the electrode edges. (iii) The vapour pressure of water is rather high at room temperature.

Liquid evaporation is therefore a critical issue. The problem is somewhat reduced by the two- plate sandwich design, but thermal treatments as required for some biochemical assays call for additional measures against evaporation. Therefore, lab-on-a-chip devices are frequently operated with oil as the surrounding medium.

Routine tasks such as moving, merging, mixing, and splitting of droplets have been demonstrated, first independently and later integrated into more complex devices and references therein). For typical droplet volumes in the microliter range, droplet motion typically sets in above a certain threshold voltage of a few tens of volts. Above that threshold, the droplet speed increases rapidly with the applied voltage, reaching values of several cm s^{-1}.

The detailed numbers depend strongly on the insulator thickness and the quality of the surfaces. Recent work aims at reducing activation voltages to approximately 20 V or less, which would simplify practical applications involving battery powered hand-held devices for medical applications.

With basic fluid manipulation techniques being established, the next step towards biotechnological applications of electrowetting-based devices is demonstrating the biocompatibility of the materials and procedures. One challenge for all lab-on-a-chip devices is the tendency of biomolecules to adsorb unspecifically onto hydrophobic surfaces. In the case of electrowetting-based devices this has a specifically detrimental effect: irreversible adsorption of biomolecules reduces the contact angle permanently, thereby compromising the performance of droplet actuation. Yoon and Garrell recently investigated the electrowetting behaviour of droplets of DNA and protein solutions in an ambient air environment. They found that both unspecific adsorption via hydrophobic interaction and electrostatic interactions contribute to the adsorption. The latter depends strongly on the charge carried by the specific protein and on the polarity as well as the waveform of the applied voltage. Biomolecular adsorption seems to be suppressed even more efficiently by using an oil phase as the ambient medium instead of air. Srinivasan et al reported not only the successful actuation of various protein solutions but that also of physiological fluids such as whole blood and urine. Even after 25000 cycles, droplets could still be actuated with only a minor increase in activation voltage. The reduced adsorption of proteins is attributed to the thin oil film wetting the hydrophobic substrate and preventing direct contact between the droplet and polymer surface. Qualitatively this strategy seems to be successful. However, detailed studies regarding its efficiency and the underlying fundamental mechanisms are lacking.

Other biotechnology-related applications use electrowetting to assist in the handling of tiny amounts of liquid. For instance, DNA and protein arrays are nowadays standard tools in genome research and drug development. Conventionally, arrays are produced using photolithography or, more recently, by spotting droplets onto surfaces using e.g. inkjet techniques. In order to reduce the typical spot sizes to 1 µm or less, new approaches have been developed, such as dip-pen nanolithography. In this technique, the ink is deposited by establishing direct mechanical contact between the pen and the surface. One challenge of dip-pen lithography is to deposit a sufficiently large amount of liquid onto the pen in a controlled fashion, in order to maximize the number of spots that can be written without refilling the pen. Belaubre et al presented a microcantilever design for dip-pen lithography, in which electrowetting was used to increase and control the amount of liquid in a reservoir on the pen. Using this approach, they were able to write arrays of more than a hundred spots from a single loading with spot sizes from the femtolitre to the picolitre range, containing fluorescence-labelled oligonucleotides and proteins. The same principle on a somewhat coarser scale was used for a glass-tube-based microinjector by Hoshino et al. Yi and Kim presented a principle which they termed 'soft printing'. In this approach tiny droplets of controlled volume (~100 nl) containing the desired biomaterial are produced on top of hydrophobic surface. They are deposited onto a hydrophilic carrier by bringing the latter close enough to the hydrophobic surface that the droplet is transferred by capillary forces. The droplet transfer is thus a rather gentle process, which does not involve splashing or excessive shear forces acting on the biomolecules. The generation and positioning of the pre-metered droplet is performed using electrowetting. Furthermore, electrowetting was used to prepare peptide and protein samples for matrix assisted laser desorption/ ionization mass spectrometry.

Huh et al presented an application in which electrowetting was used to manipulate the flow in a channel-based microfluidic system for an air–water two-phase flow. By activating the electrodes the path of the liquid jet within the channel could be controlled on a millisecond timescale. Rapid control of the stream position may be useful for sorting applications. Living cells were shown to survive transport through this system. Cheng and Hsiung presented an EW-driven valve inside a microchannel for continuous flow. The channel walls were partially made of Teflon. Using plasma etching, the Teflon coating was made hydrophilic everywhere inside the channel except for in an active area, which thus acted as a hydrophobic barrier. Upon activating electrodes embedded in the active area of the channel walls, the barrier was lowered and water could flow through the channel. Shen et al produced a chemoreceptive CMOS chip in which they also controlled the filling of closed channels using electrowetting.

Optical Applications

Microlenses: In mechanical equilibrium, the liquid–vapour interface of sessile droplets has a spherical cap shape. Depending on the refractive index contrast light passing the interface is refracted as in a classical spherical lens made from glass or some other suitable solid material. In contrast to solid lenses, however, liquid lenses are flexible. Their curvature and hence their focal length can be tuned by adjusting their shape. Obviously, this can be achieved by changing the contact angle of sessile droplets via electrowetting.

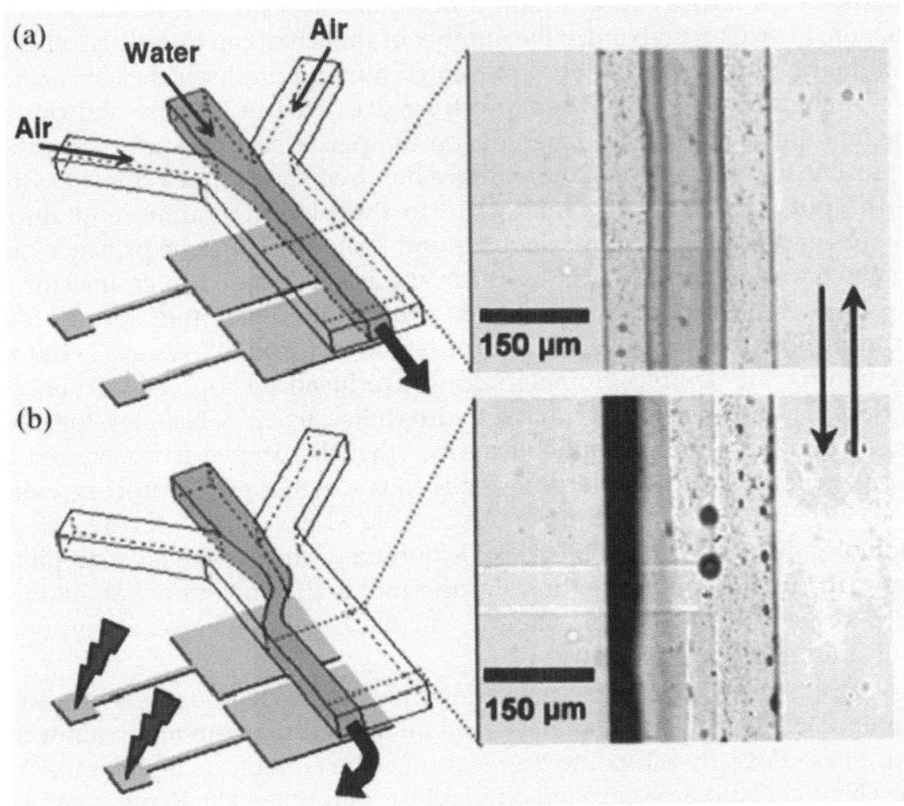

Fig. 5.26: Electrically induced switching of surface energy caused (a) a focused high speed water stream in the middle to (b) swerve to its right (relative to the direction of fluid flow), guiding theflow along the sidewall. Water was injected at 20 ml h–1, and air flows were driven by 400 mm Hg vacuum at the outlet. The channel height is 100 μm

This allows for the design of optical systems with variable focal length that can be addressed purely electrically, as first described by Peseux and Berge. These authors designed a closed cell filled with two immiscible liquids, namely a non-polar oil droplet within an aqueous salt solution. Both liquids were density matched to within 10^{-3}, both in order to eliminate the influence of gravity on the interface shape and in order to reduce the susceptibility of the lens to external mechanical shocks. At low voltage, the water contact angle is high, i.e. the oil droplet has a low contact angle and vice versa. A combination of wettability patterns on the bottom surface and gradients in the thickness of the dielectric layer were used in order to centre the droplet on the optical axis of the device.The refractive power and focal length of the lens are shown as a function of the applied voltage. The lens operated without noticeable hysteresis—presumably thanks to a thin lubricating oil film and could be switched more than 106 times without any sign of degradation. Switching speeds of the order of 10 ms were achieved for a lens with a diameter of 2.5 mm. Maximal speed requires precise adjustment of the liquid viscosity such that the drop motion is critically damped—otherwise the droplet either oscillates several times or relaxes only slowly towards the new equilibrium shape. Krupenkin et al describe a similar system with patterned electrodes that allows for lateral positioning of the lens. In their case, the activation voltage was as low as 10 V. The same authors also presented an interesting study in which they used photopolymerizable conductive liquid droplets to produce microlenses of controlled focal length. The shape and thus the desired focal length were tuned through electrowetting of the monomeric polymer solution. At fixed voltage, the droplets were cured by UV illumination. Subsequently, the voltage could be removed and the (now solidified) droplets kept their shape.

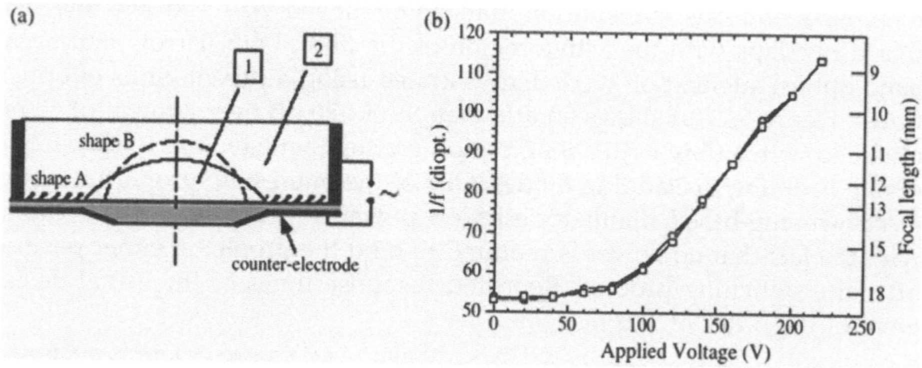

Fig. 5.27: Electrowetting lens. (a) Schematic representation of the system, not to scale. The cell is filled with water (2). A drop (1) of an insulating and non-polar liquid is deposited on the bottom wall, which is made of an insulating and transparent material, in grey. The central disc on the bottom surface is hydrophobic, in order to trap the drop. The outer zone, hatched in the figure, is hydrophilic. The optical axis is shown as a short line made up of long dashes. (b) Inverse focal length of a particular lens of 6 mm diameter, filled with α-chloronaphthalene as the insulating liquid, and a Na_2SO_4 solution in water, as a function of voltage. The two curves which correspond to increasing (o) and decreasing (□) voltage are superimposed

One potential application of interest is in variable focus systems for mobile phones with integrated CCD cameras. Challenges in this application include harsh mechanical shocks as well as a large range of required operating temperatures. Kuiper and Hendriks recently presented yet another design of an electrowetting lens system for this type of application. These authors confined the liquid laterally inside a (short) capillary with an internal diameter of 3 mm. By applying a voltage of up to 120 V, they were able to vary the refractive strength from –100 to +50 dioptres. The authors also discuss the suppression of chromatic aberrations through the addition of specific solutes to the liquids. Achromatism can thus be achieved easily and at low cost.

Fibre optics: Electrowetting was assessed in the 1980s as a possible mechanism for switching light in fibre optic applications. Mercury droplets were moved inside channels to provide either a reflective surface or to allow for the transmission of light in an optical multiplexer. More recently, the focus shifted to controlling the transmission of optical fibres that were locally stripped of their coating. For stripped fibres, the electromagnetic field of some modes, in particular so-called cladding modes, partially leaks out of the fibre into the surrounding medium. By surrounding the active (stripped) part of the fibre with liquids of suitably chosen refractive index, the transmission through the fibre can be tuned substantially. Figure 5.27(a) shows a schematic diagram of the set-up. The optical fibre passes a straight section of a racetrack-shaped channel with a rectangular cross section. The channel is filled with two immiscible liquids of controlled refractive index. One of them is an aqueous salt solution that can be moved via electrowetting such that it overlaps with the active region of the fibre. Both narrow and broad band optical attenuation were demonstrated using different kinds of optical fibres. Figure 5.27(b) shows an attenuation of >20 dB over a range of 40 nm obtained with a fibre with a long period grating that gave rise to specifically strong coupling to cladding modes. One of the interesting properties of this electrowetting-based attenuator is its low power consumption (<1 mW) along with the fact that no power is required to hold the droplet in either position after the switching process. Reported response times of the initial design were of the order of 100 ms.

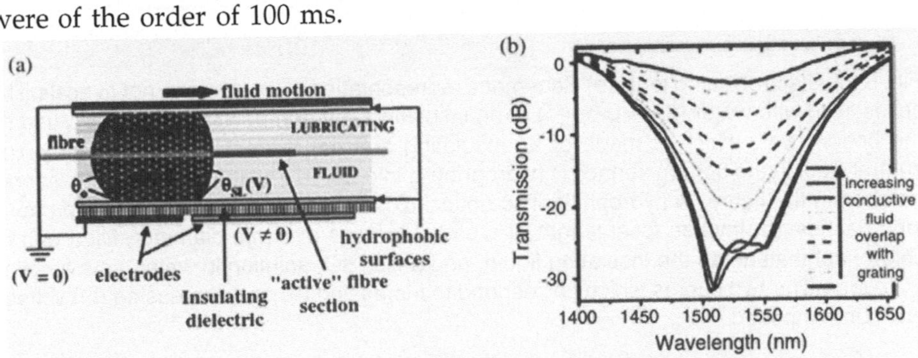

Fig. 5.28: (a) Schematic cross section of assembly utilized to tune optical fibre transmission via electrowetting actuation of a conductive fluid. (b) Evolution of the transmission spectrum as the conductive plug (water with ionic salt) advances over the fibre optimized in silicon oil

Display technology: Feenstra and Hayes presented an electrowetting-based reflective display with potential use in the field of electronic paper. The concept is very simple: an oil droplet containing dissolved dye is confined laterally to a square pixel. At zero voltage, the oil forms a continuous layer wetting the hydrophobic insulator (0.8 μm Teflon AF) at the bottom of the pixel. The rest of the pixel between the oil film and the top cover is filled with a transparent aqueous salt solution. Incoming light is strongly absorbed by the dye. Upon applying a voltage, the oil film ruptures and all the oil contracts into one corner of the pixel that can be predefined by a passive chemical wettability pattern. The dye thus covers only a small fraction of the pixel in the activated state. This gives rise to increase in reflectivity (averaged over an entire pixel) from 2.5% at zero voltage to 35% at the absorption wavelength of the dye with an activation voltage of 20 V. Any intermediate reflectivity—corresponding to a partially retracted oil film—can be stabilized by stopping at an intermediate voltage thus allowing for arbitrary grey levels. The switching speed of the display depends on the pixel size, on the thickness and on the viscosity of the oil film as well as on other geometric parameters. Figure shows that the response time of a 250 × 250 μm² pixel is sufficiently fast for video applications. The retraction and the spreading of the droplet occur on the same timescale.

By splitting each pixel into three subpixels and arranging two oil layers with different dyes in combination with a colour filter on top of each other, Feenstra and Hayes were also able to generate arbitrary colours. The reflectivity of these colour displays was four times stronger than that of liquid crystal displays.

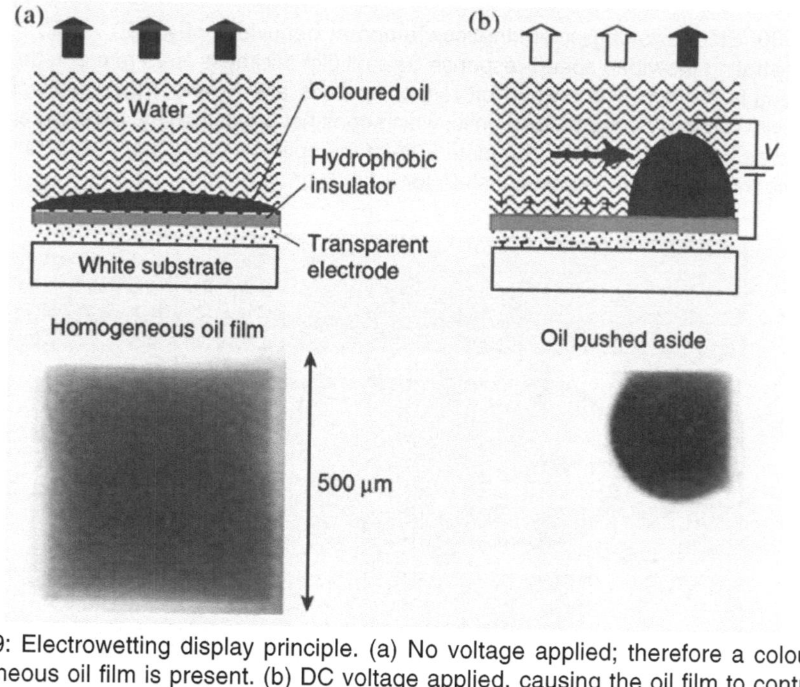

Fig. 5.29: Electrowetting display principle. (a) No voltage applied; therefore a coloured homogeneous oil film is present. (b) DC voltage applied, causing the oil film to contract. Top row, diagrams; bottom row, photographs. The photographs show typical oil motion obtained with a homogeneous pixel electrode

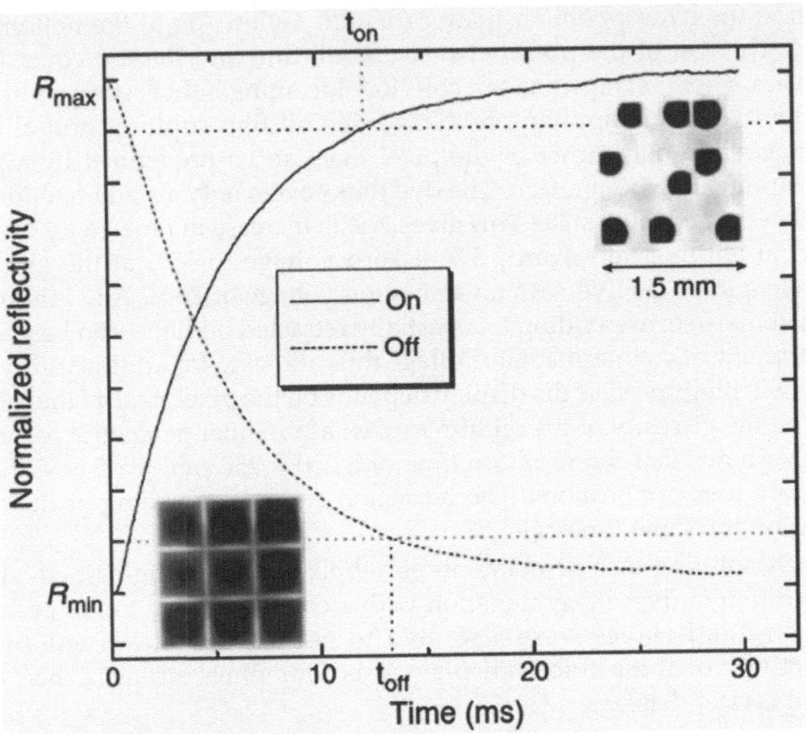

Fig. 5.30: Electrowetting pixel kinetics. Temporal behaviour of a 250 × 250 mm^2 pixel, demonstrating the video speed response. The oil film thickness is 15 mm and the insulator thickness is 0.8 mm. The on and off response times are 12 and 13 ms respectively. The reflectivity is shown in normalized units, which does not affect the time axis. ton and toff are defined as the time it takes to complete 90% of the optical modulation. Insets: photographs showing the corresponding optical state for a 3 × 3 array of 500 × 500 mm^2 pixels

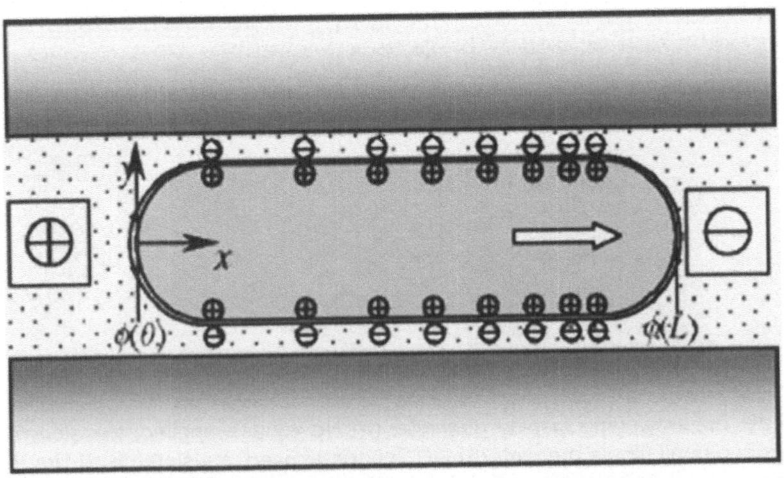

Fig. 5.31: Mercury droplet in an electrolyte-filled channel

Miscellaneous Applications

Another notable application is the optical absorber presented by Prins et al. The device was based on electrowetting-induced capillary rise. The authors designed a matrix of 4000 individually addressable capillaries with a diameter of 0.35 mm and a length of 20 mm. The capillaries were fabricated from commercially available metallized polymer foil that was laser welded to form a honeycomb structure. Electrowetting was used to switch the contact angle of aqueous salt solutions from >90° to <90° giving rise to capillary depression and capillary rise, respectively. Liquid actuation over a distance of 10 mm was achieved within ≈0.2 s. By dissolving suitable absorbers in the liquid, this device can be used as a switchable optical filter.

By dissolving heavy salts, Prins et al demonstrated this principle for the specific case of an x-ray absorber potentially useful for minimizing unnecessary exposure of patients to radiation in medical applications.

Kim et al created a number of microelectromechanical systems (MEMS) applications based on the continuous electrowetting effect that was also used earlier by Beni et al. These systems are based on mercury droplets moving in electrolyte-filled channels. By applying just a few volts along the channel, a potential gradient and, thus, a charge density and interfacial energy gradient are established along the mercury droplet, which then propels the droplet. A small micro-motor was presented, in which the mercury droplet could run continuously around a circular track with a diameter of 2 mm. At a rotation speed of 420 rpm, the power consumption was as low as 10–30 μW for an operating voltage of 2.8 V. Other applications of this principle include switches, latching relays, optical shutters, and micro-pumps.

Conclusions and Outlook

The basic principles of electrowetting and electrowetting on dielectric are well understood. If a sessile droplet of a conductive liquid is exposed to an external electric field, the distribution of charge carriers on the droplet surface redistributes and the surface morphology adjusts to reach a new equilibrium configuration. Depending on the level of accuracy that is required, different levels of complexity in the description can be chosen. On a global scale, the equilibrium surfaces remain surfaces of constant mean curvature because the electric field vanishes along the liquid–vapour interface and therefore capillarity determines the morphology. Under these conditions, electrowetting can be considered simply as a means of controlling the contact angle. Electrowetting on any surface, be it homogeneous or structured, is then equivalent to conventional wetting on a surface with an identical distribution of localcontact angles. This level of description, summarized by the basic electrowetting equation (equation (8)), proves to be sufficient for almost all practical applications of electrowetting. It has been shown to break down, however, under two related conditions. Within a range corresponding approximately to the thickness of the insulator, electric fringe fields cause distortions of the liquid–vapour interface. Upon approaching the contact line, the electric field strength and the mean curvature of the surface diverge; a result that has yet to be confirmed experimentally. The diverging electric fields are also believed to be responsible for the second limitation of the electrowetting equation, namely contact angle saturation at high voltage, which remains the fundamental unresolved problem of electrowetting. Apart from finite conductivity or finite frequency effects, most authors seem to agree that contact angle saturation is related to the onset of some non-linear response of the materials involved in the diverging electric fields. To predict the saturation angle for a given material combination, however, remains a substantial challenge.

The control of the wettability of structured surfaces, in particular topographically structured surfaces, offers rich opportunities for future work. Abrupt variation of the liquid morphology triggered by altering the wettability locally or globally can be rather dramatic, as has been demonstrated by some examples given. The full spectrum of possibilities—in particular with respect to applications—remains to be explored. The combination of electrowetting with conventional channel-based microfluidic systems offers many opportunities.

From an applied perspective, it is highly desirable to minimize the voltage required to achieve a given contact angle reduction. This is essentially a challenge for material properties. Both current approaches, composite substrates of solid state insulators (e.g. SiO_2) with hydrophobic top coatings as well as homogeneous polymeric insulators, have reached the range of sub-micrometer thickness. Activation voltages of a few tens of volts have been demonstrated in several laboratories. Future improvements will probably enable many electrowetting devices to be made with driving voltages in the range of 10–20 V.

Several applications of electrowetting have already reached or are about to reach the stage of producing commercially available products. Electrowetting-controlled variable focus lenses are commercially available. Cameras for mobile phones or hand-held PCS with EW- controlled lenses were presented at major trade shows in 2005, opening the door to a huge market. If high quality liquid lenses of larger diameter (e.g. several centimeters) can be produced, an even broader range of variable focus optics where mechanical compactness is an issue becomes accessible. Display technology and fiber optics offer opportunities for similarly broad markets. Biomedical applications for point-of-care testing of physiological fluids are also within reach. Test devices controlled by hand-held PCs are under development in several companies. Commercial products seem to be achievable within a few years from now. Additional fields of applications may exploit the overwhelming strength of capillary forces at small scales for mechanical actuation.